Java™ Management Extensions

Related titles from O'Reilly

Ant: The Definitive Guide

Building Java™ Enterprise Applications

Database Programming with JDBC and Java™

Developing JavaBeans™

Enterprise JavaBeans™

J2ME™ in a Nutshell

Java™ 2D Graphics

Java™ and SOAP

Java™ & XML

Java™ and XML Data Binding

Java™ and XSLT

Java™ Cookbook

Java™ Cryptography

Java™ Distributed Computing

Java™ Enterprise in a Nutshell

Java™ Examples in a Nutshell

Java™ Foundation Classes in a Nutshell

Java™ I/O

Java™ in a Nutshell

Java™ Internationalization

Java™ Message Service

Java™ Network Programming

Java™ Performance Tuning

Java™ Programming with Oracle JDBC

Java™ Programming with Oracle SQLJ

Java™ RMI

Java™ Security

JavaServer™ Pages

JavaServer™ Pages Pocket Reference

Java™ Servlet Programming

Java™ Swing

Java™ Threads

Java™ Web Services

Learning Java™

Learning Wireless Java™

Also available

The Java™ Enterprise CD Bookshelf

Java™ Management Extensions

J. Steven Perry

O'REILLY®

Beijing · Cambridge · Farnham · Köln · Paris · Sebastopol · Taipei · Tokyo

Java™ Management Extensions
by J. Steven Perry

Copyright © 2002 O'Reilly & Associates, Inc. All rights reserved.
Printed in the United States of America.

Published by O'Reilly & Associates, Inc., 1005 Gravenstein Highway North,
Sebastopol, CA 95472.

O'Reilly & Associates books may be purchased for educational, business, or sales promotional
use. Online editions are also available for most titles (*safari.oreilly.com*). For more information,
contact our corporate/institutional sales department: (800) 998-9938 or *corporate@oreilly.com*.

Editor:	Robert Denn
Production Editor:	Rachel Wheeler
Cover Designer:	Hanna Dyer
Interior Designer:	Melanie Wang

Printing History:

June 2002:	First Edition.

Library of Congress Cataloging-in-Publication Data

Perry, J. Steven (James Steven) 1967-
    Java Management Extensions / by J. Steven Perry.
        p. cm.
    Includes index.
    ISBN 0-596-00245-9
    1. Java (Computer program language) 2. Computer software--Development--Management.
        I. Title.

QA76.73.J38 P472 2002
005.13'3--dc21
                                                                                    2002070417

[M]

Table of Contents

Preface

As technology evolves, it enables us to write applications that are increasingly distributed and complex. Today's network technologies allow us to process units of work on physically separate machines scattered throughout the world. As the scale and complexity of today's newest applications increases, so too does the challenge of managing them. After all, it is not really beneficial to distribute an application across many different machines if the answer to a question as simple as "Is the application still running?" cannot easily be determined.

This book is about Java Management Extensions, or JMX, which is the Java standard for management of application resources. An application resource can be any piece of hardware or software that you wish to monitor and control, such as a printer, router, database connection, or queue. At the heart of JMX is the concept of a managed bean, or MBean, which is a resource that has been instrumented via JMX. The MBean gets its name from the fact that it resembles a JavaBean, in that its state is entirely maintained through the use of get and set methods for its attributes. A notification model similar to the Java notification model is also available for MBeans that need to emit notifications.

JMX provides an architecture, a set of design patterns, and a set of application programming interfaces (APIs) that allow you to instrument your application and system resources so that they can be managed. JMX was designed to be able to integrate with existing management technologies, such as the Simple Network Management Protocol (SNMP) and Web-Based Enterprise Management (WBEM). This book covers every facet of JMX as it is currently specified, from instrumentation to writing agents to using the JMX agent services. Some parts of JMX are still unspecified (most notably the JMX distributed services), so it can't cover everything; however, it is my intention that this book be the most complete reference on JMX that is available today.

Here is a summary of what this book covers:

- JMX instrumentation: standard, dynamic, model, and open MBeans
- JMX notifications: how to broadcast, filter, and listen for them

- The MBean server: a registry of MBeans and a communication broker between management applications and registered MBeans
- JMX agent services: dynamic loading, monitoring, timer, and relation services, available through the JMX agent

Audience

This is primarily a how-to book, intended for software developers who face the challenge of building management capability through JMX technology into their Java applications and want to know exactly how to go about it. However, this book can also provide software development managers with the necessary information about JMX to make decisions regarding whether or not to implement this technology in their development projects. (I assume that you are already convinced of the need to build management capabilities into your application.)

Chapter 1 looks at JMX at a high level. The JMX architecture is given the most treatment here, as it is the core of JMX. The following chapters are very meaty and are intended for developers who want to know how to use all of the aspects of JMX that are currently specified.

Organization

Chapter 1, *Java Management Extensions Concepts*, contains an overview of JMX that introduces fundamental concepts and provides an overview of the JMX architecture. It also introduces the sample application we'll use throughout the book, which demonstrates each MBean instrumentation approach. We'll see how to build and run the application and how to use a web browser to monitor what's going on inside it.

Chapter 2, *Standard MBeans*, covers how to create and use standard MBeans and discusses the inheritance patterns that they must follow. In this chapter, we will take a look at the fundamentals of a management interface and how to define one.

Chapter 3, *Dynamic MBeans*, looks at how dynamic MBeans work and the inheritance patterns you can use when creating them. It also shows how to describe a dynamic MBean using the metadata classes provided by the JMX specification.

Chapter 4, *Model MBeans*, discusses how model MBeans work and how they differ from any other MBean type. It also shows how to describe model MBeans using the metadata classes specific to model MBeans.

Chapter 5, *Open MBeans*, looks at how to describe fundamental and complex data types using the open MBean data types provided and the metadata classes specific to open MBeans.

Chapter 6, *The MBean Server*, covers the MBean server from top to bottom. The MBean server's API, its implementation, and details of how to use the MBean server to interact indirectly with MBeans are given thorough discussion.

Chapter 7, *JMX Notifications*, looks at the JMX notification model and the various interfaces and classes that are provided by the JMX Reference Implementation (RI). It also discusses how to write a notification listener, broadcaster, and filter.

Chapter 8, *Dynamic Loading*, covers dynamic loading and how to use the M-Let service to load MBeans from anywhere on the network.

Chapter 9, *The Monitoring Services*, deals with the monitoring services, which include counter, gauge, and string monitors.

Chapter 10, *The Timer Service*, discusses the timer service, an agent service that can be used to create a scheduler or simply to send repeated notifications at a specific interval.

Chapter 11, *The Relation Service*, covers the relation service and how to use it to enforce application policies regarding relationships between MBeans.

Conventions Used in This Book

The following typographical conventions are used in this book:

Italic
> Used for file and directory names, functions, methods, parameters, and URLs. Also used for emphasis and for the first use of technical terms.

Constant width
> Used for code listings and for resources, attributes, interfaces, classes, and targets where they appear in the text.

Constant width bold
> Used for emphasis in code listings.

Constant width italic
> Used for replaceable parameter names in command syntax.

 This icon indicates a tip, suggestion, or general note.

 This icon indicates a warning or caution.

Comments and Questions

Please address comments and questions concerning this book to the publisher:

O'Reilly & Associates, Inc.
1005 Gravenstein Highway North
Sebastopol, CA 95472
(800) 998-9938 (in the United States or Canada)
(707) 829-0515 (international/local)
(707) 829-0104 (fax)

There is a web page for this book, which lists errata, examples, or any additional information. You can access this page at:

http://www.oreilly.com/catalog/javamngext/

To comment or ask technical questions about this book, send email to:

bookquestions@oreilly.com

For more information about books, conferences, Resource Centers, and the O'Reilly Network, see the O'Reilly web site at:

http://www.oreilly.com

Source Code Availability

Most of the examples in the book are keyed to a sample application instrumented with JMX calls. The source code for this application is available at the book's web site (*http://www.oreilly.com/catalog/javamngext/*), along with a *README* file explaining how to build and run it.

Acknowledgments

First and foremost, I would like to thank my wife Heather, daughter Madison, and son Foster for their incredible support during the months I spent writing this book. Many late nights and long weekends writing made for a pretty tired (and grumpy, no doubt) husband and daddy. Thanks Heather, Maddie, and Foster, for putting up with me! Many thanks go to Robert Denn and Mike Loukides at O'Reilly for their great editorial support. Thanks to others at O'Reilly for all the support and help: Rob Romano, Julie Flanagan, and Kyle Hart. I would also like to thank Eamonn McManus at Sun Microsystems for his very thorough technical review of this book and the wonderful feedback. Thanks also to Joel Feraud at Sun for providing an advance look at open MBeans. Finally, thanks to Christophe Ebro at Sun for help in answering questions and putting me in touch with other extremely helpful people at Sun, such as Joel Feraud and Philippe LaLande. Thanks a million, Chris!

CHAPTER 1

Java Management Extensions Concepts

The growth of large-scale distributed applications in the past decade has been impressive. Mission-critical business applications have evolved from a sequence of programs running on a single computer to business components running on different machines scattered throughout a network. Managing one application running on a single computer is fairly straightforward; you can monitor the health of the application through the use of a single log file, or operator console, and tools provided by the operating system. The difficulty of managing today's distributed systems has increased along with the complexity of those systems. When considering a management solution for today's enterprise applications, some questions arise:

- Which management solution is best for the application?
- What standards should a management solution follow?
- How much effort is required to enable the components of the application to be managed?

Java Management Extensions (JMX), the result of the Java Community Process (JCP) Java Specification Request (JSR) 3, was designed to deal with all of these questions. JMX was designed to address the management needs of applications written for the Java platform and to be compatible with existing management standards, such as the Simple Network Management Protocol (SNMP), which is the standard for management of enterprise networks. It was also designed so that instrumentation of resources to put them under the control of a management application is as easy as possible.

Introducing JMX

A *resource* is any entity in the system that needs to be monitored and/or controlled by a management application; resources that can be monitored and controlled are called *manageable*. A *management application* is a piece of software that can be used to monitor and control manageable resources (typically remotely). Managing a system of manageable resources is what we call *system management*. The JMX architecture enables Java applications (or systems) to become manageable.

Three fundamental questions must be addressed by any complete management solution:

- How do I make my resources manageable?
- Once my resources are manageable, how do I make them available (visible) for management?
- Once my resources are visible for management, how do management applications access them?

The JMX architecture is composed of three levels, each of which answers one of these questions.

JMX Architecture

In this section, we will take a look at the three levels of the JMX architecture. The level closest to the application is called the *instrumentation level*. This level consists of four approaches for instrumenting application and system resources to be manageable (i.e., making them *managed beans*, or *MBeans*), as well as a model for sending and receiving notifications. JMX notifications are analogous to SNMP traps.

The middle level of the JMX architecture is called the *agent level*. This level contains a registry for handling manageable resources (the *MBean server*) as well as several agent services, which themselves are MBeans and thus are manageable. The combination of an instance of the MBean server, its registered MBeans, and any agent services in use within a single Java Virtual Machine (JVM) is typically referred to as a *JMX agent*.

The third level of the JMX architecture is called the *distributed services level*. This level contains the middleware that connects JMX agents to applications that manage them (*management applications*). This middleware is broken into two categories: protocol adaptors and connectors. Through a *protocol adaptor*, an application such as a web browser can connect to one or more JMX agents and manage the MBeans that are registered within it (for example, via HTTP). As long as the management application can understand the objects contained in the protocol stream, it can manage the MBeans they represent; thus, protocol adaptors do not need to be written in Java. A *connector* follows the familiar proxy pattern and is made up of a client and server pair. The server half of the connector pair is normally collocated with the JMX agent it represents (although this is not required), while the client half runs in the JVM of the management application. Issues such as security and Java serialization are understood by both the client and server components of the connector.

The JMX architecture is depicted graphically in Figure 1-1.

The Instrumentation Level

This section covers the JMX instrumentation level and includes all MBean types, with examples. This is the level that should be of most concern to developers,

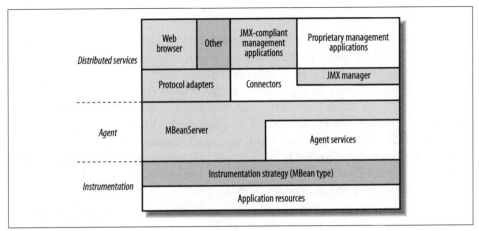

Figure 1-1. The JMX architecture (note: protocol adaptors and connectors are not currently standardized)

because this level prepares resources to be manageable. Figure 1-1 shows the two areas of concern for the instrumentation level of the JMX architecture:

- Application resources, such as a connection, a pool of connections, a printer connected to the network, or even the application itself
- The instrumentation strategy that is used to instrument application resources

An application resource that is to be manageable through JMX must provide information about five of its features:

- Attributes, which contain the state of the resource
- Constructors, which are used by management applications and other JMX agents to create instances of the resource
- Operations, which may be invoked by a management application or other JMX agent to cause the resource to perform some action
- Parameters to constructors and operations
- Notifications, which are emitted by the resource and sent via the JMX notification infrastructure to any interested agents

The combination of these five pieces of information—or *metadata*—about a resource's features is known as its *management interface*. It is through this interface alone that a management application or other JMX agent may interact with a resource.

There are four instrumentation approaches defined by JMX that we can use to describe the management interface of a resource: standard, dynamic, model, and open. Before we discuss these approaches, let's get a good working definition of an MBean, which is how we will refer to a managed resource from this point forward.

What is an MBean?

An MBean is an application or system resource that has been instrumented to be manageable through JMX. Instrumenting a resource involves writing some code. This code must follow four rules. First, the state of the resource must be completely described through getters and setters.* It is this requirement that earns the instrumented resource the "bean" moniker (from the same rule for maintaining the state of a JavaBean). Second, the resource must be instrumented (i.e., coded) according to one of the JMX MBean types (standard, dynamic, model, or open). Following this requirement earns the resource bean the "M" (for manageable) part of the MBean name. Third, the MBean must provide at least one public constructor. Finally, an MBean must be concrete (i.e., not declared abstract).

Suppose we have a resource called GenericResource that has the following attributes:

Version
> The version of the GenericResource.

ProcessingTime
> The number of milliseconds of processing time that have been consumed by this instance of GenericResource

NumberOfExceptions
> The total number of exceptions that have been thrown by this instance of GenericResource in the course of its processing

The most straightforward implementation of the state of GenericResource would look like Example 1-1.

Example 1-1. Attributes of a candidate resource

```
public class GenericResource {
// class details. . .
  // Version (read-only)
  private String _version = "1.0.1";
  public String getVersion( ) {
    return _version;
  }
  // ProcessingTime (read-only)
  private long _processingTime;
  public long getProcessingTime( ) {
    return _processingTime;
  }
  // NumberOfExceptions (read-write)
  private short _numberOfExceptions;
  public short getNumberOfExceptions( ) {
    return _numberOfExceptions;
  }
```

---

* This is not strictly true for the dynamic, model, and open MBean types. However, I highly recommend strict adherence to this pattern.

Example 1-1. Attributes of a candidate resource (continued)

```
  public void setNumberOfExceptions(short value) {
    _numberOfExceptions = value;
  }
// other class details. . .
}
```

This simple example demonstrates the fundamentals of instrumenting the attributes of a resource according to the JavaBeans state pattern. Each attribute is backed by a private member variable, so that the part of the resource's state represented by that attribute cannot be accessed directly. All attributes in this example are readable and have corresponding getters. Only the NumberOfExceptions attribute is writable, and it provides a setter for that purpose.

Standard MBeans

Standard MBeans are the simplest type of MBean to code from scratch. All you need to do is define the MBean interface as a Java interface and implement that interface on the resource MBean. If we were to instrument GenericResource (from Example 1-1) as a standard MBean, we would define a Java interface that looks like this:

```
public interface GenericResourceMBean {
  // Version (read-only)
  public String getVersion();

  // ProcessingTime (read-only)
  public long getProcessingTime();

  // NumberOfExceptions (read-write)
  public short getNumberOfExceptions();
  public void setNumberOfExceptions(short value);
}
```

We would then implement the interface on the GenericResource class:

```
public class GenericResource implements GenericResourceMBean {
// etc. (from Example 1-1)
}
```

The name assigned to this interface is very important: it must be the name of the class that implements it, followed by MBean. In other words, for any resource class XYZ that is to be instrumented as a standard MBean, a Java interface called XYZMBean must be defined, and it must be implemented by XYZ. Note that the MBean suffix is case-sensitive: Mbean is incorrect, as is mBean or mbean.

That is all the instrumentation code that must be written to make GenericResource capable of being managed! Of course, this example is more simplistic than most resources we will deal with in the real world, most of which will include one or more management operations. Suppose we want to add a method, *reset()*, to reset the state of the ProcessingTime and NumberOfExceptions attributes. We would add this method to the MBean interface, as shown in the following code.

```
public interface GenericResourceMBean {
    // Version (read-only)
    public String getVersion( );

    // ProcessingTime (read-only)
    public long getProcessingTime( );

    // NumberOfExceptions (read-write)
    public short getNumberOfExceptions( );
    public void setNumberOfExceptions(short value);

    // reset( ) operation
    public void reset( );
}
```

Then we would implement the method on the GenericResource class, as shown in Example 1-2.

Example 1-2. The GenericResource managed bean

```
public class GenericResource {
//class details. . .
  // Version (read-only)
  private String _version = "1.0.1";
  public String getVersion( ) {
    return _version;
  }
  // ProcessingTime (read-only)
  private long _processingTime;
  public long getProcessingTime( ) {
    return _processingTime;
  }
  // NumberOfExceptions (read-write)
  private short _numberOfExceptions;
  public short getNumberOfExceptions( ) {
    return _numberOfExceptions;
  }
  public void setNumberOfExceptions(short value) {
    _numberOfExceptions = value;
  }

  public void reset( ) {
    _processingTime = 0;
    setNumberOfExceptions(0);
  }
// other class details. . .
}
```

The metadata required of every MBean is created automatically by the JMX infrastructure for standard MBeans. Before an MBean can be managed, it must be registered with a JMX agent (as described in the later section, "The MBean server"). When a standard MBean is registered, it is inspected, and metadata placeholder classes are created and maintained by the JMX agent on behalf of the MBean. The

Java reflection API is used to discover the constructor(s) on the MBean class, as well as other features. The attribute and operation metadata comes from the MBean interface and is verified by the JMX agent.

We will look at creating standard MBeans in detail in Chapter 2.

 Consider instrumenting a resource as a standard MBean if:

- The management interface of the resource is fairly static (i.e., it won't change much over time).
- You want to quickly instrument the resource to be manageable.

Dynamic MBeans

In the case of standard MBeans, the JMX agent creates the metadata that describes the features of a resource. In contrast, the developer himself must provide the metadata that describes a resource as a dynamic MBean. With the increased difficulty comes a gain in flexibility, however, because the instrumentation developer controls the creation of the metadata.

Dynamic MBeans implement a JMX interface called DynamicMBean that contains methods that allow the JMX agent to discover the management interface of the resource at runtime. The DyamicMBean interface is defined in Example 1-3.

Example 1-3. The DynamicMBean interface

```
package javax.management;

public interface DynamicMBean {

  public Object getAttribute(String attribute)
    throws AttributeNotFoundException, MBeanException, ReflectionException;

  public void setAttribute(Attribute attribute)
    throws AttributeNotFoundException, InvalidAttributeValueException,
        MBeanException, ReflectionException;

  public AttributeList getAttributes(String[] attributes);

  public AttributeList setAttributes(AttributeList attributes);

  public Object invoke(String actionName, Object params[], String signature[])
    throws MBeanException, ReflectionException;

  public MBeanInfo getMBeanInfo( );

}
```

There are six types of dynamic MBean metadata (one for each type of feature), shown in Figure 1-2 in Unified Modeling Language (UML) notation.

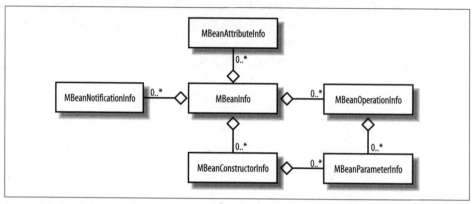

Figure 1-2. UML diagram showing the relationships between the dynamic MBean metadata classes

To describe the management interface of a resource as a dynamic MBean, we create five fundamental pieces of metadata that correspond to its five fundamental features: constructors, attributes, parameters, operations, and notifications. As we can see from Figure 1-2, these five pieces of metadata are described through instances of MBeanConstructorInfo, MBeanAttributeInfo, MBeanParameterInfo, MBeanOperationInfo, and MBeanNotificationInfo, respectively. The parameters that are passed to a constructor or operation must also be described through the JMX metadata class MBeanParameterInfo. Once all the metadata for an MBean has been described through these classes, it is contained in a single metadata class—MBeanInfo—that describes the MBean interface in its entirety. The JMX agent uses the *getMBeanInfo()* method of the DynamicMBean interface to obtain this MBeanInfo object in order to discover the management interface of a dynamic MBean.

Once the management interface has been discovered, the JMX agent uses the other methods of DynamicMBean to retrieve and set attribute values and invoke operations on the MBean.

We will look at how to instrument a resource as a dynamic MBean in detail in Chapter 3.

 Consider instrumenting a resource as a dynamic MBean if:

- You want to make a resource manageable but cannot change the source code of the resource itself (e.g., if it's third-party software). Wrapping the resource class in a DynamicMBean implementation is ideal in this case.

- The management interface of the resource changes over time as the resource evolves as part of an application.

- The management interface potentially changes each time the resource is instantiated.

Model MBeans

The features of a resource that is instrumented as a model MBean are described through the use of metadata classes that are specific to model MBeans. In addition, every model MBean must implement the ModelMBean interface, which is defined in Example 1-4.

Example 1-4. The ModelMBean interface

```
public interface ModelMBean
  extends DynamicMBean,
          PersistentMBean,
          ModelMBeanNotificationBroadcaster {

public void setModelMBeanInfo(ModelMBeanInfo inModelMBeanInfo)
  throws MBeanException, RuntimeOperationsException;

public void setManagedResource(Object mr, String mr_type)
  throws MBeanException,
         RuntimeOperationsException,
         InstanceNotFoundException,
         InvalidTargetObjectTypeException;
}
```

Notice that the ModelMBean interface extends the DynamicMBean interface, which means that a model MBean is a dynamic MBean. However, every JMX implementation is required to ship an off-the-shelf implementation of ModelMBean called RequiredModelMBean. This presents the developer with a key benefit: because a model MBean implementation already exists, the work of writing one is already done. While the instrumentation developer must still create the necessary metadata classes (which we will discuss shortly), she does not have to implement the ModelMBean interface, which significantly reduces development time.

Model MBeans introduce the concept of a *descriptor*, which is an additional set of metadata—specific to model MBeans—that allows the instrumentation developer to provide a much richer description of any MBean feature. Certain predefined descriptor values provide support for functionality such as the following:

- Automatic attribute change notifications
- Persistence of the MBean's state at a specified interval
- Logging of MBean state changes
- Caching of an MBean feature (such as an attribute value or the return value of an operation) to improve performance for static (or relatively static) MBean features

Model MBean metadata extends dynamic MBean metadata, in that each model MBean metadata class extends its dynamic MBean counterpart. This relationship is shown in Figure 1-3.

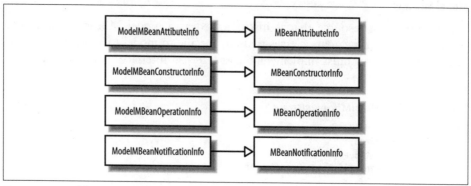

Figure 1-3. Model MBean metadata classes

`ModelMBeanInfo` is an exception, as it is an interface (implemented by a support class called `ModelMBeanInfoSupport`) that extends `MBeanInfo`. There is also no special model MBean metadata class to describe parameters, because there is no difference between a parameter to a dynamic MBean constructor or operation and a parameter to a model MBean constructor or operation.

The relationships between the model MBean metadata classes are shown in Figure 1-4.

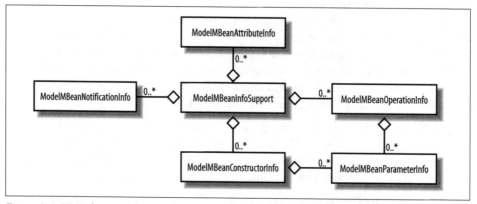

Figure 1-4. UML diagram showing the relationships between the model MBean metadata classes

We will discuss how to instrument resources as model MBeans in detail in Chapter 4.

Consider instrumenting a resource as a model MBean if:

- The benefits of instrumenting as a dynamic MBean are required, but a significant per-MBean development time investment is undesirable.

- A richer set of information about one or more of the features of the MBean (such as its attributes or operations) than can be described using dynamic MBeans is required.

Open MBeans

Using the standard, dynamic, or model MBean instrumentation approaches allows us to describe MBean features (i.e., attributes, constructors, parameters, operations, and notifications) that are one of the following types:

- A fundamental Java type, such as boolean, char, long, or float (through its corresponding JDK wrapper—Boolean, Char, Long, or Float, respectively)
- A string, as java.lang.String
- An array of fundamental types or strings

However, sometimes MBean attributes are more complex. Open MBeans were designed in an effort to make MBeans accessible to the widest possible range of management applications. Strictly speaking, you can use complex types on the management interface of standard, dynamic, and model MBeans. However, for a management application to correctly interpret the state of those types, the classes (i.e., the Java bytecode) representing those types must be available to the management application. The result is a coupling between the management application and the resources it manages, compromising the maintainability of the underlying managed resources. Open MBeans eliminate the need for management applications to understand the classes describing the complex types, deferring this intelligence instead to a predefined set of open MBean classes that can universally describe those types.

Every open MBean type is a concrete subclass of an abstract open MBean class called OpenType, and only subclasses of OpenType are allowed to describe features of open MBeans. Three new types are defined that allow the instrumentation developer to describe MBean features of arbitrary complexity:

ArrayType
> Describes an *n*-dimensional array of any open MBean type

CompositeType
> Describes an arbitrarily complex structure of open MBean types

TabularType
> Describes a tabular structure (analogous to a database table) of any number of rows, where the same CompositeType describes each row in the table

At some point, the state of an MBean (or any object, for that matter) must be resolved down to fundamental types, strings, or arrays. However, open MBeans provide us with a mechanism to describe complex links between types so that those links can be resolved indirectly. For example, if we want to instrument a class A as an MBean, and A in turn contains an instance of a class B, which contains an instance of a class C, we need some way to describe the links in the inheritance graph between A, B, and C. It is for precisely this sort of arbitrary complexity that open MBeans were designed.

Open MBeans differ from dynamic and model MBeans in that there is no special interface specifically for open MBeans that an open MBean must implement. Instead, open MBeans must implement the DynamicMBean interface; what makes them "open" is their use of special open MBean metadata classes to describe their features and their use of the `OpenType` subclasses we discussed earlier. For every open MBean feature (with the exception of notifications), JMX defines an interface/support class pair that is used to describe the feature. For example, to describe an open MBean attribute, we use the `OpenMBeanAttributeInfo` interface, which is implemented by a support class called `OpenMBeanAttributeInfoSupport`. Each support class, in turn, extends its dynamic MBean counterpart. For example, `OpenMBeanAttributeInfoSupport` extends `MBeanAttributeInfo`. These relationships are shown for all open MBean metadata classes in Figure 1-5.

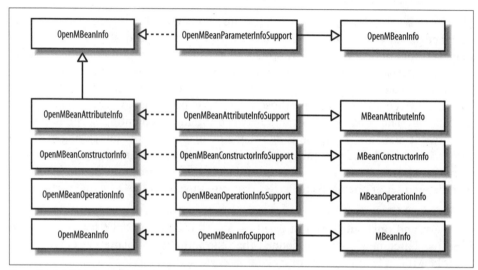

Figure 1-5. UML diagram showing the inheritance relationships between the open MBean metadata interfaces, their support classes, and the dynamic MBean metadata classes

The `OpenMBeanInfoSupport` class contains the metadata for the MBean's features (which follows the pattern for dynamic and model MBeans). The relationships between the open MBean metadata classes are shown in Figure 1-6.

We will cover open MBeans in detail in Chapter 5.

> Consider instrumenting a resource as an open MBean if:
> - The benefits of dynamic instrumentation are required.
> - One or more MBean features cannot be completely described using one of the Java fundamental types, an array, or `java.lang.String` (in other words, if the feature is a complex data structure).

JMX notifications

The JMX agent is designed so that management applications, or other components of the system, actively collect information about (i.e., query) the resources that are

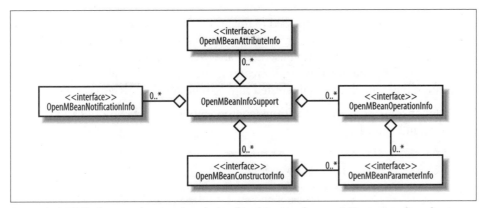

Figure 1-6. UML diagram showing the relationships between the open MBean metadata classes

being managed by that agent. This works well when this information is refreshed at reasonable intervals and the application resources are stable. However, there are times when an immediate notification of a resource fault needs to be communicated to an interested party (such as a management application) outside the JMX agent. It is for this reason that the JMX notification model was designed. A JMX notification is similar to an SNMP trap and can be used to send critical, warning, or simply system or application information when certain events occur in the system.

At the core of the notification model are two principal participants:

- A notification broadcaster, which emits notifications
- A notification listener, which registers its interest in receiving certain notifications through the JMX agent infrastructure and receives those notifications when they are broadcast

A *notification broadcaster* is an object that implements the `NotificationBroadcaster` interface. Through this interface, a notification listener can register or remove its interest in receiving notifications and can query the notification broadcaster about what notifications it emits.

A *notification listener* is an object that implements the `NotificationListener` interface, which has a single method, *handleNotification()*, that it uses to process all the notifications it receives.

To receive notifications, a notification listener must register its interest in receiving the notifications emitted by the broadcaster through the broadcaster's implementation of `NotificationBroadcaster`. When the notification listener does so, it passes references to itself, an optional *notification filter object*, and an optional *handback object*. The notification filter is an object that implements the `NotificationFilter` interface, and it is used by the broadcaster to determine which notifications it will send to the listener. Only those notification types that have been enabled in the filter will be sent to the listener. The handback object is opaque to the broadcaster and has meaning only to the listener, which uses the handback object in its processing of the notification.

If no notification filter object is passed to the notification broadcaster, the listener is in effect telling the broadcaster that it wants to receive every notification the broadcaster emits. However, if the notification listener wants to receive only a subset of the notifications emitted by the broadcaster, it creates a notification filter object and adds the notification types in which it is interested through the `NotificationFilter` interface.

The relationships between the various components of the JMX notification model are shown in Figure 1-7.

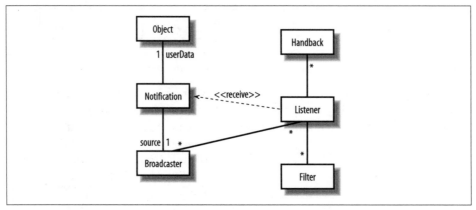

Figure 1-7. UML diagram showing the relationships between the entities that participate in the JMX notification model

A listener can receive notifications from multiple broadcasters, which in turn can send notifications to multiple listeners. In fact, a single listener may register itself multiple times with the same broadcaster, providing a different handback and/or notification filter object each time. This allows the listener a great deal of flexibility in how to process specific notifications. When the broadcaster emits a notification, an instance of `Notification` is sent, along with the handback object supplied by the listener. The notification supplied by the broadcaster must include a `userData` object. The specification does not say what this object must look like, which leaves the broadcaster free to implement it as necessary. However, the listener must be aware of this object (and what it looks like) in order to be able to determine whether to ignore it or to process it.

Notifications are a fairly advanced topic. We will take a detailed look at how to create, send, filter, and receive notifications in Chapter 7.

Consider using notifications if:

- It is necessary to alert interested parties about the inner workings of a resource in real time.
- The details of the inner workings of a resource are not of special significance (other than their business value, of course) until a particular set of circumstances occurs.

The Agent Level

The agent level of the JMX architecture is made up of the MBean server and the JMX agent services. The MBean server has two purposes: it serves as a registry of MBeans and as a communications broker between MBeans and management applications (and other JMX agents). The JMX agent services provide additional functionality that is mandated by the JMX specification, such as scheduling and dynamic loading.

In this section, we will look at the MBean server and then at each of the required JMX agent services.

The MBean server

The MBean server is at the heart of the JMX agent. The MBean server acts as a registry for MBeans, and the JMX agent accesses this registry through the MBeanServer interface. To decouple the interaction between the agent and the MBean instance, JMX introduces the concept of an *object name*, which is implemented by a JMX class called ObjectName. Before an MBean is registered, an object name that uniquely identifies the MBean within the MBean server's internal registry must be created for the MBean (this can be done by the agent who registers the MBean or by the MBean itself). If the object name is unique within the MBean server's registry, a new entry containing the object name and a reference to the MBean is created for that MBean. If the object name used to register the MBean is not unique, the registration attempt will fail because another MBean has already been registered using that object name.

Once an MBean is registered, the object name assigned to the MBean is used as the means of indirect communication between the agent and the MBean. The MBean server acts as a broker for the request through its implementation of the MBeanServer interface. If the agent wants to query an MBean for its attribute values, it invokes the appropriate method on the MBeanServer interface and passes the object name of the MBean whose values are to be retrieved. The MBean server uses the object name as a lookup into its registry, retrieves the reference to the MBean object, and makes the invocation. The results of the invocation on the MBean object are then returned to the agent. At no time does the agent have a direct reference to the MBean.

A factory class, MBeanServerFactory, is provided to obtain a reference to the MBean server. The use of a factory decouples the MBeanServer interface from its implementation. MBeanServerFactory provides two static methods that allow us to create an MBean server:

createMBeanServer()
> Creates an instance of the MBean server, holds that reference internally to the MBeanServerFactory, and returns the reference to the caller. The MBeanServerFactory internal reference to the MBean server that was created prevents it from being subject to garbage collection.

newMBeanServer( )

Creates an instance of the MBean server and returns that reference to the caller. No internal reference is maintained inside the `MBeanServerFactory`. When there are no more live references to the MBean server, it is eligible for garbage collection.

We will take a detailed look at the MBean server and how to create and use it in Chapter 6.

The M-Let service

The *M-Let* (short for *management applet*) service is a JMX agent service that allows you to load MBeans from anywhere on the network, including a local machine. The M-Let service is itself an MBean and can be managed as such. Information about MBeans to be loaded is contained in a text file called an *M-Let file*. This file has an XML-like syntax, but the syntax does not constitute well-formed XML. Using special tags called *M-Let tags*, we can encode enough information in the M-Let file that the M-Let service can locate, download the bytecode for, and instantiate MBeans.

Here's how the M-Let service works. First, we instantiate the M-Let service's MBean class and register it with the MBean server. Next, through a method call, we provide the M-Let service with the URL to the M-Let file, which retrieves the M-Let file and reads its contents. The M-Let service then instantiates all of the MBeans specified in the M-Let file.

We can also use the M-Let service, in conjunction with the MBean server, to load MBeans without the use of an M-Let file. We simply add the file's URL to the M-Let service's list of URLs that it will search when attempting to load MBeans, then call a method on the MBean server and pass the M-Let service's object name (which we created when we registered the M-Let service MBean with the MBean server) as the MBean class loader.

We will take a detailed look at how to use the M-Let service in Chapter 9.

 Consider using the M-Let service if:

- You need to be able to load MBeans into the MBean server from anywhere on the network.
- You need or desire the configuration of your application's resources to be centralized.
- You need a class loader for MBeans that is itself an MBean.

Monitoring services

A *monitor* observes the attribute value of an MBean, called the *observed object*, at specific intervals, called the *granularity period*. From this observation the monitor calculates a value called the *derived gauge*, which is either the value of the attribute or the difference in the value of the attribute (for numerical attributes only, of course) between the most recent two observations. When the derived gauge satisfies a certain condition —which varies depending on the type of monitor in use—a notification of a type that is specific to that monitor is sent to all registered notification listeners. The monitoring service can also send error notifications if a problem arises.

The JMX specification mandates that three types of monitors be provided with every compliant implementation:

Counter monitors
> Observe a continually increasing, nonnegative, integer MBean attribute (of type byte, short, int, long, or the corresponding JDK wrapper class) and send a notification when the derived gauge exceeds a certain value, known as the *threshold*

> Consider using a Counter monitor to monitor an attribute:
> - Whose type is a continually increasing, nonnegative integer
> - To send a notification when the attribute's value exceeds a certain threshold
> - When a notification must be sent each time an attribute's value is increased by some fixed amount

Gauge monitors
> Observe an arbitrarily changing numeric value (of type short, int, long, float, double, or the corresponding JDK wrapper type) and send a notification when the derived gauge exceeds an upper limit (known as the *high threshold*) or drops below a lower limit (known as the *low threshold*)

> Consider using a gauge monitor to monitor an attribute:
> - Whose type is numeric
> - Whose value can increase or decrease at any time
> - Whose value is constrained between a lower threshold and an upper threshold
> - To send a notification if the attribute's value exceeds the upper threshold or drops below the lower threshold

String monitors
> Observe a string attribute of an MBean and send a notification when the derived gauge either matches or differs from a predefined string value

> Consider using a string monitor to monitor an attribute:
> - Whose type is a string
> - To send a notification if the current value of the attribute matches a predefined string or differs from a predefined string

We will discuss the monitoring services in Chapter 9.

The timer service

The *timer service* is a special-purpose notification broadcaster designed to send notifications at specific time intervals, starting at a particular date and time. Like the other agent services, the timer service is required for all compliant JMX implementations. The timer service is itself an MBean, so it can be managed (although it does not have to be registered with the MBean server to be used). There are two primary uses of the timer service:

- To send a single notification to all listeners interested in that notification type
- To send multiple notifications that repeat at specific intervals for a set number of times, or indefinitely

The timer service is capable of sending any number of different notifications at different intervals. Each notification that is to be sent by the timer service is given a notification type, defined by the agent that instructs the timer service to send that notification. In other words, the timer service does not send a predefined set of notification types. Instead, the agent tells the timer service what notification types to send and provides other information that specifies when to start sending the notification, how many times the notification is to repeat, and the amount of time that is to elapse between each notification (for repeating notifications only).

We will discuss the timer service in Chapter 10.

Consider using the timer service if:
- Your application requires a scheduler that can also be managed (the timer service is itself an MBean).
- You need a manageable facility to send out notifications at regular intervals, either a fixed or infinite number of times.

The relation service

The *relation service* provides a facility to associate MBeans with each other and must be implemented by every compliant JMX implementation. You use the metadata classes provided by the relation service to describe *n*-ary relationships between registered MBeans as dictated by your application policies. You then use the relation service to maintain the consistency of those relationships so that those application policies are followed. The relation service formalizes the rules for describing and maintaining relationships between MBeans, resulting in two major benefits:

- The relationship between MBeans is formalized into a well-defined type that can be checked by the relation service in a way similar to how Java types are checked.
- The number of MBeans that may participate in one role of a relationship (i.e., its cardinality) can be enforced by the relation service.

To use the relation service effectively, you need to understand a few key concepts:

Roles
> A role describes the MBean objects that perform a particular role.

Role information
> Role information provides metadata about a role, such as the role name and the minimum and maximum number of MBeans that are allowed to perform that role.

Relation types
> Relation type information is also metadata, but it describes the relationship between one or more role information objects. The RelationType interface provides information about the relation type, such as the name of the relation type and the various roles that make up that type.

Relations
> A relation is an instance of a relation type. It is critical to the correct functioning of the relation service that all relation types remain *consistent*. In other words, the metadata describing the relationship between MBeans (i.e., the relation type) provides the constraints on the relation that allow the relation service to be used to ensure that the relation remains consistent at all times. Once a relation has been instantiated, it must remain consistent, or the relation service will throw an exception.

We will discuss the relation service in Chapter 11.

 Consider using the relation service if:
- There is a clearly defined policy regarding the relationship between the MBeans in your system.
- You require a facility to enforce application policies about the relationship between MBeans.

The Distributed Services Level

In this section, we will take a look at the distributed services level of the JMX architecture, which is unspecified at the time of this writing. However, significant work has already been done to create the standard. Specifically, the RMI connector client and server will be standardized soon as part of JSR 160. This will provide a standard for all subsequent connectors to follow. The protocol adaptor side will remain unspecified for a while, although significant work has been done in this area as well. The main reason to standardize on the RMI connector is to leverage existing work in the JDK regarding issues such as security, connection pools, and security.

In this section, we will briefly look at connectors and adaptors. Then we will see what is coming soon with the distributed services level of JMX architecture regarding JSR 160.

Protocol adaptors and connectors

As mentioned earlier, there is a clear difference between a connector and an adaptor. A connector consists of two parts: a client proxy and a server stub. Connectors are intended to do the following:

- Hide the specific details regarding the network location of the resources in an application under management (i.e., provide location transparency).

- Present a consistent view (via an interface) of an MBean server that is located in a different process space than the local MBean server.

Shielding the proxy client from the details of how to send and receive messages to the server stub (and vice versa) makes it unnecessary for any particular instance of the MBean server to know its location on the network, which means that this can be left as a configuration detail.

An adaptor is different from a connector in that there is no client component. The adaptor runs at the server location and renders the MBean server state in a form that is appropriate for, and can be recognized by, the client. An example of this is the HtmlAdaptorServer that ships as part of the JMX RI (note that it is not officially part of the RI, as the distributed services level has yet to be fully specified). It is unlikely that any adaptors will be mandated by the JMX specification in the near future. However, given the momentum that the adoption of JMX is enjoying, several adaptor implementations should soon be available.

We will not cover the specifics of the RMI connector or of any particular adaptor here, as those details are unspecified at the moment. However, you'll find several contributions to investigate in the contrib package of the JMX RI.

JSR 160

The next release of JMX—which is set to coincide with Release 1.4 of the Java 2 Enterprise Edition (J2EE) platform (at the time of this writing, early 2003)—will provide standards for the distributed services level of the JMX architecture. The main standardization you can expect from JMX 1.5 is the RMI connector, which provides a mechanism for handling remote agents.

 Some of the information in this section is subject to change, because JSR 160 is not final.

The RMI connector is based on the concept of a remote MBean server, which is fundamental to the model used by JMX connectors as part of the distributed services architecture. This concept is illustrated in Figure 1-8.

There are two components to a connector: the client and the server. Between the two connector components is the connection itself. In JMX 1.5, the only specified connection will be RMI. However, the remote MBean server concept can apply to other

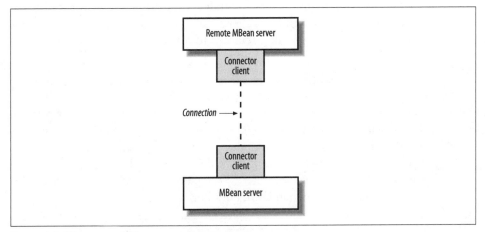

Figure 1-8. The remote MBean server concept

protocols, such as HTTP and SOAP. The connector server listens for incoming connections from connector clients. When a connector client attempts to establish a connection, the connector server handles the details of creating the connection. After the connection has been established, all of the MBeans registered in the remote MBean server can be accessed; that is, their attributes can be retrieved and set (depending on the read/write status of each particular attribute, of course) and their operations can be invoked.

This also holds true for notifications sent from MBeans in the remote agent. Notifications emitted by remote broadcasters will be sent through the RMI connection to their intended listeners. The details of how the notification is sent over the connection are unknown to both the broadcaster and the listener.

The Sample Producer/Consumer Application

In the remainder of this chapter, we will build and run a sample application that demonstrates each MBean instrumentation approach. The sections that follow look at the design of the application, where to obtain the source code, how to actually build and run the application, and how to monitor the application via a web browser.

Design

In this section, we will take a look at how the sample application is designed, so that you can better understand what is going on when you see it run. First, we will look at the pattern that is fundamental to the application's design. Then we will see how the pattern is implemented and what classes constitute the source code for the application.

The design pattern used in the application is a *monitor*. A monitor is a construct that coordinates activity between multiple threads in the system. In this pattern, the monitor coordinates activities between two categories of threads: *producer threads* and *consumer threads.* As you might imagine, a producer thread provides something that the consumer uses. That "something" is generically defined as a *unit of work*. This can be physically realized as anything relevant to a problem that is solved by this pattern.

For example, the unit of work might be an email message that is sent to the email system (the monitor) by the producer (an email client) and removed by the consumer (some agent on the incoming email server side). The producer might perform additional processing on the message before sending it to the email system, such as checking the spelling. By the same token, the consumer may perform additional processing of the message after removing it from the queue, such as applying an antivirus check. For this reason, we will refer to the pattern as "value-added producer/consumer." This pattern is shown in UML notation in Figure 1-9.

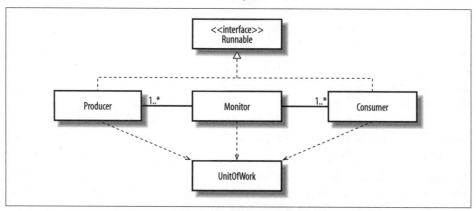

Figure 1-9. UML diagram showing the "value-added producer/consumer" pattern

As you can see in Figure 1-9, the producer and consumer are separated (decoupled) by the monitor. This pattern is best applied to systems that are inherently asynchronous in nature, where the producer and consumer are decoupled by varying degrees. This decoupling can be a separation of location as well as of synchronicity.

The implementation of the value-added producer/consumer pattern is shown in Figure 1-10. The classes in the diagram are implemented as Java classes. The stereotypes shown in the diagram are named according to the pattern shown in Figure 1-9.

Basic is the base class for all of the classes that make up the implementation (with the exception of WorkUnit, which represents the unit of work that is exchanged between Supplier and Consumer). Controller is a class that acts as the JMX agent and is responsible for creating the producer and consumer threads that run inside the application. Queue is a thread-safe queue that acts as the monitor. Producer threads place items in the queue in a thread-safe way, and consumer threads remove them. Worker is the base class for Supplier and Consumer, because much of their behavior is common.

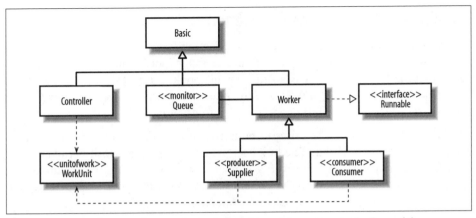

Figure 1-10. UML diagram showing the implementation of the pattern in the form of the application

In the sample application, the following resources can be managed:

- Controller
- Queue
- Supplier
- Consumer

I encourage you to look at the source code to see exactly what attributes and operations are on each of the management interfaces for these resources.

Source Code

The source code for the application is standalone with respect to each type of instrumentation approach. There are three versions of the application, each in its own package. The name of the package corresponds to the instrumentation approach. For example, with the exception of common classes such as GenericException, the application source code for standard MBeans is entirely contained in the standard package; thus, if you install the source code to *c:\jmxbook*, the path to the application source code for standard MBeans will be *c:\jmxbook\sample\standard*. All of the source code shares the contents of the exception package. Other than that, however, the application can be built and run independently of the other packages.

For each type of MBean, there is a Windows batch file and a Unix (Korn shell) script that builds and runs the code for that instrumentation strategy. The name of the script or batch file matches the instrumentation strategy: for example, the build script for dynamic MBeans is called *dynamic.sh*, and the batch file for building the source code for the version of the application instrumented as dynamic MBeans is called *dynamic.bat*. The major differences between the application versions are in the source code. The console output and the management view will show very little difference (other than output from the Ant build script) between the versions of the application.

Building and Running the Application

Before you can build and run the sample application (see "Source Code Availability" in the Preface for details on how to obtain the application's source code), you must download the JMX RI and Jakarta Ant. For this book, I used JMX RI 1.0.1 and Ant 1.4. You can obtain the JMX RI at *http://java.sun.com/products/JavaManagement/* and Jakarta Ant at *http://jakarta.apache.org/ant/index.html*.

The name of the build file Ant uses to build the application for all of the instrumentation strategies is *build.xml*. The build scripts are designed to work with very little modification on your part. However, you may have to modify either the build script or the Ant build file, depending on where you installed the JDK, the JMX RI, and Ant itself. Example 1-5 shows an excerpt from *build.xml*.

Example 1-5. Selected portions of the Ant build file for the application, build.xml

```
    .
    .
    .
<project name="jmxbook" default="standard" basedir=".">

<!-- Set global properties -->
<property name="source_root" value="c:\jmxbook\sample"/>
<property name="jmx_home" value="c:\jmx1.0.1"/>

<path id="project.general.class.path">
  <pathelement path="${jmx_home}\jmx\lib\jmxri.jar"/>
  <pathelement path="${jmx_home}\jmx\lib\jmxtools.jar"/>
  <pathelement path="."/>
</path>

<!-- Build the init target -->
<target name="init">
  <!-- create the time stamp -->
  <tstamp>
    <format property="build.start.time" pattern="MM/dd/yyyy hh:mm:ss aa"/>
  </tstamp>
  <echo message="Build started at ${build.start.time}..."/>
</target>

<!-- Build the exception target -->
<target name="build-exception" depends="init">
  <javac>
    <classpath refid="project.general.class.path"/>
    <src path="${source_root}"/>
    <include name="exception\*"/>
  </javac>
</target>

<!-- Build the "standard" target -->
<target name="build-standard" depends="build-exception">
```

Example 1-5. Selected portions of the Ant build file for the application, build.xml (continued)

```
  <javac>
    <classpath refid="project.general.class.path"/>
    <src path="${source_root}"/>
    <include name="standard\*"/>
  </javac>
</target>

<!-- Build the "dynamic" target -->
<target name="build-dynamic" depends="build-exception">
  <javac>
    <classpath refid="project.general.class.path"/>
    <src path="${source_root}"/>
    <include name="dynamic\*"/>
  </javac>
</target>

<!-- Build the "model" target -->
<target name="build-model" depends="build-exception">
  <javac>
    <classpath refid="project.general.class.path"/>
    <src path="${source_root}"/>
    <include name="model\*"/>
  </javac>
</target>
  .
  .
  .
</project>
```

As you can see, the Ant build file is an XML document. This is what sets Ant apart from other build utilities, such as *make*. Each component to be built using Ant is called a *target*. A target may have one or more dependent targets that must be built first, each of which may be dependent on other targets, and so on. Ant resolves these dependencies for you. A target is specified in an Ant build file as an XML tag called target and has the following format:

```
<target name="mytarget" depends="d1,d2">
```

in which case mytarget depends on targets d1 and d2, or:

```
<target name="mytarget">
```

if mytarget has no dependent targets. Let's look at the build-standard target from Example 1-5:

```
<!-- Build the "standard" target -->
<target name="build-standard" depends="build-exception">
  <javac>
    <classpath refid="project.general.class.path"/>
    <src path="${source_root}"/>
    <include name="standard\*"/>
  </javac>
</target>
```

You can see that the build-standard target depends on the build-exception target. Ant knows that there may be other dependencies, so it looks at build-exception:

```
<!-- Build the exception target -->
<target name="build-exception" depends="init">
  <javac>
    <classpath refid="project.general.class.path"/>
    <src path="${source_root}"/>
    <include name="exception\*"/>
  </javac>
</target>
```

and notices that build-exception depends on init. Ant then looks at init:

```
<target name="init">
  <!-- create the time stamp -->
  <tstamp>
    <format property="build.start.time" pattern="MM/dd/yyyy hh:mm:ss aa"/>
  </tstamp>
  <echo message="Build started at ${build.start.time}..."/>
</target>
```

Ant sees that init has no dependencies, so it begins the build. init is built first, followed by build-exception and finally build-standard. Notice the javac tag within build-standard and build-exception. This is known as an Ant *task*. A task is a Java class that executes within the JVM in which Ant is running (unless you tell Ant to fork a new process when executing the task). The javac task is the java compiler. The classpath, src, and include tags nested within the javac task tell the Java compiler what the CLASSPATH is, the root location of the *.java* files, and the packages (directories) to compile, respectively.

The application classes for each chapter in this book are built and run using either a batch file or a shell script. If you are running the application on Windows (as I did to produce the screen shots for this chapter), use the batch file (i.e., the *.bat* file). If you are running the application on Unix, use the shell script (i.e., the *.sh* file). Throughout the rest of this chapter, the examples will be Windows-based. There are two reasons for this. First, because of the popularity of Windows, it is likely that most developers will be running this operating system. Second, the differences in the behavior of the application when it is run on Windows versus Unix are negligible.

To build and run the application, type in the name of the batch file you want to run, based on the type of MBean instrumentation strategy you want to see in action. You will notice that there is no detectable difference between what you see when you run the build/run batch file and what you see in your browser (discussed in the next section), regardless of the instrumentation strategy. Suppose we want to run the standard MBean batch file, which will build and run the application as standard MBeans. Example 1-6 shows the batch file that builds the application.

Example 1-6. standard.bat, the batch file that builds the application as standard MBeans

```
@set TARGET_NAME=build-standard
@set JAVA_HOME=c:\jdk1.3.1
@set ANT_VERSION=1.4
@set ANT_HOME=c:\ant%ANT_VERSION%

@echo Starting Build ...

call %ANT_HOME%\bin\ant %TARGET_NAME%

if NOT "%ERRORLEVEL%"=="0" goto DONE

%JAVA_HOME%\bin\java sample.standard.Controller 100 150

:DONE
```

This batch file is very simple. Aside from setting a few environment variables, it does only two things: it builds the application by calling Ant, and, if that succeeds, it starts the application. Figure 1-11 shows the output of running the batch file. Recall our earlier discussion of how Ant resolves target dependencies; you'll see that the targets are built in the order described there.

Figure 1-11. Running the build/run batch file for standard MBeans

All of the batch files (*standard.bat*, *dynamic.bat*, and *model.bat*) operate as described below, but I've used *standard.bat* here for the purposes of illustration.

In each version of the application, Controller contains the *main()* method that starts the producer and consumer threads and is itself an MBean that can be managed and monitored. There are two command-line arguments to Controller's *main()* method: the work factor for the producer thread and the work factor for the consumer thread. Notice that in *standard.bat* values of 100 and 150, respectively, are specified for these arguments. I set these values for a reason: it is unlikely that you will find an application of the value-added producer/consumer pattern where the producer and consumer perform an equal amount of work. These command-line parameters to Controller allow you to simulate this asymmetry. When Controller is started, one producer thread and one consumer thread are created. However, Controller has a management method that allows you to start additional threads to balance out the workload (we will see how to do this later).

Figure 1-10 illustrates the relationship between the various classes in the application, where there is a single Queue object into which Supplier threads place WorkUnit objects and from which Consumer threads remove them. For a single unit of work, here is the flow of control:

1. The Supplier performs an amount of work N—where N is specified on the command line to Controller—and places a single WorkUnit object into the Queue.

2. The Consumer removes a single WorkUnit object from the Queue and performs an amount of work M—again, where M is specified on the command line to Controller.

These steps are repeated for each work unit.

 The work that is performed by Supplier and Consumer threads is to calculate prime numbers. The amount of work specified on the command line to Controller is the number of prime numbers to calculate for each WorkUnit. The Supplier calculates N primes, then places a WorkUnit object into the Queue. The Consumer removes a WorkUnit object from the Queue and then calculates M primes.

This section looked at how to run the sample application and briefly discussed what it is doing internally to simulate the production and consumption of units of work. I strongly encourage you to examine the source code for yourself to see the various attributes and operations available on the management interfaces of each resource in the application.

In the next section, we will look at how to use a web browser to monitor and manage the sample application's MBeans.

Monitoring and Managing the Application

Once the application is running, you can point your web browser to port 8090 (the default—you can change this, but if you do so, remember to point your browser to the new port number). Figure 1-12 shows the result of pointing my web browser (which happens to be Internet Explorer) to port 8090 after running *standard.bat*.

Remember the work factors that we specified on the command line to Controller for the producer and consumer threads? Because they are different (100 and 150,

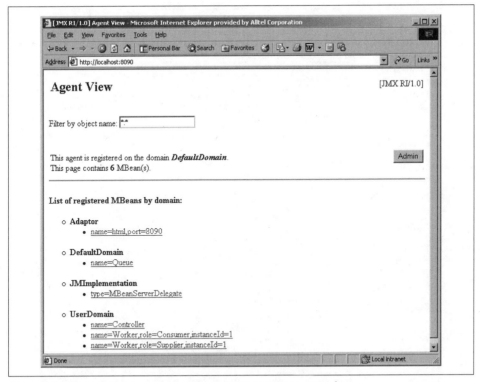

Figure 1-12. The management view of the application in Internet Explorer

respectively), and the producer thread does less work than the consumer thread for each work unit, I expect the Queue to always be full once the application reaches a steady state.

If I click on the Queue MBean in my browser, I see the screen shown in Figure 1-13. There are several interesting things about Figure 1-13. First, the AddWaitTime attribute is much larger than the RemoveWaitTime attribute. After processing 72 units of work (according to the NumberOfItemsProcessed attribute), the Supplier thread has waited a total of 3,421 milliseconds to add items to the Queue because it was full, whereas the Consumer thread has not had to wait at all to remove items (although, depending on which thread actually starts first, you may see a small amount of Consumer wait time). This is pretty much what we would expect, as the Supplier thread does only two-thirds the work of the Consumer thread.

Suppose we want to start another Consumer thread to pick up some of the slack of the other Consumer thread and balance things out a bit. For the moment, let's ignore the fact that we can control the amount of work each type of Worker thread can perform. In a real-world application, we would not have that luxury. As I mentioned earlier in this chapter, Controller acts as the JMX agent for the application, but it is also itself a managed resource (i.e., an MBean). If we look at the management interface of

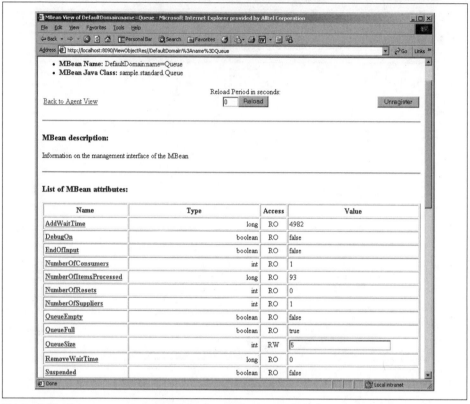

Figure 1-13. The management view of the Queue object

Controller, we'll see that there is a management operation to start new Worker threads, called *createWorker()*. Figure 1-14 shows the management view of the Controller MBean and its *createWorker()* operation.

There are two parameters to *createWorker()*: the first is a string that contains the worker type, and the second is the work factor that worker is to have (i.e., the number of primes calculated per unit of work). The valid values for the worker type are "Supplier" and "Consumer". We want to create a new Consumer thread with the same work factor as the currently running Consumer thread, so we set these parameters to Consumer and 150, respectively. Once we have entered the parameters for the management operation into the text boxes, as shown in Figure 1-14, we click the *createWorker* button to invoke the management operation. If the operation succeeds, we will see a screen that looks like Figure 1-15.

We would now expect that activity in the Queue has balanced out somewhat, and we would expect to start seeing the Supplier wait, as we now have two Consumer threads at work. Figure 1-16 shows the management view of the Queue after we start the second Consumer thread.

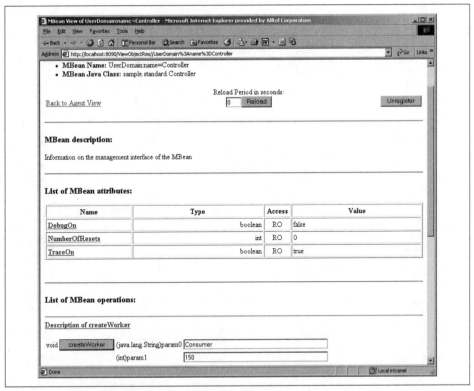

Figure 1-14. The management view of Controller showing the createWorker() operation

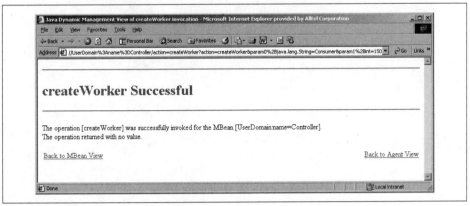

Figure 1-15. The screen we see once createWorker() has successfully been invoked

Notice that after processing 1,013 units of work (as we see from the NumberOfItems-Processed attribute), the Consumer threads have waited nearly 7 times as long as the Supplier thread. Through the use of management operations, we can give an operator at a management console the ability to tune our application at runtime.

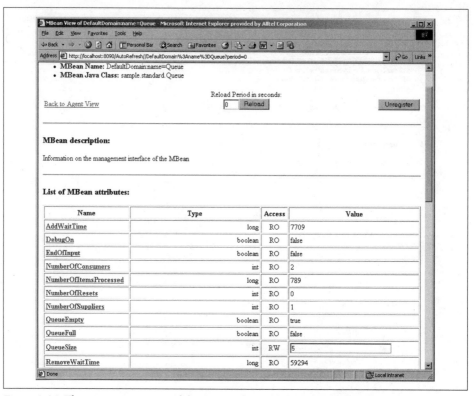

Figure 1-16. The management view of the Queue after starting a second Consumer thread

CHAPTER 2

Standard MBeans

By far the most straightforward type of MBean to create, standard MBeans are a logical starting place for our voyage into the world of JMX. In this chapter, we will begin by defining a management interface, then we will look at the design patterns we must use when building standard MBeans. Next, we will discuss some of the issues involved when using inheritance among standard MBean classes. Then we will look at some common pitfalls of using standard MBeans that might leave you scratching your head, wondering why your MBeans aren't working as expected. Finally, we will discuss some advanced topics and things to consider when creating standard MBeans. This chapter includes several examples from the sample application that is used throughout this book. When you have completed this chapter, you should be able to create standard MBeans and understand the issues involved in doing so.

What Is a Management Interface?

The idea of a management interface revolves around the notion of an application resource, which is any abstraction within an application that provides value. A resource can be, for example, a business component of the application, an infrastructure component such as a cache or queue, or even the application itself. With respect to JMX (and more broadly, system management), only those resources that must be managed are significant. Each resource that is to be managed must provide a management interface, which consists of the attributes and operations it exposes so that it can be monitored and controlled by a management application.

For example, suppose a resource we wish to manage in our application is a queue. A queue is generally used to temporarily store a logical unit of work provided by a supplier until that unit of work is removed from the queue by a consumer for further processing. This is typically done asynchronously, via a multithreaded design, so the queue must also be thread-safe. Let's suppose there is a single supplier thread in the application and a single consumer thread, and that the queue is thread-safe, so that the supplier will wait to add an item to the queue if it is full (and conversely, the consumer will wait on the queue to remove an item if the queue is empty). In monitoring the queue, we want to know two things:

- How long has the supplier waited (i.e., the accumulated wait time) to add an item to the queue because the queue is full?
- How long has the consumer waited to remove an item from the queue because the queue is empty?

Because these two pieces of information are important to us for monitoring the application, it makes sense that we expose them as two attributes on the management interface of the queue. Of course, the queue must be written so that this information is captured, so that it can be exposed in the first place! But that is very straightforward to do and will be handled by our application's Queue class.

 I won't spend a lot of time explaining all of the attributes and operations exposed on the management interface of the queue, because the goal of this chapter is to illustrate the mechanics and theory of standard MBeans, not how to design queues.

One other thing to consider is whether the values of these attributes are in milliseconds (the clock tick count, on most systems). If so, and if our application is long-running, we should probably use a long as the data type for these attributes to allow them to contain very large values.

Now that we have decided to expose these two attributes, we must decide whether to make them read-only, write-only, or read/write when we expose them on the management interface. It doesn't make much sense for these attributes to be write-only (because then we could only set them and not look at their values at any particular point in time), so we rule that option out right away. Making these attributes readable makes sense, but should we allow the management application to set their values? We could allow the management application to reset both of these values to zero by exposing an operation to handle this action, thus preventing a user of the management application from setting these values to something unreasonable.

The management interface for our queue now has the following:

- A read-only attribute whose value is the total accumulated time spent by the supplier waiting to add a unit of work to the queue because the queue is full
- A read-only attribute whose value is the total accumulated time spent by the consumer waiting to remove a unit of work from the queue because the queue is empty
- An operation that resets both attributes to zero

We may also want to be able to manage the size of the queue. To allow this, we can define an attribute on the queue and expose that attribute on the management interface as a read/write attribute. This allows us to view the current size of the queue and to modify that value to tweak the queue for maximum performance at runtime. In addition, we might be interested in the total number of work units processed by the queue, so that we can get an idea of the throughput of the application with respect to any particular instance of our queue. As long as it makes sense and fits in with the design of the queue, the sky's the limit on what we can expose on our queue's management interface. Table 2-1 summarizes the attributes we will expose on our Queue resource.

Table 2-1. Attributes exposed for management on the Queue class

Name	Data type	Read/write
Add Wait Time	`long`	Read-only
Remove Wait Time	`long`	Read-only
Queue Size	`int`	Read/write
Number of Items Processed	`long`	Read-only
Queue Full	`boolean`	Read-only
Queue Empty	`boolean`	Read-only
Suspended	`boolean`	Read-only
Number of Suppliers	`int`	Read-only
Number of Consumers	`int`	Read-only

These attributes will be discussed in detail in the next section, where we will actually implement the queue's management interface as a standard MBean.

Next, let's consider the operations to expose on the management interface of the Queue class. We touched briefly on the reset operation earlier in this chapter. Other operations we may want to include offer the management application the ability to suspend and resume activity in the queue. This allows the management application to halt processing so that, for example, an operator can look at a "snapshot" of what is happening inside the queue. It may also be helpful for the operator to be able to turn on and off tracing. Table 2-2 summarizes the operations on our queue's management interface.

Table 2-2. Operations exposed for management on the Queue class

Name	Purpose
Reset	Resets the state of the queue
Suspend	Suspends activity in the queue; all suppliers and consumers sleep until Resume is called
Resume	Signals to sleeping suppliers and consumers that activity may continue
Enable Tracing	Turns on any tracing done by the queue
Disable Tracing	Turns off tracing

Now that we have defined the management interface for our Queue class, it's time to see how to instrument our class as a standard MBean using the design patterns in the JMX specification.

How Do Standard MBeans Work?

In this section, we will learn how to instrument a Java class as a standard MBean. We will first look at how to describe the management interface according to the JMX design patterns for standard MBeans. Then we will look at how to implement the MBean interface on the Queue class touched on earlier in this chapter. Many examples will be provided. It is here that we will examine all of the classes that make up the application, showing inheritance patterns and other cool standard MBean miscellany. We will also look at the Controller class's *main()* routine, which is what drives the application, and we will discuss how to register MBeans with the MBean server, how to register and use the HTML Adaptor server, and how to build and run the example.

Describing the Management Interface

JMX provides us with a set of patterns to follow when instrumenting our application resources as standard MBeans. If we follow these patterns exactly as they are set out in the specification, our standard MBeans are said to be *compliant*. If we don't correctly follow the patterns, the MBean server (part of the reference implementation; we'll discuss the MBean server later in this chapter) will declare our MBean as *noncompliant* by throwing a javax.management.NotCompliantMBeanException at the agent that attempts to register the MBean. However, it is possible for us to correctly follow the patterns but still not expose the correct management interface on our standard MBean. We will also look at that case in this section.

There are three patterns you must follow when instrumenting your resources as standard MBeans:

- The management interface of the resource must have the same name as the resource's Java class, followed by "MBean"; it must be defined as a Java interface; and it must be implemented by the resource to be managed using the implements keyword.
- The implementing class must contain at least one public constructor.
- Getters and setters for attributes on the management interface must follow strict naming conventions.

Each of these patterns is discussed in detail in this section.

Pattern #1: Defining, naming, and implementing the MBean interface

The management interface must be defined using the Java interface keyword, it must have public visibility, and it must be strictly named. Earlier in this chapter, we looked at the thought process we might go through to define a management interface for a queue. Suppose the name of this class is Queue. Its standard MBean management interface must be defined as:

```
public interface QueueMBean {
// management interface goes here. . .
}
```

The Queue class, in turn, must implement the QueueMBean interface using the Java implements keyword:

```
public class Queue implements QueueMBean {
// implementation of QueueMBean
// and other stuff here. . .
}
```

The name of the MBean interface is case-sensitive. For example, QueueMbean is not the same as QueueMBean. Of course, the compiler will help you if you "fat-finger" the spelling of the interface in either the interface definition or the implementation. However, if you use the same misspelling in both, the compiler will chug merrily along and produce perfectly runnable bytecode. Only when you attempt to register your MBean will you receive a NotCompliantMBeanException exception!

The management interface is contained in its own *.java* file and must have the same name as its corresponding interface. Thus, every standard MBean requires at least two source code files: one for the interface and one for the class that implements the interface.

Another example from the application we use throughout this book is the Worker class. Its management interface is defined as:

```
public interface WorkerMBean {
// . . .
}
```

The Worker class, in turn, implements this interface as:

```
public class Worker implements WorkerMBean {
// . . .
}
```

 The JMX specification states that the class that implements the MBean interface must be declared public and be a concrete (i.e., not abstract) class. However, using the JMX 1.0 RI, I was able to instantiate, register, and manage an MBean with only package-level visibility. This is most likely an oversight in the RI. You should not count on being able to do this in future versions of the RI, or in other JMX implementations, because this behavior is not supported by the specification.

Pattern #2: Provide at least one public constructor

The class that implements the MBean interface must have at least one constructor declared with public visibility. This class may have any number of public constructors, but it must have *at least* one. If you do not provide a constructor, the compiler will generate a no-argument constructor with public visibility. This will work fine for your MBeans, but I recommend that you explicitly declare a no-argument constructor for these cases, as your code will follow the rule and be more readable as well. Continuing with the code snippets from earlier, then, our Queue class would look like:

```
public class Queue implements QueueMBean {
  public Queue( ) {
    // do something here. . .
  }
  // other class methods and management interface
  // implementation. . .
}
```

However, the Queue class might not have a no-argument constructor at all:

```
public class Queue implements QueueMBean {
  // no no-arg constructor provided, that's okay. . .
  public Queue(int queueSize) {
    // do something custom here. . .
  }
  // other class methods and management interface
  // implementation. . .
}
```

and still be a compliant MBean, because it provides a public constructor.

Pattern #3: Attributes and how to name their getters and setters

When defining an attribute on the management interface, you must follow strict naming standards. If the attribute is readable, it must be declared on the interface (and subsequently implemented) as *getAttributeName( )*, where *AttributeName* is the name of the attribute you want to expose, and take no parameters. This method is called a *getter*. Table 2-1 showed some of the attributes we plan to expose on the Queue class. As an example, we would define the Add Wait Time attribute on the management interface as:

```
public interface QueueMBean {
  public long getAddWaitTime( );
  // . . .
}
```

 Notice the use of "camel case" in the naming of our attribute. If an attribute's name consists of multiple words, the words are placed together and the first letter of each word is capitalized. This is a fairly common practice and will be used throughout this book.

For boolean values, preceding the attribute name with "is" is a common idiom and one that is acceptable according to the JMX standard MBean design patterns. From Table 2-1, notice that we have a boolean attribute called Suspended. We would define this attribute on the management interface as:

```
public interface QueueMBean {
  public long getAddWaitTime( );
  // . . .
```

```
public boolean isSuspended( );
// . . .
}
```

If an attribute is writable, the naming pattern is similar to that for readable attributes, only the word "get" is replaced with "set," and the attribute takes a single parameter whose type is that of the attribute to be set. This method is called a *setter*. For example, Table 2-1 shows a readable and writable attribute called QueueSize. We would define this attribute on the management interface as:

```
public interface QueueMBean {
  public long getAddWaitTime( );
  // . . .
  public boolean isSuspended( );
  // . . .
  public int getQueueSize( );
  public void setQueueSize(int value);
  // . . .
}
```

There are two rules about setters:

- The setter can take only a single parameter. If you unintentionally provide a second parameter to what you thought you were coding as a setter, the MBean server will expose your "setter" as an operation.

- The parameter types must be the same for read/write attributes, or your management interface will not be what you expect. In fact, if you have a read/write attribute where the getter returns a different data type than the setter takes as a parameter, the setter controls. For example, suppose that I mistakenly coded the setter for QueueSize to take a short data type. My management interface would then look like:

```
public interface QueueMBean {
  public long getAddWaitTime( );
  // . . .
  public boolean isSuspended( );
  // . . .
  public int getQueueSize( );
  public void setQueueSize(short value);
  // . . .
}
```

Strangely enough, what I have actually exposed is a single write-only attribute called QueueSize, of type short! Clearly, that is not what I intended. Of course, remember that with standard MBeans, the Java compiler can catch some of these mistakes for you. Let's say that I made this particular mistake on the interface definition, but on the implementing class I used the proper int type on my setter. The compiler would tell me that I should declare the implementing class abstract, because it doesn't define the setter that takes the short! That is one advantage of standard MBeans over other MBean types—the compiler can help you find mistakes before they turn into nasty bugs.

Using the information from Tables 2-1 and 2-2, the management interface is shown in Example 2-1.

Example 2-1. The QueueMBean interface

```
public interface QueueMBean {
  // attributes
  public long getAddWaitTime( );
  public long getRemoveWaitTime( );
  public int getQueueSize( );
  public void setQueueSize(int value);
  public long getNumberOfItemsProcessed( );
  public boolean isQueueFull( );
  public boolean isQueueEmpty( );
  public boolean isSuspended( );
  public int getNumberOfSuppliers( );
  public int getNumberOfConsumers( );
  // operations
  public void reset( );
  public void suspend( );
  public void resume( );
  public void enableTracing( );
  public void disableTracing( );
}
```

A word about introspection

Introspection literally means to "look inside" and is performed by the MBean server to ensure compliance on the part of your MBeans when they are registered. Because it is possible to write Java code that cleanly compiles and executes but does not follow the standard MBean design patterns we discussed earlier, the MBean server looks inside your MBean to make sure you followed the patterns correctly.

When your MBean is registered by the agent, the MBean server uses Java's reflection API to crawl around inside the MBean and make sure that the three design patterns we discussed earlier were followed. If they were, your MBean is compliant and its registration proceeds. If not, the MBean server throws an exception at the agent.

Introspection takes place only when your MBean is registered by the agent. Depending on the code paths your application takes when instantiating your MBean classes, the notification (via an exception) that one of your MBeans is not compliant will appear only when the MBean is registered.

Standard MBean Inheritance Patterns

As you are probably aware, inheritance in Java is achieved through the use of the extends keyword. When it comes to exposing a management interface, the MBean server's introspection enforces certain rules. There are some fundamental differences between Java inheritance and management interface inheritance. This section will spell out those differences.

With respect to inheritance, certain patterns are enforced by the MBean server at introspection time. If you are to successfully expose the intended management interface on your MBeans, it is important that you understand these patterns. While an MBean may inherit the public (and protected) attributes and operations of its parent class, it will not necessarily inherit its management interface.

There are five basic patterns of MBean inheritance. We will discuss each of them in this section. We will also introduce and explain the application MBean interfaces in this section, starting with the top of the inheritance hierarchy, `BasicMBean`. We will use UML diagrams to reduce ambiguity.

`BasicMBean` is the management interface that all MBeans in the inheritance graph will expose and in this section we will see exactly how to go about doing that. Along the way, I'll point out some areas to watch out for and offer some tips for avoiding potential mistakes. Example 2-2 shows the source listing for `BasicMBean`.

Example 2-2. The BasicMBean interface

```
package sample.standard;

public interface BasicMBean {
  // attributes
  public boolean isTraceOn();
  public boolean isDebugOn();
  public int getNumberOfResets();
  // operations
  public void enableTracing();
  public void disableTracing();
  public void enableDebugging();
  public void disableDebugging();
  public void reset();
}
```

Pattern #1: Basic inheritance

In the basic inheritance pattern, a class implements an MBean interface. This pattern is shown in UML notation in Figure 2-1.

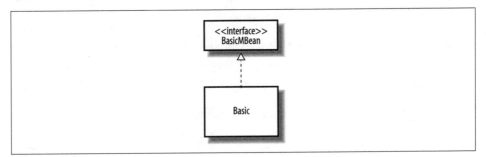

Figure 2-1. UML notation for pattern #1

In source code, this pattern is implemented using the `implements` keyword:

```
public class Basic implements BasicMBean {
// implementation of BasicMBean and other stuff. . .
}
```

Use of the `implements` keyword was explained in the previous section.

Pattern #2: Simple inheritance

With simple inheritance, one class extends another class that implements an MBean interface. This relationship is shown in Figure 2-2.

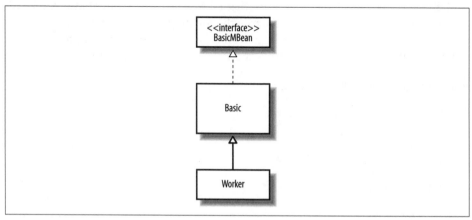

Figure 2-2. UML notation for pattern #2

In source code, this pattern is implemented using the extends keyword:

```
public class Worker extends Basic {
// implementation of Worker here. . .
}
```

In this pattern, the management interface exposed by `Worker` is `BasicMBean`. To a management application, `Worker` will appear to be a `BasicMBean`, complete with all of its attributes and operations. In other words, the management interface of `Worker` is the same as that of `Basic`.

Pattern #3: Simple inheritance with child class implementing an MBean interface

Of course, `Worker` could implement its own MBean interface and still extend `Basic`. The `WorkerMBean` interface is shown in Example 2-3.

Example 2-3. WorkerMBean management interface definition

```
package sample.standard;

public interface WorkerMBean {
```

Example 2-3. WorkerMBean management interface definition (continued)

```
// attributes
public String getWorkerName( );
public void setWorkerName(String name);
public int getWorkFactor( );
public long getNumberOfUnitsProcessed( );
public float getAverageUnitProcessingTime( );
public boolean isSuspended( );
// operations
public void stop( );
public void suspend( );
public void resume( );
}
```

According to this pattern, Worker would continue to extend Basic but would now explicitly expose its own MBean interface:

```
public class Worker extends Basic implements WorkerMBean {
// implementation of WorkerMBean. . .
}
```

This pattern is shown in UML notation in Figure 2-3.

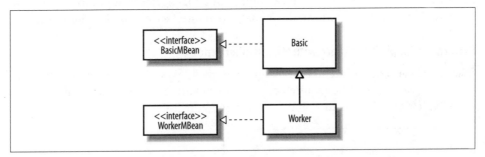

Figure 2-3. UML notation for pattern #3

After looking at pattern #3, you may think that the management interface exposed by Worker is the union of BasicMBean and WorkerMBean. However, this is not the case. When this pattern is used, the introspection performed by the MBean server proceeds up the MBean interface inheritance graph, not the implementing inheritance graph. In Example 2-3, we see that WorkerMBean stands alone at the top of the inheritance graph. Regardless of the fact that Worker extends Basic (which implements BasicMBean), the management interface exposed proceeds no further than WorkerMBean. Thus, when this pattern is used, the management interface exposed by Worker is that shown in Example 2-3. However, should a reference to Worker be obtained, methods and attribute getters and setters inherited from Basic can be invoked (Java inheritance still works!). These inherited methods and attributes are not available to a management application, though, because they are not on the management interface.

Note also that any time a class implements an MBean interface that is at the top of an MBean hierarchy, the management interface exposed by that class is that MBean interface, regardless of any attributes and methods available to that class through Java inheritance. For example, suppose I have a child class of Worker called Supplier and Supplier implements SupplierMBean, which extends nothing:

```
public interface SupplierMBean {
// management interface here. . .
}
.
.
.
public class Supplier extends Worker implements SupplierMBean {
}
```

Again, you might think that the management interface exposed by Supplier is the union of BasicMBean, WorkerMBean, and SupplierMBean. However, this is not the case. Recall that in the earlier example where Worker extended Basic but implemented WorkerMBean, the management interface exposed was WorkerMBean. Similarly, in this case, the management interface exposed by Supplier is SupplierMBean. Java inheritance still works, and a reference to Supplier will give the holder of that reference access all the way up the inheritance graph, but a management application will have access only to those methods on the management interface exposed by Supplier.

Pattern #4: Simple inheritance with MBean inheritance

If WorkerMBean were to extend BasicMBean, pattern #3 would become pattern #4, and no further work would be required on the part of Worker to implement any methods from BasicMBean. This relationship is shown in Figure 2-4.

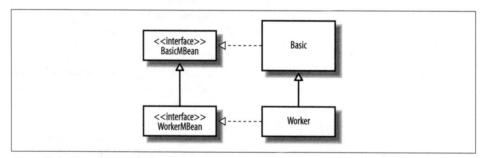

Figure 2-4. UML notation for pattern #4

The MBean interface shown in Example 2-3 would simply need to be defined as:

```
public interface WorkerMBean extends BasicMBean {
// . . .
}
```

in order to implement this pattern. No code changes to Worker are required. Now, however, the management interface exposed by Worker is the union of BasicMBean and WorkerMBean.

Suppose that the Supplier class from pattern #3 has an MBean interface that extends WorkerMBean:

```
public interface SupplierMBean extends WorkerMBean {
// . . .
}
```

This relationship is shown in UML notation in Figure 2-5.

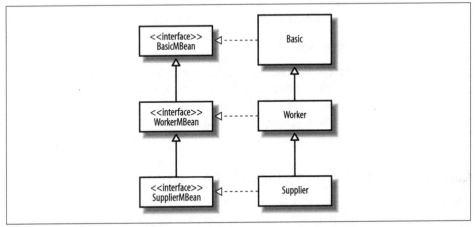

Figure 2-5. UML notation for a more complicated derivative of pattern #4

When the MBean server performs introspection, it will expose as the management interface all of the MBean interfaces until the top of the MBean inheritance graph is reached. This means that the management interface exposed by Supplier is the union of BasicMBean, WorkerMBean, and SupplierMBean.

The key to using this pattern is to remember that the MBean server uses MBean inheritance in addition to Java inheritance to determine the management interface. In other words, if you want your MBean interface to expose the management interface, you simply need to use the extends keyword when defining your MBean interface. Then your MBean interface will take advantage of Java inheritance as well.

Pattern #5: Compiler-enforced management interface inheritance

Suppose that, in pattern #4, Worker implements WorkerMBean but does not extend Basic. What then? Figure 2-6 shows this pattern in UML notation.

Clearly, the compiler will not allow Worker to inherit an interface without implementing it. In pattern #4, because Worker extended Basic, BasicMBean came along for free through Java inheritance. But if Worker does not extend Basic, it is forced to implement BasicMBean, because WorkerMBean extends BasicMBean.

This may sound like an oversight at first, but it really isn't. This pattern allows you to customize the implementation of management interfaces while keeping the definitions of those interfaces semantically consistent. Carrying the Worker example further,

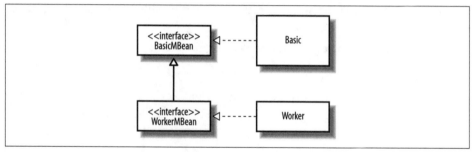

Figure 2-6. UML notation for pattern #5

suppose that you want the WorkerMBean management interface to be semantically identical to the union of WorkerMBean and BasicMBean. Logically, WorkerMBean should extend BasicMBean. However, suppose that you want to vary the implementation of BasicMBean provided by Basic. Using this pattern allows you to do this. And if you forget to implement anything from BasicMBean, the compiler will tell you!

Common Mistakes Not Caught by Introspection

The MBean server will catch and report most mistakes that you make in applying the standard MBean design patterns. However, there are mistakes you can make when applying the patterns that result in an MBean that is technically compliant but does not function as you intended. In this section, we will look at some of the most common mistakes you can make when instrumenting your application resources as standard MBeans that are not caught and reported by the MBean server. These mistakes are not caught by the Java compiler, either; your MBean simply will not work correctly. This section should aid you in troubleshooting the problem.

Mistake #1: MBean interface not given public visibility

This mistake is not caught by the compiler or reported by the MBean server. Suppose we mistakenly left off the public keyword from the interface definition for BasicMBean, using:

```
interface BasicMBean {
// . . .
}
```

instead of:

```
public interface BasicMBean {
// . . .
}
```

The Basic class implements BasicMBean as usual, and is registered by the agent:

```
public class Basic implements BasicMBean {
// . . .
}
```

To the MBean server, this MBean is compliant and is registered with no exceptions thrown. However, when the MBean server is asked to return the state of the MBean through its management interface, none of the attributes or operations can be accessed or invoked, respectively. A `javax.management.ReflectionException` is thrown by the MBean server at that time.

Mistake #2: Wrong return value type

The return value type of a getter must be never be void. Suppose we have a getter that is defined as:

```
public interface QueueMBean {
// . . .
  public void getQueueSize( );
  public void setQueueSize(int value);
// . . .
}
```

In this example, the intended getter method is not considered by the MBean server to be a getter at all and instead is exposed as an operation on the management interface. A proper getter must return the type of its attribute.

The return value of a setter, however, *must* be void. This mistake is not caught by the compiler or reported by the MBean server, and it produces some pretty strange results. Example 2-1 showed the management interface for the Queue class. Notice the read/write attribute QueueSize:

```
public interface QueueMBean {
// . . .
  public int getQueueSize( );
  public void setQueueSize(int);
// . . .
}
```

Suppose we provided a return value for *setQueueSize( )*:

```
public interface QueueMBean {
// . . .
  public int getQueueSize( );
  public int setQueueSize(int value);
// . . .
}
```

When the MBean server performs its introspection, it sees the *getQueueSize( )* method, indicating a readable attribute called QueueSize. It also notices a *setQueueSize( )* method that takes the correct number of parameters for a setter but also provides a return value. Because a setter cannot return a value, the MBean server interprets the method as a management interface operation instead of as an attribute setter. Thus, in our example, a read-only attribute called QueueSize and an operation called *setQueueSize( )* that takes an int parameter and returns an int would be exposed. (Note that the choice of int as the return value in this example was purely arbitrary. This mistake would happen if we had used any other type as well.)

If the management interface for your MBean does not show up as you expected, check the return values of all of the setter methods on your MBean interface. Any setter methods that return a value of any type other than void will be exposed as operations called *setSomething()*, where *Something* is the name of the attribute. Remember, a proper setter must return void!

What if the return value type of the getter is different from the parameter type of the setter? This is probably the least common mistake, as it is usually the result of mistyping the declaration of either the getter or the setter. Because the declaration must be typed twice (unless you copy the declaration from the interface and paste it into the implementing class), this mistake is not likely to occur often. However, because it has baffling results, I wanted to mention it here. Suppose you mistakenly define the management interface as:

```
public interface QueueMBean {
// . . .
  public int getQueueSize();
  public void setQueueSize(long value);
// . . .
}
```

Do you see the problem? Notice that the parameter type to the setter is a long. This interface definition for the QueueSize attribute certainly follows the rules: the getter takes no parameters and returns a value, while the setter returns void and takes only one parameter.

So what do you suppose is exposed as the management interface? In the JMX 1.0 RI, the management interface exposed is a write-only attribute of type long. That's it—there is no getter. Because of the conflicting types, the MBean server has to choose what is exposed, and the setter wins. Exactly what is exposed in the JMX you use depends on how the MBean server's introspection is implemented. However, the point is the same: make sure the parameter type of the setter and the return type of the getter match!

Mistake #3: Wrong number of parameters

Suppose we define a getter that takes an argument on the management interface:

```
public interface QueueMBean {
// . . .
  public int getQueueSize(int value);
  public void setQueueSize(int value);
// . . .
}
```

When the MBean server performs its introspection, it will detect that *getQueueSize()* takes a parameter and will expose it as a management operation instead of as the getter for the QueueSize attribute. A proper getter must take *zero* arguments.

A setter must take only one argument, and that argument must be of the type of the attribute it is to set. Suppose that the management interface is defined as:

```
public interface QueueMBean {
// . . .
  public int getQueueSize( );
  public void setQueueSize(int value, char someOtherValue);
// . . .
}
```

When the MBean server performs its introspection, it exposes a read-only attribute called QueueSize and an operation called *setQueueSize( )* that takes an int and a char parameter and returns void.

If the management interface for your MBean does not appear as you expected, check the number of arguments to all of the setter methods on the MBean interface. Remember, a proper setter must take only one parameter!

Implementing the MBean Interface

In this section, we will see how to implement MBean interfaces and will take a look at the application that is used throughout this book. Implementing the MBean interface is actually very straightforward, as we'll see.

The classes we will use in this chapter and their relationships to one another are shown in UML notation in Figure 2-7.

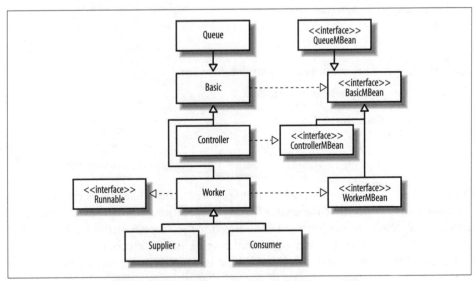

Figure 2-7. UML notation for the application classes used in this chapter

As we saw in design pattern #1, we must implement the MBean interface on the appropriately named class using the implements keyword. For the sake of review, let's take a quick look at how to do this. Example 2-2 showed the BasicMBean management interface definition. The syntax to implement this interface on the Basic class is:

```
public class Basic implements BasicMBean {
  // . . .
}
```

Notice that this interface has only getters (i.e., all attributes are read-only). Because the implementation of the getters will be hidden behind the MBean interface, we are free to implement them however we choose, as long as the implicit contract provided by the interface is obeyed. However, the most common way to implement a getter is to declare a private instance variable on the class and simply return the value of that member variable when the getter is invoked:

```
public class Basic implements BasicMBean {
  // . . .
  private boolean _traceOn;
  private int _numberOfResets;

  public boolean isTraceOn() {
    return _traceOn;
  }
  // . . .
  public int getNumberOfResets() {
    return _numberOfResets;
  }
  // . . .
}
```

Implementing an operation is equally straightforward:

```
public class Basic implements BasicMBean {
  // . . .
  public enableTracing() {
    _traceOn = true;
  }
  // . . .
}
```

When implementing the operation, we simply write code that makes the operation do something. Notice that the *enableTracing()* operation shown above resembles a setter. Why didn't we simply provide a setter for the TraceOn attribute? Notice that *enableTracing()* acts as a setter—it sets the value of the attribute—but with one important difference: it only sets the attribute to true. A setter can set the value to any value (within language limits, of course) that is acceptable for the data type of the attribute.

The full source listing of the Basic class is shown in Example 2-4.

Example 2-4. Full source listing for Basic class

```
package sample.standard;

public abstract class Basic implements BasicMBean {
  // backing stores
  private boolean _traceOn;
  private boolean _debugOn;
  private int _numberOfResets;
  // not on management interface
  public void setNumberOfResets(int value) {
    _numberOfResets = value;
  }
  // attributes on management interface
  public boolean isTraceOn() {
    return _traceOn;
  }
  public boolean isDebugOn() {
    return _debugOn;
  }
  public int getNumberOfResets() {
    return _numberOfResets;
  }
  // operations on management interface
  public void enableTracing() {
    _traceOn = true;
  }
  public void disableTracing() {
    _traceOn = false;
  }
  public void enableDebugging() {
    _debugOn = true;
  }
  public void disableDebugging() {
    _debugOn = false;
  }
  public abstract void reset();
}
```

Each child class of Basic must provide its own implementation of *reset()*. For this reason, there is a public setter (this setter also could have been protected or friendly) for the NumberOfResets attribute. Notice, however, that *setNumberOfResets()* is not included on the BasicMBean interface and hence is not part of the management interface of the MBean.

While simply returning the value of a member variable of the same type as the attribute for which the getter is provided is the most common way of writing a getter, it is not the only way. For example, without changing the interface, we might implement NumberOfResets as:

```
public class Basic implements BasicMBean {
  // . . .
```

```
    private Integer _numberOfResets = new Integer(0);
// . . .
    public void setNumberOfResets(int value) {
      _numberOfResets = new Integer(value);
    }
// . . .
    public int getNumberOfResets( ) {
      return _numberOfResets.intValue( );
    }
// . . .
}
```

Notice that in this code snippet, the backing store for the `NumberOfResets` attribute is a `java.lang.Integer` object. When *getNumberOfResets()* is called, we simply return *intValue()* on the `Integer` object. Again, the MBean interface serves as the contract between the MBean server, a management application, and your MBean. As long as your MBean implementation obeys the MBean interface, you are free to implement the interface however you choose.

A getter doesn't have to be that simple, however. For example, a getter can also be a calculated quantity. Consider the declaration of the `WorkerMBean` interface in Example 2-3. Notice the read-only attribute `AverageUnitProcessingTime`, which is of type float:

```
public class Worker extends Basic implements WorkerMBean {
// . . .
    private long _totalProcessingTime;
    private long _numberOfUnitsProcessed;
    public getNumberOfUnitsProcessed( ) {
      return _numberOfUnitsProcessed;
    }
    public float getAverageUnitProcessingTime( ) {
      return (_numberOfUnitsProcessed > 0)
        ? (float)_totalProcessingTime / (float)_numberOfUnitsProcessed
        : 0.0f;
    }
    // . . .
}
```

In designing the sample code, I decided to calculate the elapsed system time required to process a work unit and accumulate it in a private instance variable of type `long` called `_totalProcessingTime`. Then, when *getAverageUnitProcessingTime()* is called, the average is calculated by dividing `_totalProcessingTime` by the number of units processed so far (taking care not to divide by zero if no units have been processed).

Implementing a setter is equally straightforward. Consider the `WorkerName` attribute on `WorkerMBean` (see Example 2-3):

```
public class Worker extends Basic implements WorkerMBean {
// . . .
    private String _workerName;
```

```
    public String getWorkerName( ) {
      return _workerName;
    }
    public void setWorkerName(String value) {
      _workerName = value;
    }
  // . . .
  }
```

Consider the needs of your application before implementing your setters. Depending on how robust I want to make the implementation, the implementation of *setWorkerName()* shown above may be sufficient. However, I might want to set the value only if the new value is not a null reference, in which case I would make the following modification:

```
public class Worker extends Basic implements WorkerMBean {
  // . . .
    private String _workerName;
    public String getWorkerName( ) {
      return _workerName;
    }
    public void setWorkerName(String value) {
      if (value != null)
        _workerName = value;
    }
  // . . .
  }
```

An example of a more complicated setter is *setQueueSize()*, for the Queue class. This setter allows a management application to dynamically alter the size of the queue, so, as you can imagine, it is not as straightforward as simply setting an attribute value. Here is the code for *setQueueSize()*:

```
public class Queue extends Basic implements QueueMBean {
  // . . .
    public synchronized void setQueueSize(int value) {
      if (!_suspended) {
        if (value > _backingStore.length) {
          Object[] newStore = new Object[value];
          System.arraycopy(_backingStore, 0, newStore, 0, _backingStore.length);
        }
      }
      notifyAll( );
    }
  // . . .
  }
```

This code allows the queue to grow but not to shrink. Essentially, what this setter does is this: if activity in the queue is not currently suspended, and if the new queue size is greater than the current size, a new Object array is allocated and copied, then any threads in the wait state are signaled to become runnable. It's not too complicated, but it's certainly not as simple as just setting an instance variable's value.

Throwing Exceptions from Your MBeans

There will be times when you need to throw an exception from your MBeans—for example, when a setter needs to report that a bad value has been passed. Suppose that the setter for the QueueSize attribute on the Queue class needs to report when an attempt is made to shrink the queue (remember, the queue is allowed only to grow). If I want to throw such an exception, I have to change the declaration on the MBean interface:

```
public interface QueueMBean extends BasicMBean {
// . . .
  public setQueueSize(int value) throws Exception;
// . . .
}
```

as well as the implementing class:

```
// . . .
import sample.exception.*;
// . . .
public class Queue extends Basic implements QueueMBean {
// . . .
  public synchronized setQueueSize(int value) throws Exception {
    if (!_suspended) {
      if (value > _backingStore.length) {
        Object[] newStore = new Object[value];
        System.arraycopy(_backingStore, 0, newStore, 0, _backingStore.length);
      }
      else {
        throw new GenericException("Queue.setQueueSize( ): ERROR: " +
          "Queue size may not be set less than the current size of " +
          this.getQueueSize() + ". The value of " + value + " is invalid.");
      }
    }
    notifyAll( );
  }
}
```

If we attempt to set the value of the queue to be less than its current size (i.e., to shrink the queue), an exception containing a message describing the mistake will be thrown to the management application.

It is perfectly fine to use a user-defined exception. In this example, I used one called GenericException, located in the sample.exception package:

```
package sample.exception;

public class GenericException extends Exception {
  public GenericException(String message) {
    super(message);
  }
}
```

The Driver Program: Controller.main( )

As its name implies, Controller is the class that contains the *main()* method that drives the application and controls the activities that occur within it. This class has a number of interesting features. Recall that there are three levels to the JMX architecture: instrumentation, agent, and distributed services. So far, we have been concerned with only the instrumentation level. However, instrumentation by itself isn't very interesting. Controller is part of the agent level, and it performs a few duties that allow the other standard MBeans (e.g., Queue and Worker) to be plugged into the MBean server. In this section, we will discuss some of the duties of this agent program that are unrelated to standard MBeans per se but that are important for understanding JMX.

The ObjectName class

The ObjectName class is provided by the RI and is crucial to the MBean registration process. Every MBean must be represented by an ObjectName in the MBean server and no two MBeans may be represented by the same ObjectName. Each ObjectName contains a string made up of two components: the domain name and the key property list. The combination of domain name and key property list must be unique for any given MBean and has the format:

```
domain-name:key1=value1[,key2=value2,...,keyN=valueN]
```

where domain-name is the *domain name*, followed by a colon (no spaces), followed by at least one *key property*. Think of a domain name as JMX's namespace mechanism. A key property is just a name/value pair, where each property name must be unique. For example, the object name used by the Queue instance into which the Supplier places its work units is:

```
DefaultDomain:name=Queue
```

Notice the domain name. Every compliant JMX implementation must provide a default domain name. For the JMX 1.0 RI, that name is DefaultDomain, but you can't depend on this to be the case all of the time. The MBean server provides a method called *getDefaultDomain()* that returns the name of the default domain.

 As a convenience, the JMX 1.0 RI allows you to pass an empty string for the domain name if you want to use the default domain. However, the domain name you pass may never be null, or a MalformedObjectNameException will be thrown.

There is only one restriction on domain names: you cannot use JMImplementation as the domain name for your MBeans. This domain name is reserved for the implementation (hence the name) and contains a single metadata MBean that provides information about the implementation, such as its name, version, and vendor.

To create an `ObjectName` instance, use one of the three constructors provided. The simplest constructor to use takes a single `String` parameter that contains the full object name string, as described above:

```
// . . .
try {
  String myObjName = "UserDomain:Name=Worker,Role=Supplier";
  ObjectName = new ObjectName(myObjName);
} catch (MalformedObjectNameException e) {
  // . . .
}
```

In this example, you can also leave off the domain name preceding the colon if you want to use the default domain:

```
// . . .
try {
  String myObjName = ":Name=Worker,Role=Supplier";
  ObjectName = new ObjectName(myObjName);
} catch (MalformedObjectNameException e) {
  // . . .
}
```

The second constructor is provided as a convenience when you want to provide only one key property. It takes three `String` arguments: the domain name, the key property name, and the key property value.

```
// . . .
try {
  // String objName = "UserDomain:Name=Controller";
  ObjectName = new ObjectName("UserDomain", "Name", "Controller");
} catch (MalformedObjectNameException e) {
  // . . .
}
```

The third constructor is used when you want to use the contents of a `Hashtable` to set the key property list. It takes two arguments: the domain name and a `Hashtable` reference containing the name/value pairs that make up the key property list.

```
// . . .
try {
  Hashtable table = new Hashtable( );
  table.put("Name", "Worker");
  table.put("Role", "Supplier");
  ObjectName = new ObjectName("UserDomain", table);
} catch (MalformedObjectNameException e) {
  // . . .
}
```

Once the `ObjectName` instance for your MBean has been created successfully, you can use that `ObjectName` to register the MBean.

Registering the MBean with the MBean server

Without an ObjectName instance, an MBean cannot be registered with the MBean server. In fact, the ObjectName is critical to doing anything meaningful with the MBean server. In the previous section, we saw how to create an ObjectName instance using one of the three constructors provided by ObjectName. In this section, we will see how to use that ObjectName to register an MBean.

The first step in using the MBean server is to obtain a reference to it. Every compliant JMX implementation must provide an MBeanServerFactory class that contains several methods that allow you to gain access to the MBean server (these will be discussed in more detail in Chapter 6). The easiest method to use is *createMBeanServer()*, which takes no arguments and returns a reference to a newly created MBean server:

```
// . . .
MBeanServer server = MBeanServerFactory.createMBeanServer();
// now do something with the MBean server
// . . .
```

Now that we have a reference to the MBean server, we can register our MBean. The following example shows how to create an ObjectName, obtain a reference to the MBean server, and register the Controller MBean:

```
// . . .
try {
  MBeanServer server = MBeanServerFactory.createMBeanServer();
  ObjectName objName = new ObjectName("UserDomain:Name=Controller");
  Controller controller = new Controller();
  server.registerMBean(controller, objName);
} catch (MalformedObjectNameException e) {
// . . .
}
// . . .
```

There are several ways to register an MBean. In the previous example, the MBean object was created explicitly using the new keyword, and then a reference to that object was passed to the *registerMBean()* method of the MBean server. However, those two steps could have been combined into one, allowing the MBean server to create the MBean object:

```
// . . .
try {
  MBeanServer server = MBeanServerFactory.createMBeanServer();
  ObjectName objName = new ObjectName("UserDomain:Name=Controller");
  server.createMBean("sample.standard.Controller", objName);
} catch (MalformedObjectNameException e) {
// . . .
}
// . . .
```

The MBean server also provides an overloaded version of *createMBean()* that allows you to specify constructor parameters for your MBean. The various ways to create and register MBeans will be covered in more detail in Chapter 6.

Once the MBean is registered with the MBean server, it is available for management. The mechanisms used by a management application to plug into and manage an MBean server are part of the distributed services level of the JMX architecture and are not fully specified in the JMX 1.0 RI. However, provided with the RI is a class called HTMLAdaptorServer, which is used throughout this book and is described in the next section.

The HTMLAdaptorServer Class

The HTMLAdaptorServer class is located in the com.sun.jdmk.comm package, which is distributed as part of the RI in *jmxtools.jar*. This handy class allows us to manage an MBean server through a web browser. HTMLAdaptorServer ("Adaptor" for short) is itself an MBean, and as such it must have an ObjectName and be registered with the MBean server. This class is essentially an HTTP server that listens on a specified port and generates HTML forms that are sent to the web browser. It is through these forms that you can manage and monitor your MBeans.

To use the HTMLAdaptorServer class, you must create an ObjectName for it and register it with the MBean server, as you would any other MBean:

```
// . . .
   MBeanServer server = MBeanServerFactory.createMBeanServer( );
   int portNumber = 8090;
   HtmlAdaptorServer html = new HtmlAdaptorServer(portNumber);
   ObjectName html_name = null;
   try {
     html_name = new ObjectName("Adaptor:name=html,port=" + portNumber);
     server.registerMBean(html, html_name);
   } catch (Exception e) {
     System.out.println("Error creating the HTML adaptor. . .");
     e.printStackTrace( );
     return;
   }
   html.start( );
// . . .
```

In this example, the Adaptor will be listening for HTTP requests on port 8090 of the machine on which it is running. A new instance of the HTMLAdaptorServer class is created, passing the specified port number to its constructor. Then an ObjectName is created for the Adaptor, and it is registered with the MBean server. Finally, the Adaptor is started. HTMLAdaptorServer implements the Runnable interface (actually, its parent class, `CommunitorServer`, does), so it runs on its own thread. Once the thread is started (by calling the *start()* method), the Adaptor is running and awaiting HTTP requests.

Now that the Adaptor is running, all you need to do is point your browser to the machine that contains the JVM in which the MBean server is running. Assuming that the browser and the MBean server are running on the same machine, simply point your browser to *http://localhost:8090*. Figure 2-8 shows a screen shot of the form that will be displayed.

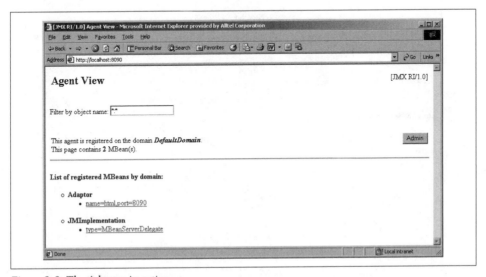

Figure 2-8. The Adaptor in action

The important elements are:

"Filter by object name:"
> This text box contains a pattern for which MBeans to show under "List of registered MBeans by domain:". The pattern starts with the domain name, followed by a colon, followed by the key property list of the MBeans to show. By default, this is "*:*", which means to show all domains and all MBeans.

"List of registered MBeans by domain:"
> This is a bulleted list of domains that match the filter (see above) and the MBeans within that domain that also match the pattern.

Notice that there are two domains, `Adaptor` and `JMIplementation`. In Figure 2-8, we see that when the `ObjectName` was created for the Adaptor MBean, "Adaptor" was provided as the domain name. The key property list consists of "name=html,port=8090".

If you click on this MBean (the key property list contains a link), you can view the attributes and operations exposed on the Adaptor MBean. The attributes are shown in Figure 2-9, and the operations are shown in Figure 2-10.

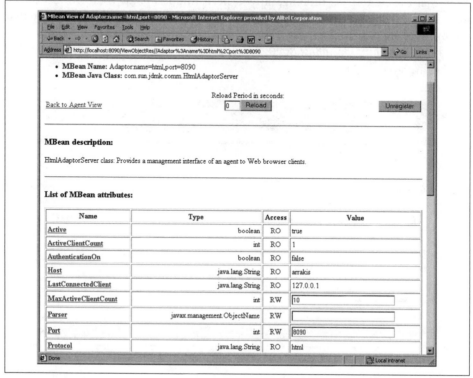

Figure 2-9. Attributes exposed for management on the HTMLAdaptorServer; scroll down to view the operations

We will use the `HTMLAdaptorServer` class throughout this book for managing all of the MBeans in the application.

Downloading and Installing the JMX Reference Implementation

Before you can build and run the application, you must first obtain the JMX RI. The easiest way to do this is to download it from Sun Microsystems at *http://java.sun.com/products/JavaManagement/*. Select either the source code or binary RI under "JMX Deliverables" and follow the instructions.

Once you've downloaded the RI, you should unzip the downloaded file directly into your *c:* drive for Windows or your home directory for Unix.

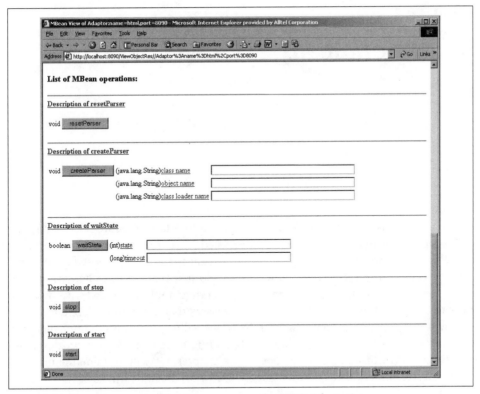

Figure 2-10. Operations exposed for management on the HTMLAdaptorServer

CHAPTER 3

Dynamic MBeans

Standard MBeans are well suited for management interfaces that are relatively static. However, if a management interface must be defined for an existing resource, is likely to evolve over time, or for some other reason needs to be exposed at runtime, JMX provides an interface that allows you to do just that. In this chapter, we will start by looking at the reasons for instrumenting application code as dynamic MBeans. Then we will look at the metadata classes that are used to define the management interface of a dynamic MBean. Next, we will explore ways to implement the DynamicMBean interface and show how the MBeanInfo metadata class is critical in making dynamic MBeans work. At the end of the chapter, we will examine the management interface inheritance patterns that are used with dynamic MBeans.

 This chapter assumes that you either are already familiar with standard MBeans or have read Chapter 2.

Why Use Dynamic MBeans?

The main reason to use dynamic MBeans is to more easily instrument existing code that is written in a manner that conflicts with the standard MBean design patterns we discussed in Chapter 2. The dynamic MBean interface is determined not through introspection, but rather through a method call on the dynamic MBean itself. This method, called *getMBeanInfo()*, returns information about the management interface and is defined on the DynamicMBean interface; it is the portal through which a management application views what has been exposed on the management interface of a resource that has been instrumented as a dynamic MBean.

Another reason to use dynamic MBeans is so that you can provide descriptions of the MBean features that are visible to the management application. An *MBean feature* is an attribute, constructor, operation, parameter, or notification of an MBean. The feature description is a brief explanation of what a particular feature means when viewed from a management application. The feature's name usually indicates what it means, but this isn't always the case. Feature descriptions are not available to standard MBeans.

Because the dynamic MBean interface is exposed at runtime, rather than at compile time (as a standard MBean is), the management interface is exposed through metadata classes. If the management interface is likely to change over time, dynamic MBeans offer a more flexible way to instrument a resource. The management interface is not statically bound to a dynamic MBean, as it is for a standard MBean. Rather, the management interface is exposed dynamically. As such, it is conceivable that a dynamic MBean could—without code changes—expose a different interface from one instance to the next by reading which attributes and operations to expose from a configuration file.

How Do Dynamic MBeans Work?

Like standard MBeans, dynamic MBeans must be created and registered with the MBean server. When the MBean server is asked to register a dynamic MBean, however, no introspection is performed. Recall that it is the strict application of the standard MBean design patterns (discussed in Chapter 2)—enforced through introspection—that tells the MBean server what management interface is exposed on an MBean. So, how does a dynamic MBean expose its management interface?

Instead of using a Java interface with the name "MBean" on it, dynamic MBeans use metadata classes to expose their management interfaces. They make that metadata available through an interface called DynamicMBean, which must be implemented by all dynamic MBeans. This interface is shown in Example 3-1.

Example 3-1. The DynamicMBean interface

```
package javax.management;

public interface DynamicMBean {

    public Object getAttribute(String attribute)
        throws AttributeNotFoundException, MBeanException, ReflectionException;

    public void setAttribute(Attribute attribute)
        throws AttributeNotFoundException, InvalidAttributeValueException,
            MBeanException, ReflectionException;

    public AttributeList getAttributes(String[] attributes);

    public AttributeList setAttributes(AttributeList attributes);

    public Object invoke(String actionName, Object params[], String signature[])
        throws MBeanException, ReflectionException;

    public MBeanInfo getMBeanInfo();

}
```

Essentially, the DynamicMBean interface provides a way for a management interface to do four things:

- Dynamically discover the management interface exposed by the MBean (*getMBeanInfo()*).
- Retrieve the value of one or more attributes on the management interface (*getAttribute()* and *getAttributes()*, respectively).
- Set the value of one or more attributes on the management interface (*setAttribute()* and *setAttributes()*, respectively).
- Invoke an operation on the management interface (*invoke()*).

Instances of the appropriate metadata classes are created by the MBean (usually in the constructor) and added to the MBeanInfo instance that is returned by *getMBeanInfo()*. Similarly, the management application, after invoking *getMBeanInfo()*, uses the metadata classes to discover that interface. In the next section, we will take a look at how a dynamic MBean uses the metadata classes to expose its management interface.

Describing the Management Interface

Dynamic MBeans tell the MBean server that they are dynamic MBeans by exposing the DynamicMBean interface, but it is the use of the dynamic MBean metadata classes that ties it all together. In this section, we will look at these classes and how a dynamic MBean uses them to describe and expose its management interface to the world.

There are six significant metadata classes:

MBeanInfo
> The top-level container of metadata; each MBean requires only one instance of this class to completely describe its management interface.

MBeanAttributeInfo
> Each instance of this class provides information about a single attribute.

MBeanParameterInfo
> Each instance of this class provides information about a single parameter.

MBeanConstructorInfo
> Each instance of this class provides information about a single constructor and may contain one or more MBeanParamaterInfo instances.

MBeanOperationInfo
> Each instance of this class provides information about a single operation and may contain one or more MBeanParameterInfo instances.

MBeanNotificationInfo
> Each instance of this class contains information about a group of notifications emitted by this MBean.

Each of these classes (except `MBeanInfo`) is a subclass of `MBeanFeatureInfo`. Figure 3-1 shows a UML diagram that describes the multiplicity (or cardinality) between `MBeanInfo` and the other metadata classes.

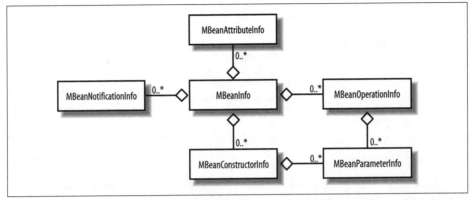

Figure 3-1. UML diagram showing the multiplicity between MBeanInfo and the other metadata classes

As you can see from Figure 3-1, there is a whole lot of aggregation going on! The aggregation mechanism used by all of the container classes is an array. Each of these classes is discussed in detail below.

MBeanAttributeInfo

This metadata class is used to describe a single attribute that is exposed on an MBean. To describe a single MBean attribute, six essential properties must be set:

name
> The name of the attribute as it appears on the management interface

type
> The string representation of the `Class` object that corresponds to the attribute's data type

description
> The description of the attribute as it should appear to a management application

isReadable
> A boolean property that indicates whether or not the attribute's value can be retrieved and viewed by a management application

isWritable
> A boolean property that indicates whether or not the attribute's value can be set by a management application

isIs
> A boolean property that indicates whether or not the attribute is a boolean and if its getter begins with *is* instead of *get*

An MBean creates an instance of this class for each attribute that it wants to expose, using one of two constructors of MBeanAttributeInfo to set its essential properties. The first constructor is defined as:

```
public class MBeanAttributeInfo extends MBeanFeatureInfo implements
  java.io.Serializable, Cloneable {
// . . .
  public MBeanAttributeInfo(String name,
                            String type,
                            String description,
                            boolean isReadable,
                            boolean isWritable,
                            boolean isIs) {
// . . .
  }
// . . .
}
```

The *name* parameter is the name of the attribute as it is exposed on the management interface and is a String. The name must match exactly what is expected by the methods on the DynamicMBean interface implementation to retrieve and set the attribute's value.

The *type* parameter is the fully qualified name of the class that is the type of the attribute's value. If *type* is an Integer, for example, this parameter will have the value "java.lang.Integer". If *type* is one of the Java fundamental types (e.g., byte, char, long), you may use either the literal string for that fundamental type or the name attribute of the TYPE member variable of the corresponding fundamental type java.lang wrapper class. The following example shows how to use this constructor for the QueueSize attribute of Queue (whose type is int) by using the literal string explicitly for type int:

```
// . . .
  public Queue(int queueSize) {
    super();
    MBeanAttributeInfo att = new MBeanAttributeInfo(
      "QueueSize",            // name
      "int",                  // type
      "Size of the Queue.",   // description
      true,                   // isReadable
      true,                   // isWritable
      false                   // isIs
      );
    // . . .
  }
// . . .
```

Here is an example that shows how to use the JDK wrapper class for the fundamental type int to create an MBeanAttributeInfo object for the same QueueSize attribute of Queue:

```
// . . .
  public Queue(int queueSize) {
```

```
    super();
    MBeanAttributeInfo att = new MBeanAttributeInfo(
      "QueueSize",              // name
      Integer.TYPE.getName(),   // type
      "Size of the Queue.",     // description
      true,                     // isReadable
      true,                     // isWritable
      false                     // isIs
      );
    // . . .
  }
// . . .
```

For each fundamental type, a JDK wrapper class has been provided as part of the java.lang package. Each wrapper class has a public static member variable called TYPE, which is a java.lang.Class object that has been initialized with a literal string that serves as the string representation of the fundamental type. Table 3-1 shows the corresponding *type* parameter values for each fundamental type, along with their JDK 1.3 string representations.

Table 3-1. type parameter values for attributes whose values are of a fundamental type

Attribute type	type parameter value	JDK 1.3 literal value
boolean	Boolean.TYPE.getName()	"boolean"
byte	Byte.TYPE.getName()	"byte"
char	Character.TYPE.getName()	"char"
short	Short.TYPE.getName()	"short"
int	Integer.TYPE.getName()	"int"
long	Long.TYPE.getName()	"long"
float	Float.TYPE.getName()	"float"
double	Double.TYPE.getName()	"double"
void	Void.TYPE.getName()	"void"

Notice in Table 3-1 that I don't use a String literal as the *type* of fundamental types. Rather, I use the appropriate TYPE member variable of the fundamental type wrapper class. Each fundamental type has a JDK wrapper class and a corresponding class-level member variable called TYPE that is a Class object whose name (accessed by the *getName()* method of Class) is a String containing the name of the fundamental type's Class. The literal values in Table 3-1 are not likely to change, but using the TYPE variable of the appropriate fundamental type's wrapper class insulates you from changes to this literal in future JDK versions.

If the attribute type is an array, the *type* string has a different format: left bracket, capital L (i.e., "[L"), followed by the fully qualified name of the attribute class, followed by a semicolon. For example, if the class is an array of String objects, the *type* string of the array is "[Ljava.lang.String;".

Using TYPE for Fundamental Types

You may have noticed in Table 3-1 that I used a rather strange-looking member variable of each of the JDK wrapper classes for the fundamental types, called TYPE. This member variable is a Class object that represents the fundamental type.

There are times when using JMX or Java's reflection API that you will need to know when to use the Class object that represents a fundamental type and when to use the string representation of that Class object.

For example, when you use the reflection API to build the signature of a method, you create a Class array and then populate the array with Class objects that correspond to the types of the parameters that constitute the signature. Let's say you're building a Class array to represent the signature of an operation that takes an int parameter, followed by a long:

```
// . . .
Class[] sign = new Class[2];
sign[0] = Integer.TYPE;
sign[1] = Long.TYPE;
// . . .
```

In this case, you want the Class object from the JDK fundamental type wrapper, so you just use its TYPE member variable.

However, in JMX you often need to express the type of an object as a string. This may seem confusing at first, but all JMX needs to know is the string representation (i.e., name) of the Class object for that type. For example, suppose that you need the string representation of the Class objects in the previous example:

```
// . . .
String sign0asString = Integer.TYPE.getName( );
String sign1asString = Long.TYPE.getName( );
// . . .
```

In fact, this is the case for all fundamental types. Hopefully, Table 3-1 makes a little more sense now.

For an array of fundamental types, the format is different still. For example, if the attribute type is an array of char, the *type* string would be "[C". Notice that there is no L and no semicolon at the end of the *type* string. Also note that the class name is not "char," as it would be if the type were simply a char. The class names for arrays of all fundamental types follow this pattern, where a single uppercase character follows the left bracket. Table 3-2 lists the literal strings that you must pass for each type of array.

Table 3-2. Class name strings for arrays of fundamental types

Attribute type	Class name literal string
boolean[]	"[Z"
byte[]	"[B"

Table 3-2. Class name strings for arrays of fundamental types (continued)

Attribute type	Class name literal string
char[]	"[C"
short[]	"[S"
int[]	"[I"
long[]	"[J"
float[]	"[F"
double[]	"[D"

Creating the MBeanAttributeInfo for a one-dimensional character array (char[]) that uses this constructor looks like this:

```
// . . .
    MBeanAttributeInfo att = new MBeanAttributeInfo(
        "StringArray",      // name
        "[C",               // type
        "2D String array.", // description
        true,               // isReadable
        true,               // isWritable
        false               // isIs
        );
// . . .
```

Creating the MBeanAttributeInfo for a one-dimensional double-precision floating point array (double[]) that uses this constructor looks like this:

```
// . . .
    MBeanAttributeInfo att = new MBeanAttributeInfo(
        "DoubleArray",      // name
        "[D",               // type
        "2D String array.", // description
        true,               // isReadable
        true,               // isWritable
        false               // isIs
        );
// . . .
```

What about multi-dimensional arrays? Simply add another left bracket to the beginning of the literal string representing the array.

A two-dimensional String array (String[][]) looks like this:

```
// . . .
    MBeanAttributeInfo att = new MBeanAttributeInfo(
        "TwoDStringArray",        // name
        "[[Ljava.lang.String;",   // type
        "2D String array.",       // description
        true,                     // isReadable
        true,                     // isWritable
        false                     // isIs
        );
// . . .
```

A three-dimensional long integer array (long[][][]) looks like this:

```
// . . .
    MBeanAttributeInfo att = new MBeanAttributeInfo(
        "ThreeDLongArray",   // name
        "[[[J",              // type
        "2D String array.",  // description
        true,                // isReadable
        true,                // isWritable
        false                // isIs
        );
// . . .
```

 The final authority on the syntax of array definitions is the Javadoc for java.lang.Class. You should consult the documentation if you run into any problems.

For attributes with user-defined types, the *type* parameter is the fully qualified class name. For example, suppose that we have an attribute called ConsumerQueue from the application's Controller class. This attribute's type is Queue. The code to create an MBeanAttributeInfo object for this attribute is:

```
// . . .
    MBeanAttributeInfo att = new MBeanAttributeInfo(
        "ConsumerQueue",       // name
        "sample.dynamic.Queue", // type
        "2D String array.",    // description
        true,                  // isReadable
        true,                  // isWritable
        false                  // isIs
        );
// . . .
```

 When using the HTMLAdaptorServer that ships with the JMX 1.0 RI (in *jmxtools.jar*), user-defined types are *not supported* for attributes. This may change without notice, however, because *jmxtools.jar* is not technically part of the RI.

The *description* parameter is simply a human-readable description of the attribute and can be anything you want. However, if you are going to use the HTMLAdaptorServer from the JMX 1.0 RI, please note that you cannot use single or double quotes in the description. This seems to mess up the Adaptor, and you will not be able to retrieve the description from your browser.

The *isReadable* parameter indicates whether or not the attribute's value can be retrieved through the management interface. Set this parameter to true if the value can be read through the management interface, and false otherwise.

The *isWritable* parameter indicates whether or not the attribute's value can be set through the management interface. Pass true if it can be, and false otherwise.

If the attribute is a boolean value and its getter starts with "is", pass *isIs* as true. Otherwise, pass false.

There is a second constructor to MBeanAttributeInfo that you may find helpful:

```
public class MBeanAttributeInfo extends MBeanFeatureInfo implements
   java.io.Serializable, Cloneable {
// . . .
   public MBeanAttributeInfo(String name,
                             String description,
                             java.lang.reflect.Method getter,
                             java.lang.reflect.Method setter)
      throws IntrospectionException {
   // . . .
   }
// . . .
}
```

This constructor is provided as a convenience if you prefer to use the Java reflection API to obtain references to the Method objects for the getter and setter and then pass those references to the constructor. The constructor then figures out whether the attribute is readable, writable, and/or boolean, and what its type is. Consequently, you don't have to worry about memorizing the information in Tables 3-1 and 3-2.

Suppose that for a particular MBean, we are creating the metadata classes to represent the attributes inside the constructor of the MBean. It is simple, then, to get a reference to the Method objects for the getter and setter:

```
// . . .
   public Queue(int queueSize) {
     super();
     Class[] setterSignature = new Class[1];
     setterSignature[0] = Integer.TYPE;

     try {
       Method getter = this.getClass().getMethod("getQueueSize", null);
       Method setter = this.getClass().getMethod("setQueueSize", setterSignature);
       MBeanAttributeInfo att = new MBeanAttributeInfo(
         "QueueSize",
         "Size of the Queue.",
         getter,
         setter
       );
     } catch (NoSuchFieldException e) {
       // oops, shouldn't really get this unless we mistyped the name
       e.printStackTrace();
     } catch (SecurityException e) {
```

```
            // you don't have access to the method. . .
            e.printStackTrace( );
      } catch (IntrospectionException e) {
            // something has gone horribly wrong. . .
            e.printStackTrace( );
      }
      // . . .
  }
  // . . .
```

If the attribute is read-only, pass null as the *setter* parameter. Conversely, if the
attribute is write-only, pass null as the *getter* parameter. This approach works well if
the attribute's name is likely to be more static than its type. If the name never
changes, the code above will not need to change, because the MBeanAttributeInfo
constructor uses Java's reflection API to determine the attribute's type.

MBeanParameterInfo

Three essential properties of a parameter to an MBean constructor or operation must
be set in order to describe that parameter:

name
> The name of the parameter as it appears to a management application

type
> The string representation of the Class object that corresponds to the parameter's data type

description
> The description of the parameter as it should appear to a management application

Each parameter to a constructor or operation must be described using the
MBeanParameterInfo class. Each instance of this class serves to completely describe a
single parameter to a single constructor or operation. Like MBeanAttributeInfo
objects, the way to create instances of MBeanParameterInfo is to use its custom constructors. In fact, there is only one constructor for MBeanParameterInfo:

```
public class MBeanParameterInfo extends MBeanFeatureInfo
  implements java.io.Serializable, Cloneable  {
// . . .
  public MBeanParameterInfo(String name,
                            String type,
                            String description) {
  // . . .
  }
// . . .
}
```

The *name* parameter is the name of the parameter as it appears to the management
application. It is good style for this name to match the name in the source code, but
the RI doesn't seem to care what you use for this parameter, including an empty

string ("") or a null reference. Note, however, that if you pass a null reference for this parameter, a NullPointerException will be thrown by the HTMLAdaptorServer when you try to access any MBean that uses this MBeanParameterInfo instance. The MBean server, on the other hand, will happily register the MBean without any glitches. This behavior indicates that Version 1.0 of the HTMLAdaptorServer doesn't much care for a null reference for the *name* parameter.

The *type* parameter for MBeanParameterInfo is exactly the same as the *type* parameter for MBeanAttributeInfo. All of the information about the *type* parameter in the previous section applies here as well.

The *description* parameter is simply a human-readable description of the attribute and can be anything you want. However, if you are going to use the HTMLAdaptorServer from the JMX 1.0 RI, note that you cannot use single or double quotes in the description. This seems to mess up the Adaptor, and you will not be able to retrieve the description from your browser.

It's time for an example from the application. The Controller class has a management operation called *createNewWorker()* that is used to start another worker thread. In order to do this, however, the worker's role (a String) and the work factor (the amount of work the worker is to perform for each work unit) must be specified. An instance of MBeanParameterInfo will be created for each of these parameters:

```
// . . .
MBeanParameterInfo param1 = new MBeanParameterInfo(
  "role",                                    // name
  "java.lang.String",                        // type
  "The role this new worker thread will take on." // description
);

MBeanParameterInfo param2 = new MBeanParameterInfo(
  "workFactor",
  Integer.TYPE.getName( ),
  "The weighted work factor for this new worker thread."
);
// . . .
```

As I stated earlier, you are not required to supply a *name* parameter to the constructor of MBeanParameterInfo. In fact, you don't have to supply a description either. Thus, you don't have to create different instances of MBeanParameterInfo for parameters that can be described in exactly the same way. In other words, if parameters have at a minimum the same type, they can share the same instance of MBeanParameterInfo. Be careful when doing this, however, because parameters can have the same type but mean different things to a management application. Also, it may confuse the person trying to manage your MBeans if he is relying on either the name or description of an operation or constructor's parameters to meaningfully manage the resources within your application.

MBeanConstructorInfo

Three essential properties must be set in order to describe an MBean constructor:

name
> The name of the constructor as it appears to a management application

description
> The description of the constructor as it should appear to a management application

signature
> An array of MBeanParameterInfo objects that describe the constructor's signature

The MBeanConstructorInfo metadata class is used to describe an MBean's public constructors. One instance of this class completely describes a single constructor. In other words, if an MBean has three public constructors, three instances of this class are required to completely describe the MBean's constructors. Like the other metadata classes, MBeanConstructorInfo provides two custom constructors that are used to set various properties of this object. The first constructor is defined as:

```
public class MBeanConstructorInfo extends MBeanFeatureInfo
   implements java.io.Serializable, Cloneable {
// . . .
   public MBeanConstructorInfo(String description,
                        java.lang.reflect.Constructor constructor) {
   }
// . . .
}
```

This constructor uses Java's reflection API to figure out what the constructor's parameters are and creates MBeanParameterInfo objects for them accordingly. However, when you use this method, you will not be able to specify a name for the constructor or a description for the constructor's parameters.

This constructor is very easy to use if you want to expose all of the constructors for an MBean. For example, the following code will expose all of the public constructors of the class of which this is an instance:

```
// . . .
   Constructor[] constructors = this.getClass().getConstructors();
   MBeanConstructorInfo[] constructorInfo = new
      MBeanConstructorInfo[constructors.length];
   for (int aa = 0; aa < constructors.length; aa++) {
     constructorInfo[aa] = new MBeanConstructorInfo(
       "Constructs a Basic MBean.", // description
       constructors[aa]             // java.lang.reflect.Constructor
     );
   }
// . . .
```

The *getConstructors()* method of the Class object associated with this returns an array of java.lang.reflect.Constructor objects. The size of the array is a value equal to the number of public constructors the class contains, and this value is used to create an equally sized array of MBeanConstructor objects. Then each Constructor object is used to create a corresponding MBeanConstructor instance.

Alternately, you can expose a specific constructor by creating an MBeanConstructorInfo object for it. Example 3-2 shows how to do this.

Example 3-2. Exposing a specific constructor

```
public class Queue extends Basic implements DynamicMBean {
// . . .
  public Queue(int QueueSize) {
    // . . .
    Class[] signature = {Integer.TYPE};
    Constructor constructor = null;
    MBeanConstructorInfo[] constructorInfo = new MBeanConstructorInfo[1];
    try {
      constructor = this.getClass().getConstructor(signature);
      constructorInfo[0] = new MBeanConstructorInfo(
        "Queue custom constructor",  // description
        constructor                  // java.lang.reflect.Constructor
      );
    } catch (Exception e) {
      e.printStackTrace();
      return;
    }
    // . . .
  }
// . . .
}
```

In this example, we explicitly exposed a single constructor whose signature consists of a single int parameter. The *getConstructor()* method of Class takes a Class array that contains the Class objects that match the signature of the constructor we want to retrieve. If the constructor is not found, a NoSuchMethodException is thrown. If the constructor is found, it's a simple matter of creating a new MBeanConstructorInfo object, passing the Constructor object we retrieved earlier.

Suppose that we have another constructor that takes an Integer parameter, instead of a fundamental int. How do we get a Class object for an Integer? There is a static method of Class called *forName()* that takes a String (actually, there are two versions of this method, but we'll use the simpler of the two), which is the fully qualified name of the class for which we want a Class object. This method does throw an exception if the class can't be found, so we have to surround our code with try/catch blocks. Using this scenario, Example 3-2 becomes:

```
public class Queue extends Basic implements DynamicMBean {
// . . .
  public Queue(int QueueSize) {
    // . . .
    Class[] signature = new Class[1];
```

```
        Constructor constructor = null;
        MBeanConstructorInfo[] constructorInfo = new MBeanConstructorInfo[1];
        try {
          signature[0] = Class.forName("java.lang.Integer");
          constructor = this.getClass().getConstructor(signature);
          constructorInfo[0] = new MBeanConstructorInfo(
            "Queue custom constructor",  // description
            constructor                  // java.lang.reflect.Constructor
          );
        } catch (Exception e) {
          e.printStackTrace();
          return;
        }
        // . . .
      }
    // . . .
    }
```

The second constructor of `MBeanConstructorInfo` requires a little more effort on our part, but it allows us to provide a name and description for each parameter of the constructor we expose. This can be helpful to the operator of a management application, as this information will be exposed if this constructor is used. The constructor is defined as:

```
public class MBeanConstructorInfo extends MBeanFeatureInfo
    implements java.io.Serializable, Cloneable  {
// . . .
    public MBeanConstructorInfo(String name,
                                String description,
                                MBeanParameterInfo[] signature) {
    }
// . . .
}
```

The extra work required on our part is that we must create an array of `MBeanParameterInfo` objects that correspond to the signature of the constructor. This is really not a big deal, though; we saw how to create `MBeanParameterInfo` objects in the previous section. Suppose that we want to expose the constructor from Example 3-2, which takes a single `int` parameter. In that case, we create a single `MBeanParameterInfo` object and pass it to the constructor of `MBeanConstructorInfo`:

```
public class Queue extends Basic implements DynamicMBean {
// . . .
    public Queue(int QueueSize) {
      // . . .
      MBeanConstructorInfo[] constructorInfo = new MBeanConstructorInfo[1];
      MBeanParameterInfo[] parms = new MBeanParameterInfo[1];
      parms[0] = new MBeanParameterInfo(
        "queueSize",
        Integer.TYPE.getName(),
        "Max number of items the Queue may contain at any time."
      );
```

```
        constructorInfo[0] = new MBeanConstructorInfo(
          "Queue",
          "Queue custom constructor",
          parms
        );
        // . . .
    }
  // . . .
  }
```

Notice how we explicitly create an instance of MBeanParameterInfo to describe the int parameter to our constructor. This object is then placed into an array consisting of a single MBeanParameterInfo element, which is passed to the second constructor of MBeanConstructorInfo.

If you are exposing the default constructor, you have two options. The first option is to simply pass null as the third parameter:

```
    // . . .
    MBeanConstructorInfo[] constructorInfo = new MBeanConstructorInfo[1];
    constructorInfo[0] = new MBeanConstructorInfo(
      "Queue",
      "Default Constructor",
      null
    );
    // . . .
```

A second, arguably more readable, way to expose the default constructor is to pass an empty array of MBeanParameterInfo objects:

```
    // . . .
    MBeanConstructorInfo[] constructorInfo = new MBeanConstructorInfo[1];
    constructorInfo[0] = new MBeanConstructorInfo(
      "Queue",
      "Default Constructor",
      new MBeanParameterInfo[0]
    );
    // . . .
```

MBeanOperationInfo

Five essential properties of an MBean operation must be set when describing the operation:

name
> The name of the constructor as it appears to a management application

description
> The description of the constructor as it should appear to a management application

signature
> An array of MBeanParameterInfo objects that describe the constructor's signature

type

 The data type of the value returned by the operation

impact

 An indicator of the type of impact to the state of the MBean following an invocation of the operation

MBeanOperationInfo is used to describe the operations that are exposed on an MBean's management interface. One instance of this class is required to completely describe a single operation. In other words, if an MBean exposes four operations on its management interface, four instances of this class are required in order to describe the operations on the management interface of the MBean. Like the other metadata classes, MBeanOperationInfo uses its constructors to set its five essential properties. The first constructor is defined as:

```
public class MBeanOperationInfo extends MBeanFeatureInfo
    implements java.io.Serializable, Cloneable  {
// . . .
    public MBeanOperationInfo(String description, java.lang.reflect.Method method) {
    // . . .
    }
// . . .
}
```

This constructor uses Java's reflection API to figure out what the constructor's parameters (and their types) are and creates MBeanParameterInfo objects for them accordingly. In addition, the return type of the operation is discovered through reflection. The *impact* property (see above) cannot be discovered, however, because there is no way to determine the impact of invoking the MBean operation through the reflection API; the impact of invoking the operation on the MBean's state is unknown, so this constructor sets *impact* to MBeanParameterInfo.UNKNOWN.

 When you use this method, you will not be able to specify a name or a description for the constructor's parameters.

You must obtain a reference to the java.lang.reflect.Method object for the operation you wish to expose:

```
public class Controller extends Basic implements DynamicMBean {
// . . .
    public Controller( ) {
        // . . .
        MBeanOperationInfo[] operationInfo = new MBeanOperationInfo[1];
        Method operation = null;
        Class[] parms = new Class[2];
        try {
            parms[0] = Class.forName("java.lang.String");
            parms[1] = Integer.TYPE;
            operation = this.getClass( ).getMethod("createWorker",parms);
```

```
            operationInfo[0] = new MBeanOperationInfo(
              "createWorker",
              operation
            );
        } catch (Exception e) {
            e.printStackTrace();
            return;
        }
        // . . .
    }
    // . . .
    // operation to be exposed on the management interface
    public void createWorker(String workerType, int workFactor) {
        // . . .
    }
}
```

In this example, we are exposing an operation called *createWorker()* that takes two parameters: a String and an int. To expose an operation using the reflection-based constructor of MBeanParameterInfo, we must accomplish the following:

- Obtain Class objects that represent the proper Class objects for the types of signatures the MBean operation has. In this example, the first parameter is a String and the second is an int. We can obtain a String Class object by using the static *forName()* method of Class. For the fundamental type int, we simply use the TYPE member, which is a Class object that represents an int:

```
    // . . .
    public Controller( ) {
        // . . .
        Method operation = null;
        Class[] parms = new Class[2];
        try {
            parms[0] = Class.forName("java.lang.String");
            parms[1] = Integer.TYPE;
            operation = this.getClass( ).getMethod("createWorker",parms);
            // . . .
        // . . .
    }
    // . . .
```

- Obtain a reference to the Method object that corresponds to the operation we want to expose. To do this, we must use the Class object of the MBean object itself. Once we obtain the Class object, we can use its *getMethod()* method to retrieve the MBean operation's Method object. Because *getMethod()* may throw an exception if the method is not found, we must use try/catch blocks:

```
    // . . .
    public Controller( ) {
        // . . .
        try {
            parms[0] = Class.forName("java.lang.String");
            parms[1] = Integer.TYPE;
            operation = this.getClass( ).getMethod("createWorker",parms);
```

```
                    operationInfo[0] = new MBeanOperationInfo(
                      "createWorker",
                      operation
                    );
                } catch (Exception e) {
                    e.printStackTrace();
                    return;
                }
                // . . .
            }
```

- Create the `MBeanOperationInfo` object:

```
        // . . .
          public Controller() {
            // . . .
            try {
                parms[0] = Class.forName("java.lang.String");
                parms[1] = Integer.TYPE;
                operation = this.getClass().getMethod("createWorker",parms);
                operationInfo[0] = new MBeanOperationInfo(
                  "createWorker",
                  operation
                );
            } catch (Exception e) {
                e.printStackTrace();
                return;
            }
            // . . .
          }
        // . . .
```

The second constructor of `MBeanOperationInfo` allows you to explicitly specify all of the essential properties of an MBean operation and is defined as:

```
    public class MBeanOperationInfo extends MBeanFeatureInfo
      implements java.io.Serializable, Cloneable  {
    // . . .
      public MBeanOperationInfo(String name,
                                String description,
                                MBeanParameterInfo[] signature,
                                String type,
                                int impact) {
        // . . .
      }
    // . . .
    }
```

This constructor is arguably easier to use than its reflection-based counterpart, because it's so easy to create `MBeanParameterInfo` objects:

```
    public class Controller extends Basic implements DynamicMBean {
    // . . .
      public Controller() {
        // . . .
        MBeanOperationInfo[] operationInfo = new MBeanOperationInfo[1];
        MBeanParameterInfo[] parms = new MBeanParameterInfo[2];
```

```
    parms[0] = new MBeanParameterInfo(
      "role",
      "java.lang.String",
      "The role this new worker thread will take on."
    );
    parms[1] = new MBeanParameterInfo(
      "workFactor",
      Integer.TYPE.getName( ),
      "The work factor for this new worker thread."
    );
    operationInfo[0] = new MBeanOperationInfo(
      "createWorker",
      "Creates a new worker thread.",
      parms,
      Void.TYPE.getName( ),
      MBeanOperationInfo.ACTION
    );
    // . . .
  }
// . . .
  // operation to be exposed on the management interface
  public void createWorker(String workerType, int workFactor) {
  // . . .
  }
}
```

In this example, we create an instance of MBeanParameterInfo for each of the parameters to the operation we want to expose and place the instances into an array. We then pass this array to the second constructor of MBeanOperationInfo.

Notice the *impact* property, which is the fifth parameter to the constructor (we used MBeanOperationInfo.ACTION). Four values for *impact* are defined on MBeanOperation:

INFO
> The state of the MBean will remain unchanged as a result of invoking this operation, because the operation will only return information.

ACTION
> The state of the MBean will be changed in some way as a result of invoking this operation. This could be as simple as an internal value changing (i.e., something not on the management interface as an attribute) or as complex as the externally visible state of the MBean changing.

ACTION_INFO
> This operation will return some information about the MBean, and the state of the MBean will change as a result of invoking this operation. This is a combination of INFO and ACTION.

UNKNOWN
> This value indicates that the impact of invoking the method is not known. When you use the reflection-based constructor of MBeanOperationInfo, this is the value to which *impact* is set.

MBeanNotificationInfo

There are three essential properties of an MBean notification:

name
> The name of the notification as it appears to a management application

description
> The description of the notification as it should appear to a management application

notifsType (notification types)
> The types of notifications that will be emitted by this MBean

MBeanNotificationInfo is the metadata class used by an MBean to indicate to the MBean server what notification types the MBean emits (we will discuss the JMX notification model in greater detail in Chapter 6). One instance of this class is necessary to completely describe a single group of notifications, but what exactly is a "group of notifications?" A group of notifications is made up of one or more notifications of the same general type. It is up to you to define what notifications belong together, depending upon the different types of notifications that are emitted by the application resource the MBean represents.

Like the other metadata classes, the essential properties for MBeanNotificationInfo are set by calling its single constructor, which is defined as:

```
public class MBeanNotificationInfo extends MBeanFeatureInfo
  implements Cloneable, java.io.Serializable {
// . . .
  public MBeanNotificationInfo(String[] notifsType,
                               String name,
                               String description) {
    // . . .
  }
// . . .
}
```

We are already familiar with the *name* and *description* parameters, but what about *notifsType*? This constructor parameter is a String array that contains a group of notifications that the MBean will emit. A notification is a String of the form:

> *vendor*[*.application*][*.component*][*.eventGroup*]*.event*

where *vendor* is the name of your company, *application* is the name of the application (optional), *component* is the name of the component (usually the name of the MBean, also optional), *eventGroup* is the name of the group to which the event belongs (optional), and *event* is the name of the event notification. The minimal notification String should contain *vendor* and *event*, but I encourage you to be as detailed as possible when naming the notifications your MBeans will emit.

For example, suppose we define a group of notifications for the Queue class from the sample application. This group of notifications will be for potential stall conditions, where for some reason the queue appears to be "asleep." Say we define one notification for the condition when the queue is continuously full for more than a preset amount of time. This may indicate that the application has stalled, perhaps by a consumer thread crashing. Then let's define another notification for the condition when the queue is continuously empty for longer than a preset period of time. This may indicate that a supplier thread has crashed. These notifications will be defined as "sample.Queue.stalled.Full" and "sample.Queue.stalled.Empty".

In this case, sample is the vendor, and we have omitted the optional *application* from the notification names. Both of these notifications indicate a potential stall condition in the queue. Now let's create an instance of MBeanNotificationInfo:

```java
public class Queue extends Basic implements DynamicMBean {
  // . . .
    public static final String NOTIF_STALLED_FULL = "sample.Queue.stalled.full";
    public static final String NOTIF_STALLED_EMPTY = "sample.Queue.stalled.empty";
  // . . .
    public Queue(int QueueSize) {
      // . . .
      String[] notificationTypes = new String[2];
      notificationTypes[0] = NOTIF_STALLED_FULL;
      notificationTypes[1] = NOTIF_STALLED_EMPTY;

      MBeanNotificationInfo[] notificationInfo = new MBeanNotificationInfo[1];

      notificationInfo[0] = new MBeanNotificationInfo(
        notificationTypes,
        "StalledQueueNotifications",
        "Potential stall notifications emitted by the Queue."
      );
      // . . .
    }
  // . . .
}
```

We declared the notification Strings as constants on the class because these literal strings will be needed by the part of the Queue that actually emits the notifications and can be referenced everywhere by their variable names. As you can see from this example, creating an MBeanNotificationInfo object for a group of notifications is quite straightforward.

The convention I suggest here regarding the use of a single instance of MBeanNotificationInfo to group similar notifications is purely my own. It's not mentioned in the JMX specification; it just seems to me to be a good idea. Strictly speaking, you don't have to use this idiom. For example, we could have created an instance of MBeanNotificationInfo for each notification the MBean will emit:

```java
public class Queue extends Basic implements DynamicMBean {
  // . . .
    public static final String NOTIF_STALLED_FULL = "sample.Queue.stalled.full";
    public static final String NOTIF_STALLED_EMPTY = "sample.Queue.stalled.empty";
  // . . .
```

```java
    public Queue(int QueueSize) {
      // . . .
      String[] notificationTypes = new String[1];
      notificationTypes[0] = NOTIF_STALLED_FULL;

      MBeanNotificationInfo[] notificationInfo = new MBeanNotificationInfo[2];

      notificationInfo[0] = new MBeanNotificationInfo(
        notificationTypes,
        "StalledFullQueueNotification",
        "Potential stall notifications emitted when the Queue is full."
      );

      notificationTypes = new String[1];
      notificationTypes[0] = NOTIF_STALLED_EMPTY;
      notificationInfo[1] = new MBeanNotificationInfo(
        notificationTypes,
        "StalledEmptyQueueNotification",
        "Potential stall notifications emitted when the Queue is empty."
      );
      // . . .
    }
  // . . .
  }
```

This is a perfectly reasonable approach to use for a small number of notifications. However, if your MBean emits a lot of notifications, you may want to consider grouping them and taking the approach shown earlier.

MBeanInfo

There are six essential properties of an MBean:

className
> The name of the MBean class

description
> A description of the MBean

attributes
> Metadata about the attributes the MBean exposes

constructors
> Metadata about the MBean's constructors

operations
> Metadata about the MBean's exposed operations

notifications
> Metadata about the notifications emitted by the MBean

A single instance of MBeanInfo is sufficient to completely describe the management interface for an MBean, because the getters provided by MBeanInfo allow a management application to drill down into, and retrieve, all of the metadata for an MBean.

Think of this class as the "magic cookie" that the distributed services level of the JMX architecture uses to expose a dynamic MBean's management interface to a management application.

When *getMBeanInfo()* is invoked on a dynamic MBean, information in the form of metadata is returned to the caller. The metadata is contained in an instance of a class called MBeanInfo, which is at the top of the dynamic MBean metadata hierarchy. It is through this metadata that the interface is both exposed by the MBean and discovered by the management application. This class should be created last, because all of the attributes, parameters, constructors, operations, and notifications must be completely described before an instance of MBeanInfo can be created.

Like all of the other metadata classes, the MBeanInfo constructor provides a way to set the essential properties. This means, of course, that you must create the metadata class instances first so that they are available at the time you create the MBeanInfo instance. Once instances of the appropriate MBeanAttributeInfo, MBeanConstructorInfo, MBeanOperationInfo, and MBeanNotificationInfo have been created, they can be added to MBeanInfo.

The constructor of the MBeanInfo class looks like this:

```
public class MBeanInfo implements Cloneable, java.io.Serializable {
// . . .
   public MBeanInfo(String className,
                    String description,
                    MBeanAttributeInfo[] attributes,
                    MBeanConstructorInfo[] constructors,
                    MBeanOperationInfo[] operations,
                    MBeanNotificationInfo[] notifications) {
// . . .
   }
// . . .
}
```

Now it's time for the metadata classes describing the attributes, constructors, operations, and notifications to be added to MBeanInfo. The way to do this is through MBeanInfo's constructor. You may have noticed in the earlier examples that we created an array of the metadata objects and then added the objects to the array. Once we create the array of metadata objects, we can simply pass the arrays to the MBeanInfo constructor.

Example 3-3 shows how to create the MBeanInfo class, using the other metadata classes. This example ties together all of the previous discussion about metadata classes.

Example 3-3. Creating an instance of MBeanInfo

```
public class Queue extends Basic implements DynamicMBean {
// . . .
   private MBeanInfo _MBeanInfo;
// . . .
```

Example 3-3. Creating an instance of MBeanInfo (continued)

```
  public static final String NOTIF_STALLED_FULL = "sample.Queue.stalled.full";
  public static final String NOTIF_STALLED_EMPTY = "sample.Queue.stalled.empty";
// . . .
  public Queue(int queueSize) {
    // . . .
    // Attributes
    attributeInfo[0] = new MBeanAttributeInfo(
      "QueueSize", Integer.TYPE.getName( ),
      "Maximum number of items the queue may contain at one time.",
      true, true, false);
    attributeInfo[1] = new MBeanAttributeInfo(
      "NumberOfConsumers", Integer.TYPE.getName( ),
      "The number of consumers pulling from this Queue.",
      true, false, false);
    attributeInfo[2] = new MBeanAttributeInfo(
      "NumberOfSuppliers", Integer.TYPE.getName( ),
      "The number of suppliers supplying to this Queue.",
      true, false, false);
    attributeInfo[3] = new MBeanAttributeInfo(
      "QueueFull", Boolean.TYPE.getName( ),
      "Indicates whether or not the Queue is full.",
      true, false, true);
    attributeInfo[4] = new MBeanAttributeInfo(
      "QueueEmpty", Boolean.TYPE.getName( ),
      "Indicates whether or not the Queue is empty.",
      true, false, true);
    attributeInfo[5] = new MBeanAttributeInfo(
      "Suspended", Boolean.TYPE.getName( ),
      "Indicates whether or not the Queue is currently suspended.",
      true, false, true);
    attributeInfo[6] = new MBeanAttributeInfo(
      "EndOfInput", Boolean.TYPE.getName( ),
      "Indicates if end-of-input has been signalled by all suppliers.",
      true, false, true);
    attributeInfo[7] = new MBeanAttributeInfo(
      "NumberOfItemsProcessed", Long.TYPE.getName( ),
      "The number of items that have been removed from the Queue.",
      true, false, false);
    attributeInfo[8] = new MBeanAttributeInfo(
      "AddWaitTime", Long.TYPE.getName( ),
      "No. Milliseconds spent waiting to add because Queue was full.",
      true, false, false);
    attributeInfo[9] = new MBeanAttributeInfo(
      "RemoveWaitTime", Long.TYPE.getName( ),
      "No. milliseconds spent waiting to remove because Queue was empty.",
      true, false, false);
    // Constructors
    Class[] signature = {Integer.TYPE};
    Constructor constructor = null;
    MBeanConstructorInfo[] constructorInfo = new MBeanConstructorInfo[1];
    try {
      constructor = this.getClass( ).getConstructor(signature);
```

Example 3-3. Creating an instance of MBeanInfo (continued)

```
      constructorInfo[0] = new MBeanConstructorInfo(
        "Custom constructor", constructor);
    } catch (Exception e) {
      e.printStackTrace( );
    }
    // Operations
    MBeanOperationInfo[] operationInfo = new MBeanOperationInfo[3];
    MBeanParameterInfo[] parms = new MBeanParameterInfo[0];
    operationInfo[0] = new MBeanOperationInfo(
      "suspend", "Suspends processing of the Queue.",
      parms, Void.TYPE.getName( ), MBeanOperationInfo.ACTION);
    operationInfo[1] = new MBeanOperationInfo(
      "resume", "Resumes processing of the Queue.",
      parms, Void.TYPE.getName( ), MBeanOperationInfo.ACTION);
    operationInfo[2] = new MBeanOperationInfo(
      "reset", "Resets the state of this MBean.",
      parms, Void.TYPE.getName( ), MBeanOperationInfo.ACTION);
    // Notifications
    MBeanNotificationInfo[] notificationInfo = new MBeanNotificationInfo[1];
    String[] notificationTypes = new String[2];
    notificationTypes[0] = NOTIF_STALLED_FULL;
    notificationTypes[1] = NOTIF_STALLED_EMPTY;
    notificationInfo[0] = new MBeanNotificationInfo(
      notificationTypes,
      "StalledQueueNotifications",
      "Potential stall notifications emitted by the Queue."
    );
    // MBeanInfo
    _MBeanInfo = new MBeanInfo(
      "Queue",
      "Queue MBean",
      attributeInfo,
      constructorInfo,
      operationInfo,
      notificationInfo
    );
  }
// . . .
}
```

In this example, 10 attributes, 1 constructor, 3 operations, and 2 notifications
describe the Queue as a managed resource. Notice the private variable _MBeanInfo,
which is used to hold an instance of the MBeanInfo object that contains the metadata
for the Queue MBean. This variable is returned by the *getMBeanInfo()* method (part
of the DynamicMBean interface) that is invoked by a management application to discover the management interface of an MBean.

In this section, we looked at how to create all of the metadata classes necessary to
fully describe the management interface of a dynamic MBean. In the next section, we
will take a closer look at how the information in the MBeanInfo object must match up
to the logic in the implementation of the DynamicMBean interface.

Implementing the DynamicMBean Interface

Example 3-1 showed the definition of the DynamicMBean interface. In this section, we will first look at some other support classes from the javax.management package that are important to properly implementing dynamic MBeans. Then we will look at how to write code to implement the methods on the dynamic MBean interface.

Attribute

This class is used to encapsulate a single attribute value. There are two important properties of this class, *name* and *value*, which represent the attribute's name and value, respectively. The following code shows the significant features of this class:

```
package javax.management;
// . . .
public class Attribute implements Serializable {
// . . .
  public Attribute(String name, Object value) {
    // . . .
  }
// . . .
  public String getName( ) {
    // . . .
  }
  public Object getValue( ) {
    // . . .
  }
// . . .
}
```

There are three significant features to this class:

Constructor
    When creating the class, pass in the name of the attribute and an object reference for the attribute's value. If the attribute's type is one of the Java fundamental types, wrap that fundamental type in the appropriate JDK wrapper class (e.g., if the type is a char, wrap it in an Character object).

Getter for the attribute name
    Returns the attribute's name.

Getter for the attribute's value
    Returns the attribute's value.

AttributeList

Instances of this class are used to hold a List of Attribute instances. The following code shows the significant features of AttributeList:

```
package javax.management;
import java.util.ArrayList;
// . . .
```

```
public class AttributeList extends ArrayList {
  public AttributeList( ) {
  }
  // . . .
  }
```

AttributeList inherits from ArrayList, which means that all of the methods you are used to using for an ArrayList—such as *get()*, *set()*, and *iterator()*—are available on AttributeList (see the JDK Javadoc for more information).

To create an instance of AttributeList, use:

```
AttributeList attributeList = new AttributeList( );
```

To set the initial capacity of the internal ArrayList to 10, use:

```
AttributeList attributeList = new AttributeList(10);
```

To add an Attribute to the AttributeList, use:

```
Attribute attribute = new Attribute("QueueSize", new Integer(10));
AttributeList attributeList = new AttributeList( );
attributeList.add(attribute);
```

AttributeList is an ArrayList, so there are two ways of getting at the contents of any AttributeList instance. The first way is to use a java.util.Iterator object:

```
// assume attributeList is an instance of AttributeList
Iterator iter = attributeList.iterator( );
while (iter.hasNext( )) {
  Attribute attribute = (Attribute)iter.next( );
  // do something with attribute. . .
}
```

The second way is to access the contents using an index. The code snippet below shows how to walk through the contents of the AttributeList from beginning to end. However, you can also access any member of the AttributeList directly by specifying its index (as long as you don't specify an invalid index, in which case an IndexOutOfBoundsException will be thrown).

```
// assume attributeList is an instance of AttributeList
for (int idx = 0; idx < attributeList.size( ); idx++) {
  Attribute attribute = (Attribute)attributeList.get(idx);
  // do something with attribute. . .
}
```

Now, let's take the example of the Queue class from the sample application. We have already looked at Queue's management interface and how we created the necessary metadata classes to expose it. Here we will look at how we implement DynamicMBean on the Queue class so that the management interface functionally corresponds to how it is exposed.

The *getMBeanInfo()* method of the DynamicMBean interface is what ties the metadata to the implementation of the DynamicMBean interface. This is a very simple method that simply returns an MBeanInfo instance that contains the definition of the management interface of the MBean. A management application uses *getMBeanInfo()* to discover what the management interface looks like. But then what? Well, now that the management interface is known, the management application uses the DynamicMBean interface to set and get attribute values and invoke methods on the MBean.

Let's take a closer look at the methods of the DynamicMBean interface and how to implement them.

getAttribute( )

This method is used to retrieve a single attribute value and is defined as:

```
public Object getAttribute(String attribute)
   throws AttributeNotFoundException,
          MBeanException,
          ReflectionException {
// . . .
}
```

Recall from the section "Describing the Management Interface" that every attribute must have a corresponding MBeanAttributeInfo instance to describe it. One of the required parameters to both of the constructors of MBeanAttributeInfo is *name*, which is the name of the attribute. This name is passed to *getAttribute()* as a String. If this parameter does not match one of the attribute names from the metadata, you must throw an AttributeNotFoundException. The following example shows one such implementation. When looking at this example, you may want to refer back to Example 3-3, which shows the metadata created for the attributes of the Queue class, so you can see how the attribute names there must match up with the code in *getAttribute()*.

```
public class Queue extends Basic implements DynamicMBean {
// . . .
   public Object getAttribute(String attributeName)
      throws AttributeNotFoundException,
             MBeanException,
             ReflectionException {
      Object ret = null;

      if (attributeName.equals("QueueSize")) {
        ret = new Integer(getQueueSize( ));
      }
      else if (attributeName.equals("NumberOfSuppliers")) {
        ret = new Integer(getNumberOfSuppliers( ));
      }
      else if (attributeName.equals("NumberOfConsumers")) {
        ret = new Integer(getNumberOfConsumers( ));
      }
      else if (attributeName.equals("QueueFull")) {
        ret = new Boolean(isQueueFull( ));
      }
      else if (attributeName.equals("QueueEmpty")) {
        ret = new Boolean(isQueueEmpty( ));
      }
```

```
      else if (attributeName.equals("Suspended")) {
        ret = new Boolean(isSuspended());
      }
      else if (attributeName.equals("EndOfInput")) {
        ret = new Boolean(isEndOfInput());
      }
      else if (attributeName.equals("NumberOfItemsProcessed")) {
        ret = new Long(getNumberOfItemsProcessed());
      }
      else if (attributeName.equals("AddWaitTime")) {
        ret = new Long(getAddWaitTime());
      }
      else if (attributeName.equals("RemoveWaitTime")) {
        ret = new Long(getRemoveWaitTime());
      }
      else throw new AttributeNotFoundException(
        "Queue.getAttribute(): ERROR: " +
        "Cannot find " + attributeName + " attribute.");
      }
      return ret;
    }
  // . . .
  }
```

The code itself is very simple: it's just a large if/else if/else construct in which we attempt to match the attribute name that is passed as a parameter. If the attribute name matches, we simply call the appropriate getter, wrap any fundamental types in their appropriate JDK wrappers, and return the value to the caller. If the attribute value cannot be found, we throw an AttributeNotFoundException with some information about the requested attribute.

What if your management interface has no attributes? In that case, the body of this method should throw an AttributeNotFoundException, because there are no attributes. For example, if Queue has no attributes, this method will look like this:

```
  public Object getAttribute(String attribute)
    throws AttributeNotFoundException,
           MBeanException,
           ReflectionException {
    throw AttributeNotFoundException("Attribute\'" + attribute +
      "\' not found.");
  }
```

setAttribute()

This method is used to set a single attribute value and is defined as:

```
  public void setAttribute(Attribute attribute)
    throws AttributeNotFoundException,
           InvalidAttributeValueException,
           MBeanException,
           ReflectionException {
  // . . .
  }
```

What is passed to this class is an `Attribute` instance, a JMX class that wraps an attribute's name and value as a pair. `Attribute` has two getters: one for the name and one for the value. The name must match one of the attribute names that has been exposed on the management interface of your MBean, or an `AttributeNotFound-Exception` will be thrown.

```java
public class Queue extends Basic implements DynamicMBean {
    // . . .
    public void setAttribute(Attribute attribute)
        throws AttributeNotFoundException,
                InvalidAttributeValueException,
                MBeanException,
                ReflectionException {
        String name = attribute.getName( );
        Object value = attribute.getValue( );
        if (name.equals("QueueSize")) {
            if (value instanceof Integer)
                setQueueSize(((Integer)value).intValue( ));
            else {
                throw new InvalidAttributeValueException(
                    "QueueSize must be an Integer."
                    );
            }
        }
        else throw new AttributeNotFoundException(
            "Queue.setAttribute( ): ERROR: " +
            "Cannot find attribute \'" + name + "\'.");
    }
    // . . .
}
```

`Queue` has only one writable attribute, `QueueSize`, so that's the only one we have to handle. But notice that we were careful to make sure the object passed inside the `Attribute` instance is of the correct type—if it isn't, we throw an `InvalidAttribute-ValueException`. This is standard practice when setting attribute values inside *setAttribute()* and prevents all sorts of nasty runtime exceptions from the JVM. Because it is possible that an ill-mannered management application may ignore the information in the metadata and pass an attribute value of the wrong type, we should always be careful and code for this contingency.

getAttributes( )

This method is used to retrieve the values of a group of attributes and is defined as:

```java
public AttributeList getAttributes(String[] attributeNames) {
    // . . .
}
```

The *attributeNames* parameter is a `String` array that contains the names of the attributes whose values are to be retrieved. It is very straightforward to implement this method by delegating to the *getAttribute()* method for each attribute in the array:

```
public class Queue extends Basic implements DynamicMBean {
// . . .
  public AttributeList getAttributes(String[] attributeNames) {

    AttributeList resultList = new AttributeList();
    for (int aa = 0; aa < attributeNames.length; aa++){
      try {
        Object value = getAttribute(attributeNames[aa]);
        resultList.add(new Attribute(attributeNames[aa], value));
      } catch (Exception e) {
        // handle the exception. . .
      }
    }
    return(resultList);
  }
// . . .
}
```

After delegating to *getAttribute()*, a new Attribute object is instantiated and initialized with the name of the attribute and its value. This is the AttributeList object that will be returned to the caller.

setAttributes( )

This method is used to set the values of a group of attributes and is defined as:

```
public AttributeList setAttributes(AttributeList attributes) {
  // . . .
}
```

The *attributes* parameter is an AttributeList object. As we discussed earlier, the AttributeList object contains a List of Attribute objects, each of which corresponds to an attribute to be set. The following example shows how to access each Attribute object from the AttributeList and set its value by delegating to *setAttribute()*:

```
public class Queue extends Basic implements DynamicMBean {
// . . .
  public AttributeList setAttributes(AttributeList attributes) {
    AttributeList attributeList = new AttributeList();
    for (int aa = 0; aa < attributes.size(); aa++) {
      try {
        Attribute attribute = (Attribute)attributes.get(aa);
        setAttribute(attribute);
        String name = attribute.getName();
        Object value = getAttribute(name);
        attributeList.add(new Attribute(name, value));
      } catch (Exception e) {
        e.printStackTrace();
      }
    }
    return attributeList;
  }
// . . .
}
```

Notice the emphasized lines. We retrieve the `Attribute` object from the `AttributeList` and delegate the actual setting of the value to *setAttribute()*. The JMX specification states that the attributes whose values were successfully set should be returned in an `AttributeList`. It is conceivable that this list could differ from the `AttributeList` that was passed into *setAttributes()*, so we must handle any exceptions thrown from *setAttribute()* gracefully and continue to process the remaining `Attribute` objects.

Because the attribute that has been set may not be readable, we delegate the retrieval of its new value to *getAttribute()*. If the attribute is not readable, *getAttribute()* throws an exception that prevents the returned `AttributeList` object from containing the `Attribute` object representing that attribute. If the attribute is readable, *getAttribute()* simply returns the value and everything proceeds.

invoke( )

This method is used to invoke an operation on an MBean's management interface and is defined as:

```
public Object invoke(String operationName,
                     Object params[],
                     String signature[])
   throws MBeanException,
          ReflectionException {
   // . . .
   }
```

operationName is the name of the management operation to invoke and must match exactly one of the operations for which there is a corresponding `MBeanOperationInfo` instance. *params* is an array of objects that contains the actual parameter values that must be passed to the operation. *signature* is an array of `Class` objects that represents the signature of the operation.

We first check to see if the *operationName* parameter matches one of the operations exposed on the MBean's management interface. If no match is found, a `ReflectionException` should be thrown. Otherwise, this method should check to make sure the signature matches the expected signature of the operation. If it does not, a `ReflectionException` should be thrown. Next, the *params* array should be checked to be sure that the objects passed are actually of the correct type. If they are not, a `ReflectionException` should be thrown. If they are of the correct type, the invocation should be made and the parameters passed. The following example shows how to implement this algorithm for *invoke()*:

```
public class Queue extends Basic implements DynamicMBean {
   // . . .
   public Object invoke(String operationName,
                        Object params[],
                        String signature[])
      throws MBeanException,
             ReflectionException {
```

```
      Object ret = null;
      if (operationName.equals("reset")) {
        reset();
      }
      else if (operationName.equals("suspend")) {
        suspend();
      }
      else if (operationName.equals("resume")) {
        resume();
      }
      else {
        throw new ReflectionException(
                new NoSuchMethodException(operationName),
                "Cannot find the operation \'" +
                operationName + " in " + dClassName);
      }
    }
  }
  // . . .
  }
```

The logic inside this method is relatively simple. We just look at the *operationName* parameter, and if it matches one of the operations for which we created an MBeanOperationInfo instance, we invoke the appropriate method. Otherwise, we throw a NoSuchMethodException wrapped inside a ReflectionException.

Dynamic MBean Inheritance Patterns

In this section, we will look at how the introspection process performed by the MBean server causes the inheritance patterns available to dynamic MBeans to differ from those available to standard MBeans.

Suppose that our application has the inheritance graph shown in Figure 3-2.

In this scenario, each class (with the exception of Supplier and Consumer) explicitly implements the DynamicMBean interface. Based on the information in the figure, what would you expect the management interface of, say, Controller to be? If you said that it would be the union of the management interface of Basic and Controller, you would be mistaken. You may recall from the previous chapter that using inheritance pattern #4 would allow a child class to augment its management interface with that of its parent class. However, no such inheritance patterns are available for dynamic MBeans.

What do you suppose the management interface of Supplier is? In fact, it may be a better question to ask whether Supplier is an MBean at all. The answer is yes, Supplier is indeed an MBean (in fact, a dynamic MBean), because it may inherit the dynamic MBean interface from its parent class. How is this possible? When Supplier is registered with the MBean server, the MBean server performs its introspection and looks to see whether Supplier exposes a management interface. Because it does not, the MBean server next looks to its parent class, Worker. The MBean server notices

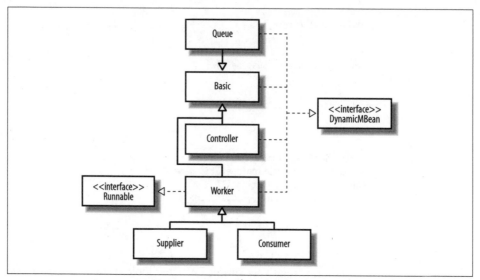

Figure 3-2. UML diagram showing a possible inheritance scenario for the sample application

that Worker does implement an MBean interface, declares Supplier to be an MBean, and delegates all MBean functionality to Worker (where the management interface is actually implemented).

Let's look at another example. Suppose that we have the inheritance scenario shown in Figure 3-3, again using the classes from the application.

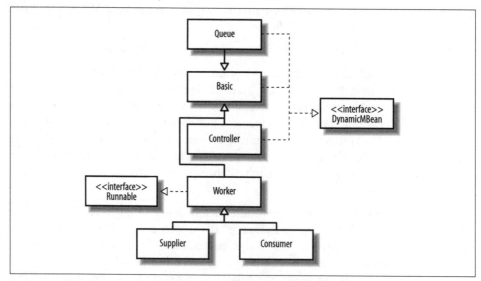

Figure 3-3. Another possible inheritance scenario, shown in UML notation

Notice that Worker does not implement DynamicMBean. What impact do you suppose that has on the management interface exposed by Supplier and Consumer? If you said that Supplier and Consumer are dynamic MBeans whose management interface looks exactly like that of Basic, you are correct. Let's look again at the introspection that is performed by the MBean server, using Supplier as an example. Supplier does not implement an MBean interface, so the MBean server moves up the inheritance graph to Worker and notices that it does not implement an MBean interface either. The MBean server continues up the inheritance graph to Worker's parent class, Basic, and notices that it implements the DynamicMBean interface, so it declares Supplier a dynamic MBean and delegates all MBean functionality to Basic. The MBean server will continue walking the inheritance graph during its introspection process either until an MBean interface is found or until the top of the inheritance tree is reached without finding an MBean interface (at which point a NotCompliantMBeanException is thrown).

A class cannot implement both DynamicMBean and a standard MBean interface. Suppose that Queue had been declared as:

```
public class Queue extends Basic
    implements QueueMBean, DynamicMBean {
// . . .
}
```

When the MBean server performs introspection, it will detect that Queue is attempting to implement both a standard and a dynamic MBean interface and will throw a NotCompliantMBeanException.

As I mentioned earlier, unlike standard MBeans, whose management interfaces can be composed from the MBean interfaces they explicitly implement as well as any MBean interfaces implemented by their parent class (and their parent's parent class, and so on), dynamic MBeans' interfaces do not aggregate. Rather, the management interface exposed by a dynamic MBean is that of the nearest implementation of DynamicMBean as the inheritance graph is traversed during introspection. If the MBean server detects an implementation of DynamicMBean, inheritance traversal stops. In other words, while a standard MBean can use the inheritance patterns discussed in Chapter 2 to create an aggregate of the management interface of its parent class, a dynamic MBean cannot.

However, all is not lost. There are two approaches that we can take to achieve the aggregation we desire, while at the same time writing perfectly compliant dynamic MBeans: explicit superclass exposure and superclass delegation.

Explicit superclass exposure means that we will write code inside the child class's implementation of DynamicMBean to explicitly expose attributes and operations from the parent class's management interface. These attributes are explicitly mentioned by name in the code. This approach offers us more control over what is exposed on the child class's management interface and allows us to selectively expose only those attributes and operations from the parent class that we deem necessary on the child class's management interface. However, this means that we are essentially writing code in the child class that has already been written in the parent class, which results in duplicate code and a larger code base.

Superclass delegation means that we will write code in the child class to delegate the attribute *set()/get()* and operation *invoke()* calls to the parent class through the super keyword, should the attribute or operation not be found on the child class. This approach results in a cleaner implementation, because we don't have to know what the management interface of the superclass looks like; we only need to know that it has one. The drawback of this approach is that it forces us into a wholesale exposure of the parent class's management interface on the child class.

Let's look at these two approaches one at a time, starting with explicit superclass exposure.

Explicit Superclass Exposure

Remember how each attribute and operation is assigned a name? Explicit superclass exposure just means that we are going to include else if blocks in the *getAttribute()*, *setAttribute()*, and *invoke()* methods that explicitly mention the names of the attributes (in the case of *getAttribute()* and *setAttribute()*) and operations (in the case of *invoke()*). These three methods will then call the appropriate getter, setter, or method, respectively. Let's look at an example from the application.

Queue inherits from Basic, and Basic implements the DynamicMBean interface for its attributes (TraceOn, DebugOn, and NumberOfResets) and its operations (*enableTracing*, *disableTracing*, *enableDebugging*, and *disableDebugging*). Recall from Example 3-3 how we created all of the metadata classes for Queue's management interface in Queue's constructor. If we are going to augment Queue's management interface with attributes and operations from Basic's management interface, we must expose those attributes and operations on the MBeanInfo instance that is returned from Queue's *getMBeanInfo()* method. Thus, we must create the metadata classes for these attributes and operations in Queue's constructor. Example 3-4 shows how to do this, showing enough of Example 3-3 to provide you some context.

Example 3-4. Creating metadata classes to expose attributes and operations from Queue's parent class, Basic, through explicit superclass exposure

```
public class Queue extends Basic implements DynamicMBean {
// . . .
  private MBeanInfo _MBeanInfo;
  // . . .
  public Queue(int queueSize) {
    // . . .
```

Example 3-4. Creating metadata classes to expose attributes and operations from Queue's parent class, Basic, through explicit superclass exposure (continued)

```
// Attributes
int numberOfParentAttributes = 2;
MBeanAttributeInfo[] attributeInfo =
  new MBeanAttributeInfo[numberOfParentAttributes + 10];
attributeInfo[0] = new MBeanAttributeInfo(
  "QueueSize", Integer.TYPE.getName( ),
  "Maximum number of items the queue may contain at one time.",
  true, true, false);
// . . .
attributeInfo[9] = new MBeanAttributeInfo(
  "RemoveWaitTime", Long.TYPE.getName( ),
  "No. milliseconds spent waiting to remove because Queue was empty.",
  true, false, false);
attributeInfo[10] = new MBeanAttributeInfo(
  "NumberOfResets", Integer.TYPE.getName( ),
  "The number of times reset( ) has been called.",
  true, false, false);
attributeInfo[11] = new MBeanAttributeInfo(
  "TraceOn", Boolean.TYPE.getName( ),
  "Indicates whether or not tracing is on.",
  true, false, true);
// . . .
// Constructors
// . . .
// Operations
int numberOfParentOperations = 2;
MBeanOperationInfo[] operationInfo =
  new MBeanOperationInfo[numberOfParentOperations+3];
MBeanParameterInfo[] parms = new MBeanParameterInfo[0];
operationInfo[0] = new MBeanOperationInfo(
  "suspend", "Suspends processing of the Queue.",
  parms, Void.TYPE.getName( ), MBeanOperationInfo.ACTION);
operationInfo[1] = new MBeanOperationInfo(
  "resume", "Resumes processing of the Queue.",
  parms, Void.TYPE.getName( ), MBeanOperationInfo.ACTION);
operationInfo[2] = new MBeanOperationInfo(
  "reset", "Resets the state of this MBean.",
  parms, Void.TYPE.getName( ), MBeanOperationInfo.ACTION);
operationInfo[3] = new MBeanOperationInfo(
  "enableTracing", "Enables tracing.",
  parms, Void.TYPE.getName( ), MBeanOperationInfo.ACTION);
operationInfo[4] = new MBeanOperationInfo(
  "disableTracing", "Disables tracing.",
  parms, Void.TYPE.getName( ), MBeanOperationInfo.ACTION);
// . . .
// Notifications
// no notifications for this MBean, also no parent notifications
MBeanNotificationInfo[] notificationInfo = new MBeanNotificationInfo[0];
// . . .
```

```
    // MBeanInfo
    _MBeanInfo = new MBeanInfo(
      "Queue",
      "Queue MBean",
      attributeInfo,
      constructorInfo,
      operationInfo,
      notificationInfo
    );
  }
// . . .
}
```

As you can see from Example 3-4, creating the necessary metadata classes requires only knowledge of the attributes and operations and extra code. Notice that we didn't create metadata for the DebugOn attribute or the *enableDebugging* and *disableDebugging* operations. This is just to show you that when you select explicit superclass exposure as the management interface inheritance approach for your dynamic MBeans, you can pick and choose which attributes and operations to expose from the parent class.

We must also make modifications to Queue's implementation of DynamicMBean, as discussed in the next section.

getAttribute( )

Implementing this method is a simple matter of adding the same number of else if blocks as the number of attributes we're exposing from the parent class:

```
    public class Queue extends Basic implements DynamicMBean {
    // . . .
      public Object getAttribute(String attributeName)
        throws AttributeNotFoundException,
               MBeanException,
               ReflectionException {
        Object ret = null;

        if (attributeName.equals("QueueSize")) {
          ret = new Integer(getQueueSize( ));
        }
        // . . .
        else if (attributeName.equals("RemoveWaitTime")) {
          ret = new Long(getRemoveWaitTime( ));
        }
        else if (attributeName.equals("NumberOfResets")) {
          ret = new Integer(getNumberOfResets( ));
        }
        else if (attributeName.equals("TraceOn")) {
          ret = new Boolean(isTraceOn( ));
        }
```

```
        else throw new AttributeNotFoundException(
          "Queue.getAttribute( ): ERROR: " +
          "Cannot find " + attributeName + " attribute.");
        }
        return ret;
      }
    // . . .
    }
```

We exposed two attributes from the parent class, so we write two else if blocks for those attributes and delegate to the appropriate method. We know we can call this method because of Java inheritance.

setAttribute( )

There are no writable attributes on Basic, but if there were, the logic would be similar to that of *getAttribute()*. Suppose, for the purposes of example, that TraceOn is a writable attribute. In that case, the implementation of *setAttribute()* would look like this:

```
public class Queue extends Basic implements DynamicMBean {
// . . .
  public void setAttribute(Attribute attribute)
    throws AttributeNotFoundException,
           InvalidAttributeValueException,
           MBeanException,
           ReflectionException {
    String name = attribute.getName( );
    Object value = attribute.getValue( );
    // See if attribute is on parent class
    if (name.equals("QueueSize")) {
      setQueueSize(((Integer)value).intValue( ));
    }
    else if (name.equals("TraceOn")) {
      setTraceOn(((Boolean)value).booleanValue( ));
    }
    else throw new AttributeNotFoundException(
      "Queue.getAttribute( ): ERROR: " +
      "Cannot find " + attributeName + " attribute.");
    }
  // . . .
  }
```

If the name of the attribute to set is "TraceOn," we simply invoke the setter for the attribute.

invoke( )

You are probably starting to see a pattern here. When you use explicit superclass exposure as the management interface inheritance mechanism for your MBeans, you simply include extra else if blocks for the attributes and, in this case, the operations that are to be exposed.

The following example shows how to use this approach to modify *invoke()* to expose
Basic's management interface methods:

```
public class Queue extends Basic implements DynamicMBean {
// . . .
   public Object invoke(String operationName,
                        Object params[],
                        String signature[])
      throws MBeanException,
             ReflectionException {
   Object ret = Void.TYPE;
   ret = Void.TYPE;
   if (operationName.equals("suspend")) {
     suspend( );
   }
   else if (operationName.equals("resume")) {
     resume( );
   }
   else if (operationName.equals("enableTracing")) {
     enableTracing( );
   }
   else if (operationName.equals("disableTracing")) {
     disableTracing( );
   }
   else {
     throw new ReflectionException(
          new NoSuchMethodException(operationName),
              "Queue.invoke( ): ERROR: " +
              "Cannot find the operation " + operationName + "!");
   }
   return ret;
 }
// . . .
}
```

One drawback of using explicit superclass exposure is that the child class must have
explicit knowledge of the parent class's management interface. Also, this approach is
more susceptible to errors when code changes to the parent class are necessary.
However, you must weigh these risks against the benefits of being able to selectively
expose attributes and operations from the parent class's management interface on
the child class and base your decision of whether or not to use this approach on that
information.

Superclass Delegation

This is the more generic of the two approaches to dynamic MBean management interface inheritance. With superclass delegation, when figuring out which attribute to
get/set or operation to invoke, the child class first looks at its own management interface and then, if the attribute or operation is not found, delegates to its parent class
(which may delegate to its parent class, and so on). This requires changes to how the
metadata is created for the child class. Let's look at an example from the application.

Queue inherits from Basic, and Basic implements the DynamicMBean interface for its attributes (TraceOn, DebugOn, and NumberOfResets) and its operations (*enableTracing*, *disableTracing*, *enableDebugging*, and *disableDebugging*). Recall from Example 3-4 how we created all of the metadata classes for Queue's management interface in Queue's constructor. If we are going to augment Queue's management interface with attributes and operations from Basic's management interface, we must expose those attributes and operations on the MBeanInfo instance that is returned from Queue's *getMBeanInfo()* method. Thus, we must create the metadata classes for these attributes and operations in Queue's constructor. Example 3-5 shows how to do this, showing enough of Example 3-4 to provide you some context.

Example 3-5. Creating metadata classes to expose attributes and operations from Queue's parent class, Basic, through superclass delegation

```java
public class Queue extends Basic implements DynamicMBean {
// . . .
  private MBeanInfo _MBeanInfo;
  // . . .
  public Queue(int queueSize) {
    MBeanInfo parentInfo = super.getMBeanInfo( );
    // . . .
    // Attributes
    MBeanAttributeInfo[] parentAttributes = parentInfo.getAttributes( );
    int numberOfParentAttributes = parentAttributes.length;
    MBeanAttributeInfo[] attributeInfo =
      new MBeanAttributeInfo[numberOfParentAttributes + 10];
    System.arraycopy(parentAttributes,0,attributeInfo,0,numberOfParentAttributes);
    attributeInfo[numParentAtts+0] = new MBeanAttributeInfo(
      "QueueSize", Integer.TYPE.getName( ),
      "Maximum number of items the queue may contain at one time.",
      true, true, false);
    attributeInfo[numParentAtts+1] = new MBeanAttributeInfo(
      "NumberOfConsumers", Integer.TYPE.getName( ),
      "The number of consumers pulling from this Queue.",
      true, false, false);
    // . . .
    // Constructors
    // . . .
    // Operations
    MBeanOperationInfo[] parentOperations = parentInfo.getOperations( );
    int numberOfParentOperations = parentOperations.length;
    MBeanOperationInfo[] operationInfo =
      new MBeanOperationInfo[numberOfParentOperations+2];
    System.arraycopy(parentOperations,0,operationInfo,0,numberOfParentOperations);
    MBeanParameterInfo[] parms = new MBeanParameterInfo[0];
    operationInfo[numParentOps+0] = new MBeanOperationInfo(
      "suspend", "Suspends processing of the Queue.",
      parms, Void.TYPE.getName( ), MBeanOperationInfo.ACTION);
    operationInfo[numParentOps+1] = new MBeanOperationInfo(
      "resume", "Resumes processing of the Queue.",
      parms, Void.TYPE.getName( ), MBeanOperationInfo.ACTION);
    // . . .
```

Example 3-5. Creating metadata classes to expose attributes and operations from Queue's parent class, Basic, through superclass delegation (continued)

```
      // Notifications
      MBeanNotificationInfo[] parentNotifications = parentInfo.getNotifications();
      int numberOfParentNotifications = parentNotifications.length;
      // no notifications for this MBean, use parent notifications
      MBeanNotificationInfo[] notificationInfo =
        new MBeanNotificationInfo[numberOfParentNotifications+0];
      System.arraycopy(parentNotifications,0,notificationInfo,0,
                      numberOfParentNotifications);
      // . . .
      // MBeanInfo
      _MBeanInfo = new MBeanInfo(
        "Queue",
        "Queue MBean",
        attributeInfo,
        constructorInfo,
        operationInfo,
        notificationInfo
      );
    }
// . . .
}
```

The highlighted lines in Example 3-5 are the lines that must be added to create the necessary metadata classes. Actually, we're only making a copy of the reference to the metadata classes that were created by the parent class. We could instead have chosen to *clone()* the instances, but this approach seemed a reasonable one for the purpose at hand. Once we get the MBeanInfo instance that contains the metadata for the parent class, it is a simple matter of making sure the attribute, operation, and notification arrays are large enough to accommodate the attributes, operations, and notifications for both the Queue class and its parent class. That's it; it's pretty straightforward.

We must also make modifications to Queue's implementation of DynamicMBean, as discussed in the next section.

getAttribute( )

This method must have the same signature as its parent method, so we first check to see if the requested attribute is available on the child class and then, if it is not, delegate to the parent class's *getAttribute()* method:

```
    public class Queue extends Basic implements DynamicMBean {
    // . . .
      public Object getAttribute(String attributeName)
        throws AttributeNotFoundException,
             MBeanException,
             ReflectionException {
```

```
      Object ret = null;
      if (attributeName.equals("QueueSize")) {
        ret = new Integer(getQueueSize( ));
      }
      // . . .
      else {
        ret = super.getAttribute(attributeName);
      }
      return ret;
    }
  // . . .
  }
```

I omitted some of the lines of code in this example, for the sake of brevity. (If you
compare this example to the corresponding example from the explicit superclass
exposure pattern, you can see how I simplified the code.) If the requested attribute is
not available on the parent class, we can simply let the AttributeNotFoundException
propagate out. The message generated will be from the parent class, but we can
always surround the superclass delegation with a try/catch block and augment or
modify any exception thrown by the superclass.

setAttribute( )

There are no writable attributes on either Queue or Basic, but superclass delegation is
a generic approach, so the child class makes no assumptions about access to the
attributes on the parent class. The following example shows how to implement
setAttribute( ) using this approach:

```
public class Queue extends Basic implements DynamicMBean {
// . . .
  public void setAttribute(Attribute attribute)
    throws AttributeNotFoundException,
           InvalidAttributeValueException,
           MBeanException,
           ReflectionException {
    String name = attribute.getName( );
    Object value = attribute.getValue( );
    if (name.equals("QueueSize")) {
      setQueueSize(((Integer)value).intValue( ));
    }
    super.setAttribute(attribute);
  }
// . . .
}
```

This example doesn't contain the contrived writable TraceOn attribute of Basic, but
notice how much simpler the code is compared to the corresponding explicit superclass exposure example from earlier in this chapter. If the attribute is not found on
the child class, we simply delegate to the parent class. If an AttributeNotFound-
Exception is thrown, we simply let it propagate out of this method.

invoke( )

Superclass delegation works the same way for this method as well. First we check to see if the method is exposed on the child class interface. If it is not, we delegate to the superclass:

```
public class Queue extends Basic implements DynamicMBean {
// . . .
  public Object invoke(String operationName,
                       Object params[],
                       String signature[])
    throws MBeanException,
           ReflectionException {
    Object ret = Void.TYPE;
    ret = Void.TYPE;
    if (operationName.equals("suspend")) {
      suspend( );
    }
    else if (operationName.equals("resume")) {
      resume( );
    }
    else {
      super.invoke(operationName, params, signature);
    }
    return ret;
  }
// . . .
}
```

Again, the code is greatly simplified because we delegate to the superclass if the method to invoke is not recognized.

One drawback of this approach is that you cannot selectively perform management interface inheritance; superclass delegation is generic and exposes the entire management interface of the parent class. However, this also means that changes to the parent class's management interface will not ripple through the child class, as is the case with explicit superclass exposure.

Mixing It Up

You may be wondering at this point why you can't simply selectively expose the desired attributes from the parent management interface and generically delegate in the DynamicMBean implementation. There is no reason that you cannot take this approach; it's entirely up to you.

CHAPTER 4

Model MBeans

Model MBeans are the most powerful type of MBean. Instrumenting your application resources as model MBeans provides you with the most features and flexibility of any of the MBean types that are fully specified by the current JMX specification. Furthermore, this power comes without a commensurate level of complexity! In this chapter, we will examine the features provided by model MBeans and why you might choose this instrumentation strategy over the others we have discussed so far. Then we will look at how model MBeans work, including a detailed look at the `Descriptor` class and the metadata classes that are used by resources instrumented as model MBeans. We will also take a look at `RequiredModelMBean`, a model MBean class that is required to be present in every JMX implementation. Finally, we will develop a working example that uses the same design as the examples of the previous chapters, so you can compare and contrast model MBeans with standard and dynamic MBeans.

An entire book could be devoted to model MBeans, as they are by far the most complex type of MBean. The objective of this chapter is simply to familiarize you sufficiently with the major issues involved in instrumenting your resources as model MBeans that you can do so.

 This chapter assumes that you have read the previous chapter, or are familiar with dynamic MBeans. You should be familiar with the `DynamicMBean` interface and how to use metadata classes to describe an MBean's management interface.

In this chapter, we will refer to MBean features, or simply features. A feature is a constituent of the management interface: an attribute, operation, constructor, parameter, or notification.

Why Use Model MBeans?

Model MBeans are dynamic MBeans and so use metadata to describe the features of the MBean. However, there is one significant difference: model MBeans offer the instrumentation developer a metadata class called `Descriptor`, which is a collection of name/value pairs in which the name is a `String` and the value is an `Object`. This allows for a much richer set of metadata to be exchanged with the agent level, other MBeans, and management applications. Model MBeans offer some significant benefits over other JMX instrumentation strategies, as described in this section.

First, instrumenting your application resources as model MBeans allows you to more quickly perform the instrumentation. You can instrument a resource as a model MBean in just a few lines of code. When a resource's attributes are accessed or changed, or when an operation is invoked, the mechanism used by model MBeans is a *callback*. In other words, when the metadata for an MBean feature (such as an attribute or operation) is created, a reference to the instance of the resource is stored with the metadata, along with the name of the attribute getter/setter or operation. When a management application manages the MBean, it simply uses this information to call back into the resource.

A second benefit of model MBeans is the feature set that comes along with them. Model MBeans have a rich set of features, including support for:

- Automatic attribute-change notifications
- Persistence of the MBean's state at predefined intervals
- Logging of certain significant events in state changes of the MBean
- Accessing MBean state from a cache to improve performance for attributes whose values have a relatively long freshness

A third benefit of model MBeans is that the resource you are instrumenting does not require any code changes. This is a significant advantage when instrumenting existing application or third-party resources that provide a well-defined API. Unlike standard or dynamic MBeans, the resource itself does not have to implement anything to be a perfectly compliant JMX resource. All that is required is that somewhere in the code execution stream there must be code that creates the necessary `Descriptor` and other metadata classes to instrument the resource. A logical place for this code is in the resource itself, but JMX does not require this.

So how can model MBeans offer so much ease of use, flexibility, and power without a corresponding boost in complexity over standard and dynamic MBeans? We will discuss that and much more in the next section.

How Do Model MBeans Work?

Like all other MBean types, model MBeans must be created and registered with the MBean server, and, as with dynamic MBeans, the management interface of your resource is exposed through metadata classes. The similarities end there.

Every compliant JMX implementation must ship a class called `RequiredModelMBean`. This class is instantiated and registered with the MBean server, and it implements several interfaces (including DynamicMBean) that make the life of the instrumentation developer easier. But what is it that makes a model MBean tick? What makes a model MBean work and live up to its reputation (which we discussed in the previous section)? The rest of this section is devoted to answering those questions.

Model MBean Descriptors

The key difference between instrumenting a resource as a model MBean versus as a dynamic MBean is the Descriptor interface. A class implementing this interface describes certain properties of the MBean to the agent level of the JMX architecture, other MBeans, and management applications. Each *descriptor* contains one or more *fields*, which have corresponding Object values. Think of a field as a property of the MBean that gives some other party in the system (usually a management application) a little "nugget" of information about the MBean or one of its features (such as an attribute or operation). Of course, in order to exploit the full power of a descriptor, the management application must know about model MBeans. If the management application knows nothing of model MBeans, it simply treats the MBean as it would any other. Unfortunately, it is then unable to exploit the additional metadata contained in the descriptor. Example 4-1 shows the Descriptor interface.

Example 4-1. The Descriptor interface

```
public interface Descriptor extends java.io.Serializable {

  public Object getFieldValue(String fieldName)
    throws RuntimeOperationsException;

  public void setField(String fieldName, Object fieldValue)
    throws RuntimeOperationsException;

  public String[] getFields();

  public String[] getFieldNames();

  public Object[] getFieldValues(String[] fieldNames);

  public void removeField(String fieldName);

  public void setFields(String[] fieldNames, Object[] fieldValues)
    throws RuntimeOperationsException;

  public Object clone() throws RuntimeOperationsException;

  public boolean isValid() throws RuntimeOperationsException;
}
```

As you can see from Example 4-1, the Descriptor interface revolves around the idea of a field. A field is a name/value pair in which the name is a String that contains the name of the field and the value is an Object that is the value of the field.

Fields have two uses. First, field values are used internally by the JMX implementation—for example, to determine when to retrieve the value of an attribute from the internal cache or when to invoke the getter for that attribute. The second use of Descriptor fields is to provide more information to the agent level or a management application about an MBean or one of its features. This information can then be exploited by any agent or management application that is aware of model MBeans. We will discuss these two types of fields separately, starting with those fields that are used by the JMX implementation (which, for the purposes of this discussion, is the JMX RI). Among the fields used by the JMX RI are several that are required, which will be pointed out when they are presented. None of the fields used by the agent level or management applications are required for JMX compliance, but some of those fields have constraints on the possible values they may have. These will also be pointed out when they are presented.

The fields used by the JMX RI are:

- class
- currencyTimeLimit
- default
- descriptorType (required)
- export
- getMethod
- log
- logFile
- name (required)
- persistPeriod
- persistPolicy
- role
- setMethod
- severity
- value
- visibility

All of these fields are predefined by the JMX specification and are considered to be reserved. They are discussed in detail in the sections that follow.

class

This field is not required and applies only to operations. The value of this field is the string representation of the Class object of the managed resource. For example, if an instance of the application class Queue is instrumented as a model MBean, the value of this field would be "sample.model.Queue". If the object is an Integer, the string representation of its Class object would be "java.lang.Integer". Remember, the string representation of a Class object is always fully qualified.

Example: "class=java.lang.Integer"

currencyTimeLimit

This field is not required and applies to attributes and operations. The value of this field is a String containing the number of seconds that the value field of an attribute or the lastReturnedValue field of an operation is valid. Each time an attribute's getter is called, the value field is updated with the latest value for the attribute, and the lastUpdatedTimeStamp field is set to the current system time.

Once the number of seconds specified by currencyTimeLimit plus the value of lastUpdatedTimeStamp exceeds the current system time, the attribute's value is considered *stale*. At any time before that, however, when the attribute's value is requested, the value field is simply returned to the caller.

By the same token, when an operation is invoked, the lastReturnedValue field is updated and lastReturnedTimeStamp is set to the current system time. Once the number of seconds specified by currentTimeLimit plus the value of lastReturnedTimeStamp exceeds the current system time, the lastReturnedValue is considered stale and the operation is invoked.

This is how caching is performed in the JMX RI. It minimizes the impact of the management infrastructure on application performance for attributes and operations whose values and returned values, respectively, do not necessarily need to be accessed in real time.

If the value of this field is 0, the getter for the attribute is always called. If the value of this field is -1, the attribute's value is never considered to be stale.

Example: "currencyTimeLimit=5"

default

This field is not required and applies only to attributes. The value of this field is a reference to an object of the same type as the attribute. For example, suppose that the attribute's type is Float. The value of default would then be a Float object that contains the default value.

This value is returned only if no getMethod field is defined. If a getMethod is defined, this field is ignored by the RI. This field can be set only by using the *setField()* method of the Descriptor object.

descriptorType

This field is required and applies to the MBean, attributes, operations (including constructors), and notifications. The value of this field is a String that contains one of the following fixed values:

MBean
> The descriptor is for an MBean.

attribute
> The descriptor is for an attribute.

operation
> The descriptor is for an operation or constructor, or for the getter or setter for an attribute.

notification
> The descriptor is for a notification.

Any other value will result in an exception being thrown when you attempt to register the model MBean with the MBean server.

Example: "descriptorType=attribute"

export

The meaning of this field is somewhat vague, as it relates to the export policy of an MBean in a distributed environment (and the distributed services level of the JMX architecture has yet to be specified). The value of the field is the fully qualified class name of an object that is capable of making the MBean locatable—that is, an object that allows the MBean to be found in a distributed environment. If the MBean is not locatable, or if this behavior is not supported, the value of this field should be set to F.

Example: "export=F"

getMethod

This field is not required and applies only to attributes. Although it is not required, if you want to be able to access the value of an attribute, this field is a must. If this field is not provided, the MBean server tries to use the default field value or the value field value to provide a value. The value of getMethod is a String that contains the name of the method on the managed resource that acts as the getter for the attribute.

Example: "getMethod=isQueueFull"

log

This field is not required and applies only to notifications in the current RI. The value of this field is a Boolean object that contains true if notifications are to be logged or false if they are not. If you want to set this field value to a Boolean object, you must use the *setField()* method of the Descriptor object. The value of this field may also be T for true or F for false.

Example: "log=T"

logFile

This field is not required and applies only to notifications in the current RI. However, this field is required if log is set to true. If log is true but the logFile field either is not set or is set to an invalid value, no logging will be performed. The value of this field is a String that contains the full path to the log file to which notifications will be logged. If the value of logFile is not fully qualified, the log file will be written to the current directory.

Example: "logFile=/usr/home/steve/jmxlog"

name

This field is required and applies to the MBean, attributes, operations (including constructors) and notifications. The value of this field is a String that must match exactly what is passed as the *name* parameter to the appropriate metadata constructor. For example, suppose we have an attribute called WorkFactor. When we create the ModelMBeanAttributeInfo object, we must pass WorkFactor as the *name* parameter (which happens to be the first parameter) to the constructor.

Example: "name=WorkFactor"

 The JMX specification states that this field's value is case-sensitive. However, in the JMX 1.0 RI, this does not appear to be the case. When instrumenting your resources, be careful to ensure that you match the case between this field and the *name* parameter of the metadata object. In future releases of the RI, case-sensitivity may be in place, causing your instrumentation to break.

persistPeriod

This field is not required and applies to the MBean and attributes. The value of this field is a String containing the number of seconds that should elapse before the attribute value is written to persistent storage. The value of this field may also be a reference to an Integer object. If you want to set this field value to an Object reference, you must use the *setField()* method of the Descriptor object. This field is valid only if persistPolicy is set to OnTimer or NoMoreOftenThan; otherwise, it is ignored.

Example: "persistPeriod=10"

persistPolicy

This field is not required and applies to the MBean and attributes. The value of this field is a `String` that contains one of the following values:

`Never`
> The attribute is never written to persistent storage.

`OnTimer`
> The attribute value is persisted whenever the number of seconds specified by the `persistPeriod` field expires.

`OnUpdate`
> The attribute value is persisted whenever the attribute's value changes.

`NoMoreOftenThan`
> The attribute value is persisted only when the minimum number of seconds that should expire, as specified by the `persistPeriod` field, have elapsed.

Example: `"persistPolicy=OnTimer"`

role

This field is not required and applies only to operations. The following values for this field are currently recognized by the JMX RI:

`operation`
> Used for operations only

`constructor`
> Used for constructors only

`getter`
> Used if the operation to be invoked is the getter for an attribute

`setter`
> Used if the operation to be invoked is the setter for an attribute

Example: `"role=getter"`

setMethod

This field is not required and applies only to attributes. Although it is not required, if you want to be able to modify the value of an attribute, this field is a must. The value of `setMethod` is a `String` that contains the name of the method on the managed resource that acts as the setter for the attribute.

Example: `"setMethod=setQueueSize"`

severity

This field is not required and applies only to notifications. The JMX specification defines seven numeric `String` values, ranging from 0 to 6, as shown in Table 4-1.

Table 4-1. Predefined severity values and meanings

Value	Meaning
0	Unknown or indeterminate
1	Nonrecoverable
2	Critical or failure
3	Major or severe
4	Minor, marginal, or error
5	Warning
6	Normal or informative

You may create your own values for severity, but consider those summarized in Table 4-1 to be reserved. This helps to ensure compatibility between vendors.

Example: "severity=3"

value

This field is not required and applies only to attributes. This field acts as a cache for the current value of the attribute. Each time an attribute's value is accessed or changed, this field is updated to reflect the current value. This field can be used in conjunction with currencyTimeLimit to minimize the impact of instrumentation on application performance, by acting as a cache for get requests of the attribute's current value. When currencyTimeLimit expires, the next get request for the attribute invokes the attribute's getter and the value is updated. If you want to set this field value to an Object reference, you must use the *setField()* method of the Descriptor object.

Example: "value=SomeStringValue"

visibility

This field is not required and provides a built-in abstraction mechanism for MBeans. There are four predefined values, ranging from 1 to 4. At the least abstract level, 1, the MBean is nearly always visible to any management application. At the greatest abstraction level, 4, the MBean is the least visible. The concrete meanings of "nearly always visible" and "least visible" are not clear in the specification. The meaning of this field will certainly require some sort of agreement between instrumentation developers and management application developers and will most likely be firmed up in a future version (or maintenance release) of the specification.

Example: "visibility=1"

Other fields

Three additional fields are predefined by the JMX specification and are considered to be reserved: presentationString, iterable, and messageID.

The interpretation of the values of each of these fields is covered fairly well (if somewhat necessarily vaguely) in the JMX specification, and we won't discuss them further here. Why not? Remember, one of the strengths of descriptors (and hence of model MBeans) is that they provide a richer set of metadata than is available for dynamic MBeans. The JMX specification provides general guidelines for interpreting predefined field values, but it does not constrain the model MBean instrumentation developer or the management application in terms of exactly how they are to interpret these values.

This openness of field values leads us into our next topic of discussion: user-defined field values. Are they allowed? Absolutely. The JMX specification does not prohibit the model MBean instrumentation developer, the agent level developer, or the management application developer from agreeing on a specific set of field values, as long as they do not conflict with the reserved field names we have already discussed.

So, how do you create a descriptor? As we have already seen, the Descriptor interface defines the contract between the instrumentation level and any other level of the JMX architecture. The JMX implementation must ship with at least one concrete class that implements the Descriptor interface. In the RI, this class is called DescriptorSupport. (It is a common pattern in the RI for interfaces to be implemented by classes named by adding "Support" to the name of the interface.) DescriptorSupport provides several constructors, but we will only look at a few of the more interesting ones here. Note that in the following discussion we'll use the terms descriptor, Descriptor, and DescriptorSupport synonymously (descriptor is a generic term for the Descriptor interface or a class such as DescriptorSupport that implements it, respectively).

The easiest way to create a descriptor is to use the default constructor:

```
// . . .
  Descriptor desc = new DescriptorSupport( );
// . . .
```

What then? The next step is to set the fields that make up the descriptor, using the *setField()* method:

```
// . . .
import javax.management.Descriptor;
import javax.management.modelmbean.DescriptorSupport;
// . . .
  Descriptor desc = new DescriptorSupport( );
  desc.setField("name", "WorkFactor");
  desc.setField("descriptorType", "attribute");
  desc.setField("getMethod", "getWorkFactor");
// . . .
```

DescriptorSupport also provides three constructors that let you do all of this at once. One lets you pass an XML-like String object that contains the field names and values. Its signature is:

```
public DescriptorSupport(String inStr)
  throws MBeanException,
```

```
              RuntimeOperationsException,
              XMLParseException {
     // . . .
     }
```

This XML-like String must be of the format:

```
<descriptor>
   <field name=fieldname1 value=fieldvalue1></field>
   <field name=fieldname2 value=fieldvalue2></field>
     . . .
   <field name=fieldnameN value=fieldvalueN></field>
</descriptor>
```

where *fieldname1* is the name of the first field, *fieldvalue1* is its corresponding value, and so on. Let's use the WorkFactor attribute described earlier to demonstrate how to use the DescriptorSupport constructor:

```
   // . . .
   import javax.management.Descriptor;
   import javax.management.modelmbean.DescriptorSupport;
   // . . .
     String xmlString =
       "<descriptor>" +
         "<field name=name value=WorkFactor></field>" +
         "<field name=descriptorType value=attribute></field>" +
         "<field name=getMethod value=getWorkFactor></field>" +
       "</descriptor>";
     Descriptor desc = new DescriptorSupport(xmlString);
   // . . .
```

 If you think this XML String is not well formed, you are correct; notice that what appear to be XML attributes in the field tag are not surrounded by single or double quotes. I am not certain if this is intentional—if it's simply an oversight, it will certainly be fixed in a future version of the JMX RI. Regardless, this is how the JMX RI behaves, so it deserves mention.

If you need to set a number of fields whose values are String objects, you can create a String array and pass it to another DescriptorSupport constructor. This constructor's signature is:

```
   public DescriptorSupport(String[] fields) {
   // . . .
   }
```

The String objects in the array are of the format *name=value*, where *name* is the name of the field and *value* is its String value. Using the WorkFactor example again, here's how to create a descriptor with this constructor:

```
   // . . .
   import javax.management.Descriptor;
   import javax.management.modelmbean.DescriptorSupport;
   // . . .
```

```
    String[] fields = new String[] {
      "name=WorkFactor",
      "descriptorType=attribute",
      "getMethod=getWorkFactor"
    };
    Descriptor desc = new DescriptorSupport(fields);
    // . . .
```

This constructor parses through the String objects in the array and sets each field accordingly.

The third and final constructor we'll look at in this section takes two arguments: a String array containing the names of the fields and an Object array containing references to the objects that represent the field values. The signature for this constructor is:

```
public DescriptorSupport(String[] fieldNames, Object[] fieldValues)
   throws RuntimeOperationsException {
   // . . .
   }
```

Note that the number of items in the String array must match the number of items in the Object array, or none of the fields will be set for the descriptor you are trying to create. Let's again use the WorkFactor attribute from earlier to demonstrate how to use this constructor:

```
// . . .
import javax.management.Descriptor;
import javax.management.modelmbean.DescriptorSupport;
// . . .
   String[] fieldNames = new String[] {
     "name", "descriptorType", "getMethod"
   };
   Object[] fieldValues = new Object[] {
     "WorkFactor", "attribute", "getWorkFactor"
   };
   Descriptor desc = new DescriptorSupport(fieldNames, fieldValues);
   // . . .
```

We used an attribute here to demonstrate how to create descriptor objects, but the principles are exactly the same for an MBean, operation (including a constructor), or notification. The only differences are the allowable field names.

A final note about the DescriptorSupport constructors: all of these constructors are valid ways to create DescriptorSupport objects, and none is preferable over another. However, the following two constructors will be used most often throughout the rest of this book:

1. Default constructor, *setField()* approach

2. String array parameter constructor

Every attempt will be made to give these two constructors equal treatment in the examples that follow. However, bear in mind that you are free to use any of the constructors (that is, after all, why they are there) as your needs dictate.

By now you should be familiar with the `DescriptorSupport` constructors available to you to create descriptors for your MBeans, attributes, operations, and notifications. While descriptors provide metadata to other levels of the JMX architecture, as well as to management applications, we must still provide the MBean server with metadata classes that satisfy the `DynamicMBean` behavior of our model MBeans. In the next section, we will look at how to create the metadata classes that are required to describe the management interface to the MBean server.

Describing the Management Interface

As with dynamic MBeans, every feature of a model MBean, including the MBean itself, must have a corresponding metadata class. Furthermore, for model MBeans, each metadata class must contain a descriptor. In this section, we will examine the metadata classes that are used to describe the management interface of your managed resource. You may notice a similarity between the layout of this section and the corresponding section in Chapter 3. Recall that a model MBean implements the `DynamicMBean` interface, so it should be no surprise that model MBean metadata classes resemble their dynamic MBean counterparts. In fact, as we will see, each of the model MBean metadata classes (with the exception of `ModelMBeanInfo`, which is an interface) extends the corresponding dynamic MBean metadata class.

There are five metadata classes of interest:

`ModelMBeanAttributeInfo`
> Each instance of this class describes one attribute of the MBean's management interface.

`ModelMBeanContructorInfo`
> Each instance of this class describes one of the MBean's public constructors and may contain one or more `MBeanParameterInfo` instances (`MBeanParameterInfo` was discussed in detail in the previous chapter).

`ModelMBeanOperationInfo`
> Each instance of this class describes one of the operations on the MBean's management interface and may contain one or more `MBeanParameterInfo` instances.

`ModelMBeanNotificationInfo`
> Each instance of this class describes one group of notifications emitted by the MBean.

`ModelMBeanInfoSupport`
> The top-level container of metadata. This class implements the `ModelMBeanInfo` interface, which is how the agent level and management applications access the metadata for a model MBean. Each MBean requires only one instance of this class to completely describe its management interface.

As mentioned earlier, each of these metadata classes (with the exception of `ModelMBeanInfo`) extends its dynamic MBean counterpart. These relationships are shown in Figure 4-1 in UML notation.

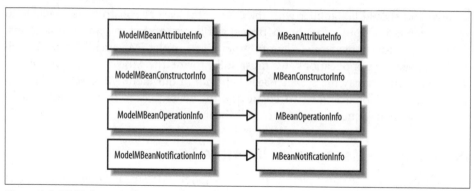

Figure 4-1. UML diagram showing inheritance of model MBean metadata classes from dynamic MBean metadata classes

As shown in Figure 4-2, the relationships between model MBean metadata classes are similar to those between dynamic MBean metadata classes.

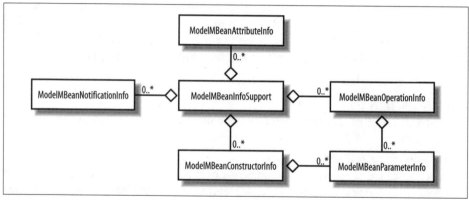

Figure 4-2. UML diagram showing the relationships between ModelMBeanInfoSupport and the other model MBean metadata classes

As with dynamic MBeans, the aggregation mechanism used in `MBeanInfoSupport` for each MBean feature is an array. As we saw in Figure 4-1, all of the model MBean metadata classes extend their dynamic MBean counterparts and are able to take advantage of the basic structure contained in them. We will discuss each of the model MBean classes below. `MBeanParameterInfo` is discussed at length in the previous chapter, so we will not cover it here.

Recall from our discussion of the `DescriptorSupport` class and the `Descriptor` interface that it does not matter whether the descriptor fields are created in a `String` array and passed to the `DescriptorSupport` constructor or created with the *setField()* method of `Descriptor`. Both approaches will be used in the examples throughout the rest of this chapter to demonstrate that they are equally valid.

ModelMBeanAttributeInfo

All but one of the essential properties that must be set for a model MBean attribute are the same as those that must be set for a dynamic MBean attribute, so they will not be discussed here. The lone exception is the descriptor that must be set for a model MBean attribute. Recall from the previous chapter that there are two constructors that are used to set the essential properties for an MBeanAttributeInfo instance. One of these constructors uses the Java reflection API, and the other explicitly sets all of the essential properties. These same properties (in addition to the descriptor) exist on ModelMBeanAttributeInfo, which inherits from MBeanAttributeInfo. Four constructors are available to you on ModelMBeanAttributeInfo, as shown in Example 4-2.

Example 4-2. The significant constructors of ModelMBeanAttributeInfo

```
// . . .
public class ModelMBeanAttributeInfo extends MBeanAttributeInfo
  implements DescriptorAccess, Cloneable {
  // . . .
  public ModelMBeanAttributeInfo(String name,
                                 String description,
                                 Method getter,
                                 Method setter)
    throws javax.management.IntrospectionException {
    // . . .
  }
  public ModelMBeanAttributeInfo(String name,
                                 String description,
                                 Method getter,
                                 Method setter,
                                 Descriptor descriptor)
    throws javax.management.IntrospectionException {
    // . . .
  }
  public ModelMBeanAttributeInfo(String name,
                                 String type,
                                 String description,
                                 boolean isReadable,
                                 boolean isWritable,
                                 boolean isIs) {
    // . . .
  }
  public ModelMBeanAttributeInfo(String name,
                                 String type,
                                 String description,
                                 boolean isReadable,
                                 boolean isWritable,
                                 boolean isIs,
                                 Descriptor descriptor) {
    // . . .
  }
  // . . .
}
```

Notice the emphasized lines in Example 4-2. The second and fourth constructors are each passed a reference to a `Descriptor` object. The first and second constructors are otherwise identical, as are the third and fourth. As mentioned earlier, every model MBean attribute contains a `Descriptor` object that provides a richer set of metadata than that of the metadata class.

In the first and third constructors in Example 4-2, a *default descriptor* is created by `ModelMBeanAttributeInfo`. The default descriptor contains the following predefined fields:

- `descriptorType`
- `displayName`
- `iterable`
- `name`

Each of these fields (with the exception of `iterable`) was discussed in a previous section. For two of these fields, the values are literal strings: the value for `descriptorType` is `"attribute"`, and the value for `iterable` is `"F"`. The values for both `displayName` and `name` are set to the *name* parameter that was passed to the constructor. Consider the following example, which results in a descriptor whose `name` and `displayName` fields are set to `"WorkFactor"`:

```
// . . .
    ModelMBeanAttributeInfo[] attributeInfo = new ModelMBeanAttributeInfo[1];
    attributeInfo[0] = new ModelMBeanAttributeInfo(
      "WorkFactor",
      "java.lang.Integer",
      "Amount of work performed per work unit.",
      true,
      false,
      false
    );
// . . .
```

This example uses the third constructor from Example 4-2 (use of the first constructor requires more code). For more information on the use of the reflection API for this constructor, see the "MBeanAttributeInfo" section in the previous chapter.

Notice the second parameter to the `MBeanAttributeInfo` constructor in this example. Even though the attribute type for `WorkFactor` is the fundamental type `int`, we pass `"java.lang.Integer"` to the `ModelMBeanAttributeInfo` constructor. There appears to be an oversight in the JMX 1.0 RI: when the getter for an attribute whose return value is a fundamental type is invoked, the return value is wrapped in its corresponding JDK wrapper class. Thus, even though the getter for `WorkFactor` returns an `int`, the reflection API (which is what the JMX RI uses under the hood to perform the invocation) wraps the return value in a `java.lang.Integer`. However, the RI does not take this into account, and upon returning from the getter, the RI checks to see if the return value matches what was expected.

Say we create the metadata using the proper value (notice parameter #2):

```
// . . .
   attributeInfo[0] =
     new ModelMBeanAttributeInfo(
       "WorkFactor",
       Integer.TYPE.getName( ),
       "Amount of work performed per work unit.",
       true,
       false,
       false
     );
// . . .
```

The RI looks at the return value from the getter (which has been wrapped in a java.
lang.Integer), compares it to what is in the metadata (which is the string representation of a fundamental int), declares the return value to be bad, and throws an exception. This is clearly not what we intended—to work around the problem, we have to
specify the JDK wrapper class name when we create the metadata class.

If you would like to create your own descriptor instead of using the default descriptor, you can use the second and fourth constructors shown in Example 4-2. The second constructor uses Method objects and the Java reflection API and differs from the
fourth constructor only in that regard. Use of this constructor is otherwise identical
to that of the corresponding MBeanAttributeInfo constructor, which was covered in
the previous chapter, and will not be presented here. The following example shows
how to create a ModelMBeanAttributeInfo object using the fourth constructor for the
read-only attribute WorkFactor:

```
// . . .
   Descriptor desc = new DescriptorSupport( );
   desc.setField("name", "WorkFactor");
   desc.setField("descriptorType", "attribute");
   desc.setField("getMethod", "getWorkFactor");

   ModelMBeanAttributeInfo[] attributeInfo = new ModelMBeanAttributeInfo[1];
   attributeInfo[0] = new ModelMBeanAttributeInfo(
     "WorkFactor",
     "java.lang.Integer",
     "Amount of work performed per work unit.",
     true,
     false,
     false,
     desc
   );
// . . .
```

Notice that we create the Descriptor object by instantiating the DescriptorSupport
class, as we discussed earlier in this chapter. We used the *setField()* method in this
example, but there are many ways to set the fields of the descriptor. The use of the
other DescriptorSupport constructors was discussed at length earlier in this chapter.

ModelMBeanConstructorInfo

All but one of the essential properties that must be set for a model MBean constructor are the same as those that must be set for a dynamic MBean constructor, so they will not be discussed here. The lone exception is the descriptor that must be set for a model MBean constructor. Recall from the previous chapter that there are two constructors that are used to set the essential properties for an MBeanConstructorInfo instance. One of these constructors uses the Java reflection API, and the other explicitly sets all of the essential properties. These same properties (in addition to the descriptor) exist on ModelMBeanConstructorInfo, which inherits from MBean-ConstructorInfo. Four constructors are available to you on ModelMBeanConstructor-Info, as shown in Example 4-3.

Example 4-3. The significant constructors of ModelMBeanConstructorInfo

```
public class ModelMBeanConstructorInfo extends MBeanConstructorInfo
  implements DescriptorAccess, Cloneable {
// . . .
  public ModelMBeanConstructorInfo(String description,
                                   Constructor constructorMethod) {
  // . . .
  }
  public ModelMBeanConstructorInfo(String description,
                                   Constructor constructorMethod,
                                   Descriptor descriptor) {
  // . . .
  }
  public ModelMBeanConstructorInfo(String name,
                                   String description,
                                   MBeanParameterInfo[] signature) {
  // . . .
  }
  public ModelMBeanConstructorInfo(String name,
                                   String description,
                                   MBeanParameterInfo[] signature,
                                   Descriptor descriptor) {
  // . . .
  }
// . . .
}
```

Notice the emphasized lines in Example 4-3. The second and fourth constructors are each passed a reference to a Descriptor object. The first and second constructors are otherwise identical, as are the third and fourth.

In the first and third constructors in Example 4-3, a default descriptor containing the following predefined fields is created by ModelMBeanConstructorInfo:

- descriptorType
- displayName

- name
- role

Each of these fields was discussed in a previous section. For two of these fields, the values are literal strings: the value for descriptorType is "operation", and the value for role is "constructor". The values for both displayName and name are set to the *name* parameter that was passed to the constructor. Consider the following example:

```
// . . .
    ModelMBeanConstructorInfo[] constructorInfo = new ModelMBeanConstructorInfo[1];
    constructorInfo[0] = new ModelMBeanConstructorInfo(
      "DefaultConstructor",
      "The default constructor",
      new MBeanParameterInfo[0]
    );
// . . .
```

This example uses the third constructor from Example 4-3. The ModelMBean-ConstructorInfo object created here results in a descriptor whose name and displayName fields are set to "DefaultConstructor".

If you would like to create your own descriptor, you can use the second and fourth constructors shown in Example 4-3. The second constructor uses Constructor objects and the Java reflection API and differs from the fourth constructor only in that regard. The following example shows how to create a ModelMBeanConstructorInfo object using the fourth constructor for an MBean's default constructor:

```
// . . .
    Descriptor desc = new DescriptorSupport( );
    desc.setField("name", "DefaultConstructor");
    desc.setField("descriptorType", "operation");
    desc.setField("role", "constructor");
    desc.setField("displayName", "The Default Constructor");

    ModelMBeanConstructorInfo[] constructorInfo = new ModelMBeanConstructorInfo[1];
    constructorInfo[0] = new ModelMBeanConstructorInfo(
      "DefaultConstructor",
      "The default constructor",
      new MBeanParameterInfo[0],
      desc
    );
```

Notice that in this example the name and displayName fields do not have the same value, as is the case when a default descriptor is created for a ModelMBean-ConstructorInfo object. This is one advantage of creating your own descriptor.

What if you simply want to expose all of the public constructors for your MBean? This method was covered thoroughly in the previous chapter; however, it bears repeating here, because this is by far the simplest way to create ModelMBean-ConstructorInfo objects.

In the following example, we create a descriptor and pass it explicitly to the `ModelMBeanConstructorInfo`'s second constructor:

```
// . . .
    Constructor[] constructors = this.getClass().getConstructors( );
    ModelMBeanConstructorInfo[] constructorInfo = new
      ModelMBeanConstructorInfo[constructors.length];
    for (int aa = 0; aa < constructors.length; aa++) {
      Descriptor desc = new DescriptorSupport(
        new String[] {
          ("name=" + constructors[aa].getName( )),
          "descriptorType=operation",
          "role=constructor"
        };
      );
      constructorInfo[aa] = new ModelMBeanConstructorInfo(
        "Constructs a Basic MBean.", // description
        constructors[aa]             // java.lang.reflect.Constructor
        desc
      );
    }
// . . .
```

Notice that the `displayName` field has been omitted from this example. Recall from our discussion of the required descriptor fields that only `name` and `descriptorType` are required, so we are free to omit `displayName`.

ModelMBeanOperationInfo

All but one of the essential properties that must be set for a model MBean operation are exactly the same as those that must be set for a dynamic MBean operation, so they will not be discussed here. The lone exception is the descriptor that must be set for a model MBean operation. Recall from the previous chapter that there are two constructors that are used to set the essential properties for an `MBeanOperationInfo` instance. One of these constructors uses the Java reflection API, and the other explicitly sets all of the essential properties. These same properties (in addition to the descriptor) exist on `ModelMBeanOperationInfo`, which inherits from `ModelMBeanOperationInfo`. There are four constructors of interest on `ModelMBeanOperationInfo`, as shown in Example 4-4.

Example 4-4. The significant constructors of ModelMBeanOperationInfo

```
public class ModelMBeanOperationInfo extends MBeanOperationInfo
  implements DescriptorAccess {
// . . .
  public ModelMBeanOperationInfo(String description,
                                 Method operationMethod) {
  // . . .
  }
  public ModelMBeanOperationInfo (String description,
                                  Method operationMethod,
                                  Descriptor descriptor) }
```

Example 4-4. The significant constructors of ModelMBeanOperationInfo (continued)

```
    // . . .
    }
    public ModelMBeanOperationInfo(String name,
                                   String description,
                                   MBeanParameterInfo[] signature,
                                   String type,
                                   int impact) {
    // . . .
    }
    public ModelMBeanOperationInfo(String name,
                                   String description,
                                   MBeanParameterInfo[] signature,
                                   String type,
                                   int impact,
                                   Descriptor descriptor) {
    // . . .
    }
// . . .
}
```

Notice the emphasized lines in Example 4-4. The second and fourth constructors are each passed a reference to a Descriptor object. The first and second constructors are otherwise identical, as are the third and fourth.

In the first and third constructors in Example 4-4, a default descriptor containing the following predefined fields is created by ModelMBeanOperationInfo:

- descriptorType
- displayName
- name
- role

Each of these fields was discussed in a previous section. For two of these fields, the values are literal strings: the value for descriptorType is "operation", and the value for role is "operation". The values for both displayName and name are set to the *name* parameter that was passed to the constructor. Consider the following example:

```
    // . . .
    ModelMBeanOperationInfo[] operationInfo = new ModelMBeanOperationInfo[1];
    operationInfo[0] = new ModelMBeanOperationInfo(
      "reset",
      "Resets the state of this MBean.",
      new MBeanParameterInfo[0],
      Void.TYPE.getName( ),
      MBeanOperationInfo.ACTION
    );
    // . . .
```

This example uses the third constructor from Example 4-4. The ModelMBean-OperationInfo object created here results in a descriptor whose name and displayName fields are set to "reset".

If you would like to create your own descriptor, you can use the second and fourth constructors shown in Example 4-4. The second constructor uses Constructor objects and the Java reflection API and differs from the fourth constructor only in that regard. Use of this constructor is otherwise identical to that of the corresponding constructor of MBeanOperationInfo—covered in the previous chapter—and will not be presented here. The following example shows how to create a ModelMBeanOperationInfo object using the fourth constructor:

```
// . . .
    Descriptor desc = new DescriptorSupport(
      new String[] {
        "name=reset",
        "descriptorType=operation",
        "role=operation",
        ("class=" + this.getClass().getName())
      }
    );

    ModelMBeanOperationInfo[] operationInfo = new ModelMBeanOperationInfo[1];
    operationInfo[0] = new ModelMBeanOperationInfo(
      "reset",
      "Resets the state of this MBean.",
      new MBeanParameterInfo[0],
      Void.TYPE.getName(),
      MBeanOperationInfo.ACTION,
      desc
    );
```

The only difference between the previous two examples is that we created our own descriptor in the second. There are several advantages to creating your own descriptors, not the least of which is improved code readability. Notice that the class field was set to this.getClass().getName(). This information is used by RequiredModelMBean when making the actual invocation of the *reset()* method.

 At the time of this writing, there is a bug in the JMX 1.0 RI when allowing ModelMBeanOperationInfo to create a default descriptor for a management operation that causes any invocation of that operation to fail. If you create a descriptor and pass it to ModelMBeanOperationInfo's constructor, you will avoid this problem.

ModelMBeanNotificationInfo

All but one of the essential properties that must be set for a model MBean notification are exactly the same as those that must be set for a dynamic MBean notification, so they will not be discussed here. The lone exception is the descriptor that must be set for a model MBean notification. Recall from the previous chapter that there is a single constructor that is used to set the essential properties for an MBeanNotificationInfo instance. These same properties (in addition to the descriptor) exist on ModelMBeanNotificationInfo, which inherits from MBeanNotificationInfo. There are two constructors of interest on ModelMBeanNotificationInfo, as shown in Example 4-5.

Example 4-5. The significant constructors of ModelMBeanNotificationInfo

```
public class ModelMBeanNotificationInfo extends MBeanNotificationInfo
  implements DescriptorAccess, Cloneable {
// . . .
  public ModelMBeanNotificationInfo(String[] notifTypes,
                                    String name,
                                    String description) {
  // . . .
  }
  public ModelMBeanNotificationInfo(String[] notifTypes,
                                    String name,
                                    String description,
                                    Descriptor descriptor) {
  // . . .
  }
// . . .
}
```

Notice the emphasized line in Example 4-5. The second constructor is passed a reference to a Descriptor object, but the two constructors are otherwise identical.

In the first constructor, a default descriptor containing the following predefined fields is created by ModelMBeanNotificationInfo:

- descriptorType
- displayName
- name
- severity

Each of these fields was discussed in a previous section. For two of these fields, the values are literal strings: the value for descriptorType is "notification", and the value for severity is "5" (i.e., Warning). The values for both displayName and name are set to the *name* parameter that was passed to the constructor. Consider the following example, which uses the same notification types that we discussed in the previous chapter (refer to the "MBeanNotificationInfo" section for more information):

```
// . . .
  String[] notificationTypes = new String[] {
    "sample.Queue.stalled.queueFull",
    "sample.Queue.stalled.queueEmpty"
  };
  ModelMBeanNotificationInfo[] notificationInfo = new ModelMBeanNotificationInfo[1];
  notificationInfo[0] = new ModelMBeanNotificationInfo(
    notificationTypes,
    "StalledQueueNotifications",
    "Potential stall notifications emitted by the Queue."
  );
  // . . .
```

In this example, the first constructor of ModelMBeanNotificationInfo is called, resulting in a default descriptor whose name and displayName fields are set to "StalledQueueNotifications".

If you would like to create your own descriptor, use the second constructor. The only difference between the two constructors is the addition of a `Descriptor` parameter. Creating a descriptor is very straightforward, as we have already seen. The following example shows how to use the second constructor, which allows you to pass a `Descriptor`:

```
// . . .
  String[] notificationTypes = new String[] {
    "sample.Queue.stalled.queueFull",
    "sample.Queue.stalled.queueEmpty"
  };
  ModelMBeanNotificationInfo[] notificationInfo = new ModelMBeanNotificationInfo[1];
  Descriptor desc = new DescriptorSupport(
    new String[] {
      "name=StalledQueueNotifications",
      "descriptorType=notification",
      "severity=3"
    };
  );
  notificationInfo[0] = new ModelMBeanNotificationInfo(
    notificationTypes,
    "StalledQueueNotifications",
    "Potential stall notifications emitted by the Queue.",
    desc
  );
// . . .
```

In this example, a descriptor is created for potential stall conditions of the `Queue` class. The severity field is set to `"3"`, indicating that a stall condition is very serious and may require immediate operator intervention. Other than the creation of the descriptor, the previous two examples are effectively identical.

ModelMBeanInfo

All but one of the essential properties that must be set for a model MBean are the same as those that must be set for a dynamic MBean, so they will not be discussed here. The lone exception is the descriptor that must be set for a model MBean. Recall from the previous chapter that there is a single constructor that is used to set the essential properties for an `MBeanInfo` instance. These same properties (in addition to the descriptor) exist on `ModelMBeanInfo`. The difference between `MBeanInfo` and `ModelMBeanInfo` is that `ModelMBeanInfo` is an interface and cannot be instantiated.

There is a class in the RI called `ModelMBeanInfoSupport` that provides an implementation of the `ModelMBeanInfo` interface and constructors to create it in exactly the same fashion as the other metadata classes. These constructors are shown in Example 4-6.

Example 4-6. The significant constructors of ModelMBeanInfoSupport

```
public class ModelMBeanInfoSupport extends MBeanInfo
  implements ModelMBeanInfo, java.io.Serializable {
// . . .
```

```
public ModelMBeanInfoSupport(String className,
                             String description,
                             ModelMBeanAttributeInfo[] attributes,
                             ModelMBeanConstructorInfo[] constructors,
                             ModelMBeanOperationInfo[] operations,
                             ModelMBeanNotificationInfo[] notifications) {
// . . .
}
public ModelMBeanInfoSupport(String className,
                             String description,
                             ModelMBeanAttributeInfo[] attributes,
                             ModelMBeanConstructorInfo[] constructors,
                             ModelMBeanOperationInfo[] operations,
                             ModelMBeanNotificationInfo[] notifications,
                             Descriptor mbeandescriptor) {
// . . .
 }
// . . .
}
```

In the first constructor, a default descriptor is created by `ModelMBeanInfoSupport`. The default descriptor contains the predefined fields and values listed in Table 4-2.

Table 4-2. Fields and corresponding values for a model MBean default descriptor

Field	Value
descriptorType	"mbean"
displayName	"ModelMBeanInfoSupport"
export	"F"
log	"F"
name	"ModelMBeanInfoSupport"
visibility	"1"

Like the other model MBean metadata classes, the second constructor of `ModelMBeanInfoSupport` takes as its last parameter a `Descriptor` object. The following example shows how to create a `ModelMBeanInfoSupport` object using the second constructor. This example also shows relevant portions of the previous examples to provide you with some context.

```
// . . .
   ModelMBeanAttributeInfo[] attributeInfo =
     new ModelMBeanAttributeInfo[1];
   // create attribute metadata
   ModelMBeanConstructorInfo[] constructorInfo =
     new ModelMBeanConstructorInfo[1];
   // create constructor metadata
   ModelMBeanOperationInfo[] operationInfo =
     new ModelMBeanOperationInfo[1];
```

```
// create operation metadata
ModelMBeanNotificationInfo[] notificationInfo =
// create notification metadata
ModelMBeanInfo mbeanInfo = new ModelMBeanInfoSupport(
  "ModeMBean",
  "A Model MBean",
  attributeInfo,
  constructorInfo,
  operationInfo,
  notificationInfo
);
// . . .
```

As you can imagine, this example would be quite lengthy if all of the code necessary
to create the ModelMBeanInfo object were shown. However, we have already discussed at length how to create the other metadata classes (with their optional
descriptors), so you should be adequately prepared to create ModelMBeanInfo objects.

DescriptorAccess

DescriptorAccess is a simple interface that must be implemented by each of the
metadata classes so that access to the descriptor is available. The DescriptorAccess
interface is defined as:

```
public interface DescriptorAccess
{
  public Descriptor getDescriptor();
  public void setDescriptor(Descriptor inDescriptor);
}
```

By implementing this interface, metadata classes provide a means to access or even
replace their existing descriptors. Recall from earlier in this chapter, when we discussed how to create the metadata classes, that each metadata class provides a
default descriptor if none is specified when the class is instantiated. At first glance, it
may appear that you must either create your own descriptor or put up with the
default descriptor. However, through the DescriptorAccess interface, you can create
a metadata object, access its descriptor, and modify or add fields to it. Consider the
following code snippet, where we create a ModelMBeanAttributeInfo object without
specifying a Descriptor on the constructor call:

```
ModelMBeanAttributeInfo[] attributeInfo = new ModelMBeanAttributeInfo[1];
attributeInfo[0] = new ModelMBeanAttributeInfo(
  "WorkFactor",
  "java.lang.Integer",
  "Amount of work performed per work unit.",
  true,
  false,
  false
);
```

As you may recall, this will result in a default descriptor with certain predefined
fields. What if you want to modify or add fields to the default descriptor? Because

ModelMBeanAttributeInfo implements the DescriptorAccess interface, this is straight-forward. Suppose that after the previous code snippet executes, we want to modify the displayName property and add a persistPolicy property. Here's what we would do:

```
// . . .
ModelMBeanAttributeInfo[] attributeInfo = new ModelMBeanAttributeInfo[1];
attributeInfo[0] = new ModelMBeanAttributeInfo(
  "WorkFactor",
  "java.lang.Integer",
  "Amount of work performed per work unit.",
  true,
  false,
  false
);
Descriptor desc = attributeInfo[0].getDescriptor();
desc.setField("displayName", "Work Factor");
desc.setField("persistPolicy=never");
// . . .
```

The DescriptorAccess interface gives you the option of modifying a default descriptor. If you are happy with most of the field values that are set with a default descriptor, this approach may save you a few lines of code per metadata object.

RequiredModelMBean

Every compliant JMX implementation is required to implement a model MBean called RequiredModelMBean. The managed resource that wishes itself to be instrumented using the RequiredModelMBean (or possibly even another model MBean, if the implementation provides more than the one concrete model MBean) obtains a reference to the MBean server, and then a reference to a new instance of the model MBean. Once the resource has the model MBean reference, it uses the metadata classes to configure the management interface it wants to expose. In this section, most of the information comes straight from the JMX RI.

RequiredModelMBean must implement at least three interfaces in order to be compliant. These interfaces are discussed below.

ModelMBean

This interface must be implemented by every concrete model MBean and is defined as:

```
public interface ModelMBean
  extends DynamicMBean,
          PersistentMBean,
          ModelMBeanNotificationBroadcaster {

public void setModelMBeanInfo(ModelMBeanInfo inModelMBeanInfo)
  throws MBeanException, RuntimeOperationsException;

public void setManagedResource(Object mr, String mr_type)
```

```
        throws MBeanException,
                RuntimeOperationsException,
                InstanceNotFoundException,
                InvalidTargetObjectTypeException;
    }
```

The model MBean metadata and the resource to be managed are set through this interface. Once the `ModelMBeanInfo` object has been created, *setModelMBeanInfo()* is called. This establishes the management interface of the resource to be managed, which is set through a call to *setManagedResource()*. The second argument to *setManagedResource()* is a `String` and must be one of the following predefined values:

- `ObjectReference`
- `Handle`
- `IOR`
- `EJBHandle`
- `RMIReference`

The only value we will use in the examples in this book is `ObjectReference`. We will see later in this chapter how to use this interface.

DynamicMBean

We discussed the `DynamicMBean` interface at length in the previous chapter, so we won't discuss it here. Note, however, that every compliant concrete model MBean (such as `RequiredModelMBean`) must also implement `DynamicMBean`.

PersistentMBean

This interface provides a persistence mechanism for every model MBean and is defined as:

```
    public interface PersistentMBean {
        public void load( ) throws MBeanException,
                                RuntimeOperationsException,
                                InstanceNotFoundException;
        public void store( ) throws MBeanException,
                                RuntimeOperationsException,
                                InstanceNotFoundException;
    }
```

Once a reference to a model MBean is obtained by the agent level, the state of the model MBean may be persisted or restored from a persistent store by invoking *store()* or *load()*, respectively.

Instrumenting Resources as Model MBeans

In this chapter, we have seen how to create `Descriptor` objects and the necessary metadata classes for a model MBean, and we have looked at `RequiredModelMBean` and the interfaces that it must implement. In this section, we will see how to tie all of this information together to instrument resources as model MBeans.

The steps you must go through to instrument each of your resources as model MBeans are:

1. Create an instance of the resource to be managed.

2. Create an instance of `RequiredModelMBean`.

3. Create the necessary metadata classes and optional descriptors for the features of the management interface.

4. Create the metadata for the resource (i.e., the `ModelMBeanInfo` object).

5. Set the metadata of `RequiredModelMBean` to the metadata for the resource (from Step 3) and the resource to be managed through the `ModelMBean` interface.

As in the previous chapters, we will use the sample application for all of our examples. This will allow you to compare and contrast the other MBean types with model MBeans.

In the examples presented here we will look at the application class `Controller`, which acts as the JMX agent. For the example code in this chapter, the `Controller` class is responsible for creating the resources to be managed, instrumenting them as model MBeans, and registering them with the MBean server.

The first two steps are to create an instance of the managed resource (in this example, the `Queue`) and to create the `RequiredModelMBean` instance:

```
// . . .
Queue queue = new Queue( );
RequiredModelMBean queueModelMBean = new RequiredModelMBean( );
// . . .
```

Next, we must create the necessary model MBean metadata classes (only some of the attributes and operations are shown, as the examples can be quite lengthy). First we'll create the attributes:

```
// There are 10 attributes . . .
ModelMBeanAttributeInfo[] attributeInfo = new ModelMBeanAttributeInfo[10];
attributeInfo[0] = new ModelMBeanAttributeInfo(
  "QueueSize",
  "java.lang.Integer",
  "The maximum size of the queue.",
  true,
  true,
  false,
);
DescriptorSupport desc = attributeInfo[0].getDescriptor( );
desc.setField("getMethod", "getQueueSize");
desc.setField("setMethod", "setQueueSize");
desc = new DescriptorSupport(
  new String[] {
    "name=NumberOfItemsProcessed",
```

```
      "descriptorType=attribute",
      "getMethod=getNumberOfItemsProcessed",
    }
);
attributeInfo[1] = new ModelMBeanAttributeInfo(
  "NumberOfItemsProcessed",
  "java.lang.Long",
  "The number of work units processed.",
  true,
  false,
  false,
);
// . . . other attributes . . .
desc = new DescriptorSupport(
  new String[] {
    "name=NumberOfConsumers",
    "descriptorType=attribute",
    "getMethod=getNumberOfConsumers",
  }
);
attributeInfo[9] = new ModelMBeanAttributeInfo(
  "NumberOfConsumers",
  "java.lang.Integer",
  "No. of consumer threads currently feeding the queue.",
  true,
  false,
  false,
);
```

Then we'll create the metadata for the operations:

```
// . . .
ModelMBeanOperationInfo[] operationInfo = new ModelMBeanOperationInfo[13];
desc = new DescriptorSupport(
  new String[] {
    "name=suspend",
    "descriptorType=operation",
    "role=operation",
  }
);
operationInfo[0] = new ModelMBeanOperationInfo(
  "suspend",
  "Suspends activity in the queue.",
  new MBeanParameterInfo[0],
  Void.TYPE.getName(),
  MBeanOperationInfo.ACTION,
);
desc = new DescriptorSupport(
  new String[] {
    "name=resume",
    "descriptorType=operation",
  }
);
```

```
operationInfo[1] = new ModelMBeanOperationInfo(
  "resume",
  "Resumes activity in the queue.",
  new MBeanParameterInfo[0],
  Void.TYPE.getName( ),
  MBeanOperationInfo.ACTION,
  desc
);
// . . .
```

One difference between model MBeans and other MBean types is that operation metadata must be created for attribute getters and setters. This is probably an oversight of the JMX RI, but one that you must deal with if you wish to use it. For each getter and setter, you must create a ModelMBeanOperationInfo instance, such that a writable attribute has two ModelMBeanOperationInfo instances (one for the getter and one for the setter). A read-only attribute will have only one (for the getter). The following example shows how to create the ModelMBeanOperationInfo objects for the getters and setters for the attributes for Queue. Note that only QueueSize has a setter.

```
// . . .
desc = new DescriptorSupport(
  new String[] {
    "name=getQueueSize",
    "descriptorType=operation",
    "role=getter"
  }
);
operationInfo[2] = new ModelMBeanOperationInfo(
  "getQueueSize",
  "Getter for QueueSize",
  new MBeanParameterInfo[0],
  Integer.TYPE.getName( ),
  MBeanOperationInfo.INFO,
  desc
);
desc = new DescriptorSupport(
  new String[] {
    "name=setQueueSize",
    "descriptorType=operation",
    "role=setter"
  }
);
MBeanParameterInfo[] parms = new MBeanParameterInfo[1];
parms[0] = new MBeanParameterInfo(
  "value",
  "java.lang.Integer",
  "value"
);
operationInfo[3] = new ModelMBeanOperationInfo(
  "setQueueSize",
  "Setter for QueueSize",
```

```
    parms,
    Void.TYPE.getName( ),
    MBeanOperationInfo.ACTION,
    desc
);
// . . . other getters. ..
desc = new DescriptorSupport(
  new String[] {
    "name=getNumberOfSuppliers",
    "descriptorType=operation",
    "role=getter"
  }
);
// . . .other getters/setters. . .
operationInfo[12] = new ModelMBeanOperationInfo(
  "getNumberOfSuppliers",
  "Getter for NumberOfSuppliers",
  new MBeanParameterInfo[0],
  Integer.TYPE.getName( ),
  MBeanOperationInfo.INFO,
  desc
);
```

Because no explicit constructors are required and there are no notifications, the
ModelMBeanInfo object can be created:

```
// . . .
ModelMBeanInfo mbeanInfo = new ModelMBeanInfoSupport(
  queue.getClass().getName( ),
  "Queue Model MBean",
  attributeInfo,
  null,
  operationInfo,
  null
);
queueModelMBean.setModelMBeanInfo(mbeanInfo);
queueModelMBean.setManagedResource(queue, "ObjectReference");
MBeanServer mbeanServer = MBeanServerFactory.createMBeanServer( );
mbeanServer.registerMBean(queueModelMBean, objName);
// . . .
```

Notice the emphasized line in this example. The managed resource isn't the instance
of RequiredModelMBean (whose instance variable is queueModelMBean), but the instance
of the Queue (whose instance variable is queue). When we were creating standard and
dynamic MBeans, the managed resource and the MBean were physically the same
object. Although they are *logically* still one entity, with model MBeans the managed
resource and the MBean (i.e., the instance of RequiredModelMBean) are not *physically*
the same object.

In creating the metadata for the model MBean itself, we have allowed the
ModelMBeanInfoSupport constructor to create a default descriptor. If you would like
to create a descriptor for the ModelMBeanInfo object that represents your MBean,
there should be sufficient information in this chapter to help you do that.

Notice that we can pass `null` as parameter values for the constructors and notification metadata (we can also pass `null` for attribute or operation metadata if there are no attributes or operations, respectively). In previous sections (and the previous chapter), we covered at length how to create constructor and notification metadata. If you need to create these metadata classes, simply pass them as the appropriate parameters to the `ModelMBeanInfoSupport` constructor.

CHAPTER 5

Open MBeans

So far, we have looked at three ways to instrument resources to be manageable. Now we will look at a way to instrument resources so that they are the most open to management applications. In this chapter, we will discuss how to instrument resources whose attributes are more complex than the fundamental types and whose operations take complex parameters. The key to this more open means of instrumentation lies in the set of data types defined by the JMX specification called *open MBeans*. By using open MBeans, we can instrument application resources of any type and make them available to any agent or management application that does not have access to the bytecode for either the resource, attribute, or operation parameter. The agent or management application can even be a non-Java program!

We will first look at the various open MBean types. Those types include the fundamental types, such as int, long, and char, as well as new types, such as structural and tabular data. All of the open MBean types are classes that derive from a single open MBean type, OpenType.

Next, we will examine the various open MBean metadata classes that allow us to instrument our resources as open MBeans. At the time of this writing, open MBeans are newly finalized (they were not part of the JMX 1.0 specification), so some of the information in this chapter may be subject to change.

Open MBean Types

The open MBean types are at the heart of what makes open MBeans "open." The JMX RI defines a base class, OpenType, from which all open MBean types are derived. This ensures consistency among all of the subsequent types. In this section, we will look at the basic types, most of which are fundamental and correspond to their JDK wrapper types. We will first look at OpenType, then we will take a look at SimpleType, an RI class that provides static methods to obtain references to the various fundamental open types. Then we will look briefly at the basic types that allow us to describe complex data.

This section also describes how to represent complex data using the JMX classes CompositeData and TabularData and discusses their type definition classes (CompositeType and TabularType, respectively). Finally, we will look at the JMX support classes that implement these complex type enablers.

Basic Types

All of the open MBean types are one of the basic types. There are two categories of basic types: those types that are fundamental and those that may be used to describe arbitrarily complex types. In this section, we will look at all of the open MBean basic types. We will start with the base class for all open MBean types, OpenType. Then we will look at SimpleType, a subclass of OpenType, which is used to obtain instances of the fundamental open MBean types. Finally, we will take a quick look at the open MBean types that are used to represent complex data, saving the bulk of the discussion for the next section, "Complex Data."

OpenType

This class is the base class for all open MBean types. OpenType is abstract, so it cannot be instantiated. However, the essential characteristics for all open MBean types are defined in the protected constructor for OpenType, to which subclasses must delegate:

Class name
> The fully qualified name of the Java class that the OpenType instance represents (e.g., java.lang.Integer is the class name for integer data types).

Type name
> The name that has been assigned to the data type represented by this OpenType instance. Must be unique across all other open MBean types.

Description
> A human-readable description (suitable for display on a management console, for example) of the type represented by this OpenType instance.

These three attributes are read-only and are common to all open MBean types. The values for these attributes may not be null, all spaces, or an empty string, or the OpenType constructor will throw an IllegalArgumentException.

In addition to these attributes, OpenType provides a few helper methods that agent and management application developers may find useful when interrogating open MBeans:

isArray()
> Returns true if the open type represented by this instance of OpenType is an instance of ArrayType (see below)

isValue()
> Returns true if the class name of the specified Object argument is the same as this instance of OpenType

SimpleType

This class is a subclass of OpenType (as are all valid open MBean types) that is used to represent the following open MBean types:

- java.lang.Void
- java.lang.Boolean
- java.lang.Character
- java.lang.Byte
- java.lang.Short
- java.lang.Integer
- java.lang.Long
- java.lang.Float
- java.lang.Double
- java.lang.String
- java.math.BigDecimal
- java.math.BigInteger
- javax.management.ObjectName

The constructor for SimpleType is explicitly declared with private visibility, so it cannot be instantiated. Publicly declared static fields are provided to obtain an instance of an open type corresponding to each of the above types. For example, to obtain an instance of a SimpleType object that represents the open type for java.lang.Long, use:

```
OpenType openType = SimpleType.LONG;
```

Notice that the field name is the unqualified name of the corresponding Java class in capital letters. Thus, the open type for java.lang.Integer is obtained through SimpleType.INTEGER, and so on.

Other basic types

There are three other basic types that are currently part of the JMX specification:

ArrayType
: Describes *n*-dimensional arrays of open types.

CompositeType
: Describes structural (i.e., inherently nonuniform) data of arbitrary complexity. A CompositeData object is logically an "instance" of CompositeType.

TabularType
: Describes tables of CompositeData objects. The same CompositeType object describes every row of the table, so the table is homogeneous. A TabularData object is logically an "instance" of TabularType.

All of these classes are subclasses of OpenType. If one of the attributes on an open MBean is an array type, it can be completely described by an ArrayType instance and understood by a management application. CompositeType and TabularType are used to describe complex data. We will look at these types in detail in the next section.

Complex Data

As implemented in the JMX RI, the basic data types for representing complex data are implemented by a type class, an interface, and a support class. We saw the support-class idiom when we looked at model MBeans. In this section, we will see how the type/interface/support-class idiom works for open MBeans for the two basic open MBean types, CompositeType and TabularType. While the JMX specification addresses CompositeData and TabularData (which are interfaces) and their underlying support classes, it makes sense to talk first about the classes provided by the RI that describe them.

CompositeType

CompositeType is a concrete class provided by the JMX RI that allows us to describe complex data that is composed of other basic open MBean types (including other complex types). There is no limit to the complexity of a complex type in open MBeans. With CompositeType, we are able to describe attributes, parameters, and return value types that are objects of arbitrary complexity. You can think of a CompositeType as providing metadata about a complex type, similar to the way the source code for a struct in C/C++ describes a complex data structure.

CompositeType includes the following parameters:

typeName
> The name assigned to the new complex type. Continuing with the C/C++ analogy, this is similar to the name of the struct.

description
> A human-readable text description of the type described by this CompositeType, suitable for display on a management console.

itemNames
> A String array of names for the members of the CompositeType. This is similar to the variable names of a C/C++ struct. When dealing with a CompositeData object, the item names are referred to as the *keys* for accessing the corresponding values in the CompositeData object.

itemDescriptions
> A String array of human-readable descriptions that correspond to the *itemNames* array.

itemTypes
> An array of OpenType objects that describe the basic type of each item that comprises the data structure described by this CompositeType object.

Note that the indexes of the *itemNames*, *itemDescriptions*, and *item-Types* arrays must match each other exactly.

The CompositeType class provides a constructor that allows us to set the values of the above attributes; its constructor is defined as:

```
public CompositeType(String typeName,
                     String description,
                     String[] itemNames,
                     String[] itemDescriptions,
                     OpenType[] itemTypes)
    throws OpenDataException {
    // . . .
}
```

When creating a CompositeData object, we must first create a CompositeType object to describe it. Let's look at a simple example that deviates somewhat from the sample application. Suppose we have to represent a simple (and not very object-oriented) data structure that looks like the following:

```
public class Building {
    public String name;
    public short numberOfFloors;
    public int height;
    public boolean undergroundParking;
    public short numberOfElevators;
    public long officeSpace;
}
```

We might then create a CompositeType object to represent all possible instances of Building, as shown in Example 5-1.

Example 5-1. Describing a complex data type using CompositeType

```
try {
    // first describe the attribute names
    String[] itemNames = {
      "Name",
      "NumberOfFloors",
      "Height",
      "UndergroundParking",
      "NumberOfElevators",
      "OfficeSpace"
    };
    // next describe the attribute descriptions
    String[] itemDescriptions = {
      "Name of the building",
      "The number of floors (stories) the building has",
      "The height of the building in feet",
      "Whether or not the building has underground parking",
      "The total number of elevators in the building",
      "The amount of office space in square feet"
    };
```

```
    // next describe the data type of each item
    OpenType[] itemTypes = {
      SimpleType.STRING,
      SimpleType.SHORT,
      SimpleType.INTEGER,
      SimpleType.BOOLEAN,
      SimpleType.SHORT,
      SimpleType.LONG
    };
  CompositeType buildingType = new CompositeType(
    "BuildingCompositeType",
    "CompositeType that represents a Building.",
    itemNames,
    itemDescriptions,
    itemTypes
  );
} catch (OpenDataException e) {
  // . . .
}
```

What we have done, in essence, is to create an entirely new data type. Because we used the open MBean class CompositeType to do it, the new type can be instrumented in an application and be managed by a JMX-compliant management application.

CompositeData

The CompositeData interface describes how to access the contents of a complex object. This interface is defined as:

```
public interface CompositeData {
    public CompositeType getCompositeType( );
    public Object get(String key);
    public Object[] getAll(String[] keys);
    public boolean containsKey(String key);
    public boolean containsValue(Object value);
    public Collection values( );
    public boolean equals(Object obj);
    public int hashCode( );
    public String toString( );
}
```

Whereas CompositeType describes one or more instances of CompositeData, the CompositeData class itself contains values. Two methods are provided to access the values inside a CompositeData object:

get()
Retrieves the object (i.e., the value) of a complex data structure that has the specified key

getAll()
Retrieves an array of objects of a complex data structure that have the specified keys

Recall from our discussion of CompositeType that each member of a complex structure—at a particular index—described by a CompositeType object is assigned a name, located in the item names attribute at that index. That name is the key for retrieval. In Example 5-1, we saw how to create a CompositeType object for a complex data type called Building. Suppose that we need to manipulate an instance of a CompositeData object that is based on BuildingCompositeType (the name given to the new type in Example 5-1) and that this instance is passed to some method we have created. If we needed to access the Name attribute, we would use the *get()* method:

```
public void someMethod(CompositeData buildingData) {
  String buildingName = (String)buildingData.get("Name");
  // . . .
}
```

By the same token, we could retrieve several attributes at once by using the *getAll()* method:

```
public void someMethod(CompositeData buildingData) {
  String[] attributeNames = {
    "Name",
    "Height",
    "OfficeSpace"
  };
  Object[] attributeValues = buildingData.getAll(attributeNames);
  String name = (String)attributeValues[0];
  int height = ((Integer)attributeValues[1]).intValue();
  long officeSpace = ((Long)attributeValues[2]).longValue();
  // . . .
}
```

The order of the values in the array is the same as the order in which the keys were specified. Notice that we must unwrap any fundamental types (after casting them out of the Object array) to get the Java primitive.

The *get()* and *getAll()* methods will probably be the ones you use most often to manipulate CompositeData objects. However, the following methods may also come in handy:

getCompositeType()

Retrieves the CompositeType object that describes this CompositeData instance. This might be useful, for example, when you need to display descriptions of the item names.

containsKey()

Returns a boolean indicating whether or not the specified key value is one of the item names of the CompositeType. For example, the following code from our Building example would return true:

```
public void someMethod(CompositeData buildingData) {
  if (buildingData.containsKey("Height"))
    doSomething();
}
```

and the *doSomething()* method would be invoked. This code would return false:

```
public void someMethod(CompositeData buildingData) {
  if (buildingData.containsKey("Width"))
    doSomething( );
}
```

and *doSomething()* would not be executed, because Width is not a valid key.

containsValue()

Returns true if any value in the CompositeData object contains the specified value.

values()

Returns an object that implements the Collection interface and contains all of the values in the CompositeData object. The values are in the same order as their corresponding keys (i.e., in alphabetical, ascending key order).

equals()

Tests the equality of this instance of a CompositeData object with another. For this method to return true, the two CompositeData objects must be of the same CompositeType, and all of their item values must be equal. If the specified object does not implement the CompositeData interface, or is a null reference, this method returns false.

hashCode()

Returns a hashcode for this CompositeData object.

toString()

Returns a string representation of this CompositeData object. The format of the representation depends on the implementation.

CompositeDataSupport

This class implements the CompositeData interface. If we need to create a CompositeData object, we use one of this class's constructors:

```
public CompositeDataSupport(CompositeType compositeType,
                          String[] itemNames, Object[] itemValues)
  throws OpenDataException {
  // . . .
}
public CompositeDataSupport(CompositeType compositeType, Map items)
  throws OpenDataException {
  // . . .
}
```

The first constructor takes a CompositeType object, a String array of item names, and an Object array of item values in the exact order of the item names. Each of the item names in *itemNames* must be the same as one of the item names in the CompositeType object, but the order does not have to be the same.

The RI checks the parameters to make sure that all of the following are true:

- *compositeType* is not null.
- *itemNames* and *itemValues* are not empty arrays or null, none of their elements are empty strings or null, and *itemNames* and *itemValues* are of the same length.
- *itemNames* and *itemValues* are both of the size specified in *compositeType* (as its *itemNames* attribute).
- Each of the elements in *itemNames* is one of the elements in the *itemNames* attribute of *compositeType* and is of the correct type for that item name.

If the first two conditions are not true, an IllegalArgumentException will be thrown. If either of the last two is not true, an OpenDataException will be thrown. Using our Building example, suppose we wanted to create an instance of CompositeDataSupport using the attribute values listed in Table 5-1.

Table 5-1. Attribute values for new CompositeDataSupport instance

Attribute name	Attribute value
Name	"Fictitious Life Building"
NumberOfFloors	3
Height	45
UndergroundParking	false
NumberOfElevators	1
OfficeSpace	10000

Using these values, we can create an instance of CompositeDataSupport (as shown in Example 5-2), using the *buildingType* CompositeType created in Example 5-1.

Example 5-2. Creating a CompositeData object using CompositeDataSupport

```
public CompositeData createCompositeDataObject() {
  try {
    String[] itemNames = {
      "Name",
      "NumberOfFloors",
      "Height",
      "UndergroundParking",
      "NumberOfElevators",
      "OfficeSpace"
    };
    Object[] itemValues = {
      "Building A",
      new Short(3),
      new Integer(45),
      new Boolean(false),
      new Short(1),
      new Long(10000)
    };
```

```
      CompositeData buildingData = new CompositeDataSupport(
        buildingType, // See Example 5-1
        itemNames,
        itemValues
      );
      return buildingData;
    } catch (Exception e) {
    // . . .
    }
}
```

We can also create a `CompositeData` object through `CompositeDataSupport`'s second constructor, passing a `Map` object that contains the name/value pairs:

```
    public CompositeData createCompositeDataObject( ) {
      try {
        Map items = new HashMap( );
        items.put("Name", "Building A");
        items.put("NumberOfFloors", new Short(3));
        items.put("Height", new Integer(45));
        items.put("UndergroundParking", new Boolean(false));
        items.put("NumberOfElevators", new Short(1));
        items.put("OfficeSpace", new Long(10000));
        CompositeData buildingData = new CompositeDataSupport(
          buildingType, // see Example 5-1
          items
        );
        return buildingData;
      } catch (Exception e) {
      // . . .
      }
    }
```

TabularType

This open MBean type class represents tabular data, which consists of rows of `CompositeType` elements. As we've seen, while a `CompositeType` data structure can have an arbitrarily complex structure, each `CompositeData` object that follows the structure is only a single object. However, with `TabularType`, we can further compose `CompositeData` objects into a table view, from which rows can be added or deleted. Each row of the `TabularData` object that adheres to its corresponding `TabularType` object must be of the same `CompositeType`, so that the rows are homogeneous. Beyond that, there is no limit to the complexity of the structure of a `TabularType` object.

You can think of the elements (items) of the `CompositeData` objects that make up the rows in a `TabularData` object as columns in a database table. As with a database table, you can define a set of keys, each of which is composed of one or more of the items in the `CompositeData` object that makes up each row. You can then use these keys to access (i.e., update, add, or remove) rows of the table.

TabularType is a concrete class provided with the JMX RI. It provides a constructor with which to create instances, defined as:

```
public TabularType(String typeName, String description,
                   CompositeType rowType, String[] indexNames)
  throws OpenDataException {
  // . . .
  }
```

The *typeName* parameter allows us to give a name to the new TabularType object. *description* lets us provide a human-readable description of the type. Each row of a TabularData object described by the TabularType we are creating must be of the same CompositeType, given by the *rowType* parameter. Finally, the *indexNames* parameter is an array of Strings that specify the item names from the CompositeType; this array forms the key that lets us access the elements of a TabularData object described by the TabularType we are creating.

Suppose we want to create a new TabularType object that describes a table of Building objects (from our earlier example). Example 5-3 shows how we would do this.

Example 5-3. Creating a TabularType object

```
try {
  TabularType buildingTableType = new TabularType(
    "BuildingTabularType",
    "Tabular view of BuildingCompositeTypes",
    buildingType,
    new String[] {
      "Name",
      "Height"
    }
  );
} catch (Exception e) {
  // . . .
}
```

In this example, we create a new TabularType object where each row is of type BuildingCompositeType (see Example 5-1) and is keyed by the Name and Height items of BuildingCompsiteType.

TabularData

This is an interface that describes how to access data structured in tabular format. It must be implemented by a concrete class (most likely TabularDataSupport, which we will discuss later). TabularData provides a convenient way to manipulate objects that are in tabular format. In discussing TabularData in this section, we will assume that an instance of the concrete class that implements this interface has been created elsewhere. In the next section, we will see how to create TabularData objects by using TabularDataSupport. The TabularData interface is defined as:

```
public interface TabularData {
  public TabularType getTabularType( );
  public Object[] calculateIndex(CompositeData value);
  public String toString( );
  // Map interface
  public void clear( );
  public boolean containsKey(Object[] key);
  public boolean containsValue(CompositeData value);
  public boolean equals(Object obj);
  public CompositeData get(Object[] key);
  public int hashCode( );
  public boolean isEmpty( );
  public Set keySet( );
  public void put(CompositeData value);
  public void putAll(CompositeData[] values);
  public CompositeData remove(Object[] key);
  public int size( );
  public Collection values( );
}
```

As we can see from the methods on the interface, TabularData is structured much like a Map object. With the exception of *entrySet( )*, TabularData implements methods with the same names as those on the JDK Map interface. However, the Map behavior required of TabularData necessitates different parameters from those of the corresponding Map interface method. For example, the *containsKey( )* method of the Map interface takes a single Object parameter, whereas the TabularData version takes an Object array. For that reason, we will take a look at all of these methods in this section. In addition to the Map-like methods of TabularData, there are several other methods on this interface, and we'll look at each one. If you've worked much with Java's Map implementations (HashMap, TreeMap, etc.), much of this section will look very familiar.

We will use the following example to demonstrate how these methods work. In Example 5-3, we created a TabularType object to describe a table of Building-CompositeType objects (see Example 5-1). This TabularType object has as its key the BuildingCompositeType items Name and Height. Recall that the elements (columns) of the underlying CompositeType that makes up each row have the following format (in the specified order):

1. Name
2. NumberOfFloors
3. Height
4. UndergroundParking
5. NumberOfElevators
6. OfficeSpace

Table 5-2 summarizes the rows in our hypothetical example.

Table 5-2. Rows of tabular data for our example

Name	NumberOfFloors	Height	UndergroundParking	NumberOfElevators	OfficeSpace
Building A	3	45	false	1	10000
Building B	7	90	false	3	70000
Building C	42	478	true	5	335000

getTabularType() returns the `TabularType` object that describes this `TabularData` object. In our example, this method returns the `BuildingCompositeType` object created in Example 5-3.

calculateIndex() takes a `CompositeData` object and returns an array of `Objects` that contains the data items of the `CompositeData` object that correspond to the key of the `TabularType` on which this `TabularData` object is based. In our example, this method would return array containing the `Name` (at element 0) and `Height` (at element 1) values for the `CompositeData` object parameter. In Example 5-2, we created a `CompositeData` object that looks like the first row in Table 5-1.

```
public void someMethod(TabularData buildingData) {
  try {
    CompositeData cd = createCompositeDataObject( );  //from Example 5-2
    Object[] index = buildingData.calculateIndex(cd);
    // . . .
  } catch (Exception e) {
    // . . .
  }
}
```

The index array returned by this method contains two elements: at index 0 is a `String` containing "Building A", and at index 1 is an `Integer` containing the value 3. This method is handy if the caller is aware of the structure of the `CompositeType` of which each row is constituted but wants to retrieve key values of a particular row without necessarily having to know what the key structure looks like. If the `CompositeData` parameter is `null`, an `IllegalArgumentException` is thrown. If the `CompositeData` parameter does not conform to this `TabularData` object's `CompositeType` structure, an `InvalidOpenTypeException` is thrown.

toString() returns a string representation of this `TabularData` object. The format of the representation is implementation-dependent.

Now let's look at each of the `Map`-like methods of `TabularData`.

clear() removes all rows from this `TabularData` object.

containsKey() takes an `Object` array that contains values that correspond to the key type of the `CompositeData` object and returns true if there is a row containing that key. Using our example, suppose we pass an `Object` array that contains "Building A" (at element 0) and 3 (at element 1):

```
public someMethod(TabularData buildingData) {
  try {
    Object[] key = {
      "Building A",
      new Short(3)
    };
    if (buildingData.containsKey(key))
      doSomething( ); // gets executed
    key = new Object[2];
    key[0] = "No Such Building";
    key[1] = new Short(3);
    if (buildingData.containsKey(key))
      doSomethingElse( ); // does NOT get executed
  } catch (Exception e) {
    // . . .
  }
}
```

As we can see from Table 5-2, the first call to *containsKey()* in this example will return true, because the key specified corresponds to a row that exists in the TabularData object. The second call will return false, because no row contains a name of "No Such Building." In addition, if the key does not conform to the structure of the key specified when the TabularType object was created, this method returns false. It does not throw an exception. This method is useful when the caller needs to know whether a particular row exists in the table but doesn't necessarily have to retrieve and process that row.

containsValue() functions in exactly the same manner as *containsKey()*, except it takes a CompositeData object as a parameter. If all fields of the row specified by the CompositeData object passed as a parameter match the contents of one row of this TabularData object exactly, this method returns true. If not, or if the CompositeData object has a different structure than the rows of this TabularData object, this method returns false. It does not throw an exception.

equals() takes an Object parameter and returns true if the specified Object is a TabularData object and each row is a match for at least one other row in this TabularData object. If the specified Object parameter is null, is not a TabularType object, or has at least one row that is different from this TabularData object, this method returns false. It does not throw an exception.

get() takes an Object array that contains a key to this TabularData object and returns the corresponding CompositeData object for the row that matches the specified key. If the specified key is null, a NullPointerException is thrown. If the specified key does not conform to this TabularData object's TabularType definition, an InvalidKeyException is thrown.

hashcode() returns the hashcode for this TabularData object.

isEmpty() returns a boolean indicating whether or not this `TabularData` object contains any rows. If it contains at least one `CompositeData` object (i.e., a row), this method returns true. Otherwise, it returns false.

keySet() returns a `Set` that contains all of the keys in the underlying `Map`-like implementation. The returned `Set` can then be iterated over by calling the *iterator()* method of the `Set`. Each item in the `Set` is a `List` object that contains the objects that constitute the key, which in the current implementation are `Strings`.

```
public void someMethod(TabularData buildingData) {
  try {
    Set set = buildingData.keySet();
    Iterator iter = set.iterator();
    while (iter.hasNext()) {
      List key = (List)iter.next();
      String name = (String)key.get(0);
      int height = ((Integer)key.get(1)).intValue();
      // now do something with these values. . .
    }
  } catch (Exception e) {
    // . . .
  }
}
```

Because a `List` is used to maintain the keys internally, the order of the items follows exactly the order in which the keys were specified when the `TabularType` object was created for this `TabularData` object.

put() takes a `CompositeData` object and stores it in its internal `Map`-like implementation. No key needs to be specified (as is the case with the *put()* method of the `Map` interface, for example), because the key is calculated based on the index names specified in the `TabularType` object that describes this `TabularData` object. However, `TabularData` does not allow duplicate keys. In our example, the index names are the `Name` and `Height` fields of the `BuildingCompositeType` object. If the `CompositeData` object we want to store in this `TabularType` object looks like the second row from Table 5-2, the key is calculated to be "Building B" and 90. Consider the following example:

```
public void addCompositeDataObject(TabularData buildingData)
  try {
    String[] itemNames = {
      "Name",
      "NumberOfFloors",
      "Height",
      "UndergroundParking",
      "NumberOfElevators",
      "OfficeSpace"
    };
    Object[] itemValues = {
      "Building B",
      new Short(7),
      new Integer(90),
      new Boolean(false),
```

```
      new Short(3),
      new Long(70000)
   };
   CompositeData building = new CompositeDataSupport(
      buildingType, // See Example 5-1
      itemNames,
      itemValues
   );
   buildingData.put(building);
} catch (Exception e) {
   // . . .
}
```

The emphasized line shows the method call to add a CompositeData object. As in the previous examples, we have assumed that the TabularData object with which we're working has already been created (we haven't seen how to do this yet—if you suspect that we use TabularDataSupport to create the object, you're correct; we'll look at this in the next section). The following code shows how to retrieve the row we added in the previous example:

```
public void addCompositeDataObject(TabularData buildingData)
   try {
      // see above example. . .
      buildingData.put(building);
      // now retrieve the row just added:
      Object[] key = {
         "Building B",
         new Integer(90)
      };
      CompositeData newRow = buildingData.get(key);
      // . . .
   } catch (Exception e) {
      // . . .
   }
}
```

If the CompositeData object reference passed to this method is null, a NullPointer-Exception is thrown. If the CompositeData object doesn't conform to the CompositeType object that dictates the row structure of this TabularData object, an InvalidOpenType-Exception is thrown. As we mentioned earlier, the key for the CompositeData row to be added is calculated internally, based on the contents of the CompositeData object and the key structure specified when the TabularType object for this TabularData object was created. If the key already exists in the TabularData object, a KeyAlreadyExists-Exception will be thrown. The key for each row must be unique.

putAll() functions in exactly the same manner as *put()*, except that *putAll()* allows us to store more than one CompositeData object in a single method call. *putAll()* takes an array of CompositeData objects and stores them all inside the internal Map-like implementation. When an attempt is made to put each CompositeData element into the array that is passed to this method, that *putAll()* attempt is subject to the same conditions as a *put()* attempt. This means that the same exceptions can be thrown.

remove() takes an Object array containing the key of a CompositeData row to be removed. If the key does not exist, this method returns null; otherwise, it returns a reference to the CompositeData object that was removed. If the Object array reference is null, a NullPointerException will be thrown. If the reference is to an object that does not conform to the CompositeType that specifies the structure of rows in this TabularData object, an InvalidKeyException will be thrown.

size() returns the number of CompositeData elements, or rows, that are contained within this TabularData object.

values() returns a Collection that contains all of the CompositeData elements that are contained in the underlying Map-like implementation. The returned Collection can then be used to iterate through the CompositeData objects.

TabularDataSupport

This class implements the TabularData interface. If we need to create a TabularData object, we use one of this class's two constructors:

```
public TabularDataSupport(TabularType tabularType) {
  // . . .
}
public TabularDataSupport(TabularType tabularType,
                          int initialCapacity,
                          float loadFactor) {
  // . . .
}
```

The first parameter to both constructors is a TabularType object that describes the key structure for the TabularData object to be created, as well as the structure of the CompositeData elements that make up each row in this TabularData object. As we've already seen, the underlying implementation TabularData is a Map (in fact, it's a HashMap). The *initialCapacity* and *loadFactor* parameters of the second constructor allow us to set the initial size of the Map and the load factor, which must be a floating-point number between zero and one in other words, it's a percentage). Once the number of entries in the Map exceeds this percentage, the capacity of the Map is increased.

Both constructors verify the validity of the *tabularType* parameter. If it is null, an IllegalArgumentException is thrown. When using the second constructor, an IllegalArgumentException is also thrown if the *initialCapacity* or the *loadFactor* is less than zero.

Unlike CompositeDataSupport, for which we must specify the constituents when we create an instance, TabularDataSupport can be created empty. Once we create an instance of TabularDataSupport, we can use the *put()* or *putAll()* method to add CompositeData rows.

Open MBean Metadata Classes

Now that we've seen how open MBean types work and how they are defined, let's take a look at creating the metadata classes that describe resources that are instrumented as open MBeans. We will start by seeing how to describe parameters, attributes, constructors, operations, notifications, and finally OpenMBeanInfo. Each of these is described by an interface and implemented by a support class. This is similar to model MBeans—the focus of the previous chapter—and the open MBean types we looked at earlier in this chapter.

As with the open MBean type classes, when we talk about an object that implements the interface (e.g., an OpenMBeanParameterInfo object) we have presupposed the creation of the object using a support class. This is because we generally work with a particular open MBean metadata type through its interface and use the corresponding support class only to create instances of those objects.

A common theme for all of the OpenMBean*Info objects (where * is Parameter, Attribute, etc.) is that the support classes provided extend their javax.management. MBean*Info counterparts—for example, OpenMBeanParameterInfoSupport extends MBeanParameterInfo. The relationships between the open MBean classes are shown in Figure 5-1.

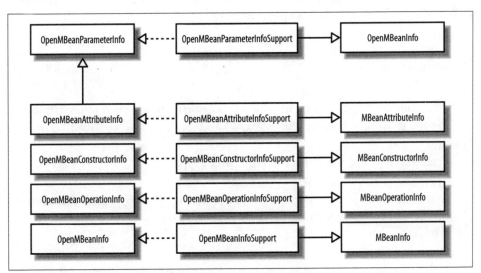

Figure 5-1. Relationships between the open MBean metadata classes

As we saw with dynamic MBeans in Figure 3-1, a single instance of OpenMBeanInfo-Support completely describes an MBean. The relationship between OpenMBeanInfo-Support and the other open MBean interfaces is shown in Figure 5-2.

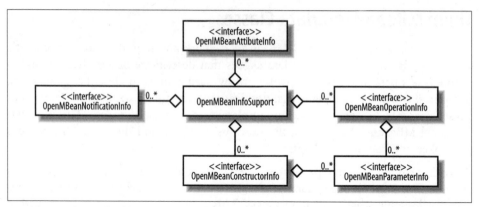

Figure 5-2. Relationships between OpenMBeanInfoSupport and the other open MBean metadata interfaces

In the rest of this section we will look at each of the open MBean metadata interfaces and classes, starting with `OpenMBeanParameterInfo`.

OpenMBeanParameterInfo

This interface deals with open MBean parameter information. There are several read-only attributes of an open MBean parameter:

Description
> A human-readable description of the parameter described by this `OpenMBean-ParameterInfo` object.

Name
> The name of the parameter; usually the variable name assigned to the parameter in the signature of the method, of which this parameter is a constituent.

OpenType
> The `OpenType` subclass that is this parameter's type.

DefaultValue
> A default value for the parameter represented by this `OpenMBeanParamaterInfo` object, to be used if one is not provided for the parameter. This attribute is `null` if it has not been set.

LegalValues
> A `Set` of values that specifies the only values the parameter represented by this `OpenMBeanParameterInfo` object may have. This attribute is `null` if it has not been set. If this attribute has been set, `MinValue` and `MaxValue` will be `null`, as this attribute is mutually exclusive with the use of minimum and maximum values.

MinValue
> The minimum value that a parameter represented by this `OpenMBeanParameter-Info` object may have. This attribute is an object that implements the `Comparable`

interface, such as String, Short, Integer, Long, or Float. This attribute is null if it has not been set. MinValue and LegalValues are mutually exclusive.

MaxValue

The maximum value that a parameter represented by this OpenMBeanParameterInfo object may have. This attribute is an object that implements the Comparable interface. This attribute is null if it has not been set. MaxValue and LegalValues are mutually exclusive.

In addition to these read-only attributes, the OpenMBeanParameterInfo interface provides some other utility methods, which we will look at in this section. OpenMBeanParameterInfo is defined as:

```
public interface OpenMBeanParameterInfo {
    public String getDescription();
    public String getName();
    public OpenType getOpenType();
    public Object getDefaultValue();
    public Set getLegalValues();
    public Comparable getMinValue();
    public Comparable getMaxValue();
    public boolean hasDefaultValue();
    public boolean hasLegalValues();
    public boolean hasMinValue();
    public boolean hasMaxValue();
    public boolean equals(Object obj);
    public int hashCode();
    public String toString();
}
```

This interface provides four methods that allow us to determine whether the DefaultValue, LegalValues, MinValue, and MaxValue attributes have been set. Each of these methods begins with "has" followed by the name of the attribute and returns a boolean indicating whether that attribute has been set. For example, *hasDefaultValue()* returns true if the parameter has a default value.

equals() is used to test for equality between this OpenMBeanParameterInfo object and another that also implements this interface. A field-by-field comparison is made, and if all fields contain the same values, this method returns true. Otherwise, it returns false.

hashCode() returns the hashcode for this OpenMBeanParameterInfo object.

toString() returns a string representation of this OpenMBeanParameterInfo object. The physical representation produced by calling this method depends on the underlying implementation of the OpenMBeanParameterInfo interface.

OpenMBeanParameterInfoSupport

This is the support class for OpenMBeanParameterInfo and subsequently implements that interface. This class is provided so that instrumentation developers (i.e., the developers who are instrumenting their code as open MBeans) can create OpenMBeanParameterInfo objects to describe parameters. This class is declared as:

```
public class OpenMBeanParameterInfoSuport
  extends MBeanParameterInfo
  implements OpenMBeanParameterInfo, java.io.Serializable {
// . . .
}
```

As mentioned in the introduction to this section, all of the open MBean support classes extend their MBean*Info counterparts. As we can see, OpenMBeanParameter-InfoSupport extends MBeanParameterInfo. OpenMBeanParameterInfoSupport provides four constructors that we can use to create an OpenMBeanParameterInfo object:

```
public OpenMBeanParameterInfoSupport(String name,
                                     String description,
                                     OpenType openType) {
  // . . .
}

public OpenMBeanParameterInfoSupport(String name,
                                     String description,
                                     OpenType openType,
                                     Object defaultValue)
  throws OpenDataException {
  // . . .
}

public OpenMBeanParameterInfoSupport(String name,
                                     String description,
                                     OpenType openType,
                                     Object defaultValue,
                                     Object[] legalValues)
  throws OpenDataException {
  // . . .
}

public OpenMBeanParameterInfoSupport(String name,
                                     String description,
                                     OpenType openType,
                                     Object defaultValue,
                                     Comparable minValue,
                                     Comparable maxValue)
  throws OpenDataException {
  // . . .
}
```

The minimum amount of information we must supply to fully describe an open MBean parameter is:

- Name
- Description
- OpenType

Each of the constructors for OpenMBeanParameterInfoSupport takes these three arguments. The first constructor takes only these arguments and creates an OpenMBeanParameterInfoSupport instance (or, as we've been referring to it, an OpenMBeanParameterInfo object) in which the DefaultValue, LegalValues, MinValue, and MaxValue attributes are all set to null.

The second constructor allows us to set the DefaultValue attribute, which must be of the same OpenType subclass as the *openType* parameter, or an OpenDataException will be thrown. If the OpenType of the OpenMBeanParameterInfo object we are creating is TabularType or ArrayType, this constructor will throw an exception, because this class does not support the concept of a default value for those types. For SimpleType, it is sufficient that the OpenType of *openType* and *defaultValue* be the same Java class (e.g., both may be java.lang.Integer). However, for CompositeType, their contents (i.e., their item names and corresponding OpenTypes) must also be equal, or an OpenDataException will be thrown. Using this constructor sets the LegalValues, MinValue, and MaxValue attributes to null. Passing null as the *defaultValue* parameter does not cause an exception to be thrown, because null is a valid value for the DefaultValue attribute.

The third constructor allows us to set the DefaultValue attribute (subject to the same checks we discussed in the previous paragraph) and the LegalValues attribute. null is an acceptable value for both attributes. The *legalValues* parameter that allows us to set the LegalValues attribute is an Object array that contains the values that constrain the values of the parameters that are specified by the OpenMBeanParameterInfo object we are creating. If the OpenType of the OpenMBeanParameterInfo object we are creating is TabularType or ArrayType, this constructor will throw an exception, because this class does not support the concept of legal values for those types. If we are using a default value, it must be included in the array of legal values, or an OpenDataException will be thrown.

The fourth constructor allows us to set the DefaultValue attribute and the MinValue and MaxValue attributes. null is an acceptable value for all three attributes. Also, we can set either MinValue or MaxValue without the other, allowing us to specify a minimum value (by setting MinValue) but no maximum, for example. Whatever minimum and/or maximum values we use, the classes used to define the types must implement the appropriate Comparable interface, as listed here:

- java.lang.Byte
- java.lang.Character
- java.lang.Short
- java.lang.Integer
- java.lang.Long
- java.lang.Float
- java.lang.Double

- `java.lang.String`
- `java.math.BigInteger`
- `java.math.BigDecimal`

This constructor performs checks on the values of *defaultValue*, *minValue*, and *max-Value*, such that all of the following must be true, or an `OpenDataException` will be thrown:

- The `OpenType` of the *minValue* and/or *maxValue* parameters must be the same as that of the *openType* parameter.

- *minValue* must be less than *maxValue*, if both *minValue* and *maxValue* are specified.

- If specified, *defaultValue* must be greater than or equal to *minValue* (if *minValue* is specified) and less than or equal to *maxValue* (if *maxValue* is specified).

Once we have created an instance of `OpenMBeanParameterInfoSupport`, we can pass it around through its interface, `OpenMBeanParameterInfo`, as we saw in the previous section.

Let's look at a couple of examples of how to use this class. The `Controller` class (from the sample application) has a method on it called *createWorker()* that has the following declaration:

```
public void createWorker(String role, int workFactor) {
    // . . .
}
```

There are two parameters to this method: a `String` and an `int`. We will see later in this chapter how to create open MBean metadata for an operation such as *createWorker()*, but for now we will focus on describing its parameters (which we must do before describing the operation anyway).

```
OpenMBeanParameterInfo[] params = new OpenMBeanParameterInfo[2];
params[0] = new OpenMBeanParameterInfoSupport(
    "role",
    "The type of worker to create.",
    SimpleType.STRING
);
params[1] = new OpenMBeanParameterInfoSupport(
    "workFactor",
    "The weighted work factor for this new worker thread.",
    SimpleType.INTEGER
);
// . . .
```

This is the simplest example of creating open MBean parameter metadata, where we create `OpenMBeanParameterInfo` objects using the first constructor of `OpenMBean-ParameterInfoSupport`. The `DefaultValue`, `LegalValues`, `MinValue`, and `MaxValue` attributes are all set to `null` in this case. Now suppose we want to define a set of legal values for the *role* parameter and a range of values for the *workFactor* parameter, along with a default value for each parameter:

```
OpenMBeanParameterInfo[] params = new OpenMBeanParameterInfo[2];
params[0] = new OpenMBeanParameterInfoSupport(
  "role",
  "The type of worker to create.",
  SimpleType.STRING,
  "Supplier",    // default role
  new Object[] { // legal values
    "Supplier",
    "Consumer"
  }
);
params[1] = new OpenMBeanParameterInfoSupport(
  "workFactor",
  "The weighted work factor for this new worker thread.",
  SimpleType.INTEGER,
  new Integer(100), // default work factor
  new Integer(50),  // minimum work factor
  new Integer(200)  // maximum work factor
);
// . . .
```

The default value for the *role* parameter is "Supplier", and two valid values are defined: "Supplier" and "Consumer". Notice that the default value is one of the legal values. Had this not been the case, the constructor for OpenMBeanParameterInfo-Support would have thrown an OpenDataException. If no default value had been defined (i.e., if the parameter value passed was null), this check would not have been made, as we are not required to provide a default parameter value.

The default value for *workFactor* is 100, and the work factor specified may be in the range of 50 to 200, inclusive. Notice that the default value lies in this range—had this not been the case (e.g., if the default value was specified to be 49), the OpenMBeanParameterInfoSupport constructor would have thrown an OpenData-Exception. If no default value had been defined (i.e., if the parameter value passed was null), this check would not have been made, as we are not required to provide a default parameter value.

OpenMBeanAttributeInfo

This interface describes an attribute of an open MBean and is defined as:

```
public interface OpenMBeanAttributeInfo extends OpenMBeanParameterInfo {
    public boolean isReadable();
    public boolean isWritable();
    public boolean isIs();
    public boolean equals(Object obj);
    public int hashCode();
    public String toString();
}
```

Notice that OpenMBeanAttributeInfo is a subclass of OpenMBeanParameterInfo, so all of the methods of OpenMBeanParameterInfo must be implemented on OpenMBean-AttributeInfoSupport. There are three fundamental boolean properties[*] of an OpenMBeanAttribute:

isReadable

    Indicates whether or not the value of the attribute described by this OpenMBeanAttributeInfo can be accessed

isWritable

    Indicates whether or not the value of the attribute described by this OpenMBeanAttributeInfo can be modified

isIs

    Indicates whether or not the value of the attribute described by this OpenMBeanAttributeInfo is a boolean attribute whose getter starts with is instead of get

There are three other methods that we will describe briefly, as they function exactly the same as they do for OpenMBeanParameterInfo.

equals() takes a parameter to an Object reference and returns true if the reference is to an object that implements OpenMBeanAttributeInfo and if the Name, OpenType, access properties (isReadable, isWritable, and isIs), DefaultValue, MinimumValue, MaximumValue, and LegalValues values are the same. Otherwise, this method returns false.

hashCode() returns the hashcode for this OpenMBeanAttributeInfo object.

toString() returns a string representation of this OpenMBeanAttributeInfo object. The physical representation is dependent upon the underlying implementation.

OpenMBeanAttributeInfoSupport

This is the support class for OpenMBeanAttributeInfo and subsequently implements that interface. This class is provided so that instrumentation developers can create OpenMBeanAttributeInfo objects to describe attributes. It is declared as:

```
public class OpenMBeanAttributeInfoSupport extends MBeanAttributeInfo
  implements OpenMBeanAttributeInfo, java.io.Serializable {
  // . . .
  }
```

As we mentioned in the introduction to this section, all of the open MBean support classes extend their MBean*Info counterparts. Thus, OpenMBeanAttributeInfoSupport

---

[*] I've chosen to call them properties instead of attributes to avoid any confusion while we discuss open MBean attributes.

extends `MBeanAttributeInfo`. `OpenMBeanAttributeInfoSupport` provides four constructors that we can use to create an `OpenMBeanAttributeInfo` object:

```
public OpenMBeanAttributeInfoSupport(String name,
                                     String description,
                                     OpenType openType,
                                     boolean isReadable,
                                     boolean isWritable,
                                     boolean isIs) {
// . . .
}

public OpenMBeanAttributeInfoSupport(String name,
                                     String description,
                                     OpenType openType,
                                     boolean isReadable,
                                     boolean isWritable,
                                     boolean isIs,
                                     Object  defaultValue)
   throws OpenDataException {
// . . .
}

public OpenMBeanAttributeInfoSupport(String name,
                                     String description,
                                     OpenType openType,
                                     boolean isReadable,
                                     boolean isWritable,
                                     boolean isIs,
                                     Object defaultValue,
                                     Object[] legalValues)
   throws OpenDataException {
// . . .
}

public OpenMBeanAttributeInfoSupport(String name,
                                     String description,
                                     OpenType openType,
                                     boolean isReadable,
                                     boolean isWritable,
                                     boolean isIs,
                                     Object defaultValue,
                                     Comparable minValue,
                                     Comparable maxValue)
   throws OpenDataException {
// . . .
}
```

The minimum amount of information we must supply to fully describe an open MBean attribute is:

- Name
- Description

- OpenType
- isReadable
- isWritable
- isIs

Each of the constructors of OpenMBeanAttributeInfoSupport takes these six arguments. The first constructor takes only these arguments and creates an OpenMBeanAttributeInfoSupport instance (or, as we've been referring to it, an OpenMBeanAttributeInfo object) in which the DefaultValue, LegalValues, MinValue, and MaxValue properties are set to null.

The second constructor allows us to set the DefaultValue attribute, which must be of the same OpenType subclass as the *openType* parameter, or an OpenDataException will be thrown. If the OpenType of the OpenMBeanAttributeInfo object we are creating is TabularType or ArrayType, this constructor will throw an OpenDataException, because this class does not support the concept of a default value for those types. For SimpleType, it is sufficient that the OpenType of *openType* and *defaultValue* be the same Java class (e.g., both may be java.lang.Integer). However, for CompositeType, their contents (i.e., their item names and corresponding OpenTypes) must also be equal, or an OpenDataException will be thrown. Using this constructor sets the LegalValues, MinValue, and MaxValue attributes to null. Passing null as the *default-Value* parameter does not cause an exception to be thrown, because null is a valid value for the DefaultValue attribute.

The third constructor allows us to set the DefaultValue attribute (subject to the same checks we discussed in the previous paragraph) and the LegalValues attribute. null is an acceptable value for both parameters. The *legalValues* parameter that allows us to set the LegalValues attribute is an Object array that contains the values that constrain the values of the parameters that are specified by the OpenMBeanAttributeInfo object we are creating. If the OpenType of the OpenMBeanAttributeInfo object we are creating is TabularType or ArrayType, this constructor will throw an exception, because this support class does not support the concept of legal values for those types. If we are using a default value, it must be included in the array of legal values, or an OpenDataException will be thrown.

The fourth constructor allows us to set the DefaultValue attribute and the MinValue and MaxValue attributes. null is an acceptable value for all three parameters. Also, we can set either MinValue or MaxValue without the other, allowing us to specify a minimum value (by setting MinValue) but no maximum, for example. Whatever minimum and/or maximum values we use, they must implement the appropriate Comparable interface.

Let's look at a couple of examples of how to use this class. The Queue class (from the sample application) has several attributes, and we will look at how to create open MBean metadata to describe two of them: QueueSize and NumberOfItemsProcessed.

```
OpenMBeanAttributeInfo[] attributes = new OpenMBeanAttributeInfo[2];
attributes[0] = new OpenMBeanAttributeInfoSupport(
  "QueueSize",
  "Number of items the Queue can hold.",
  SimpleType.INTEGER,
  true,
  true,
  false
);
attributes[1] = new OpenMBeanAttributeInfoSupport(
  "NumberOfItemsProcessed",
  "The number of items processed.",
  SimpleType.LONG,
  true,
  false,
  false
);
// . . .
```

This is the simplest example of creating open MBean parameter metadata, where we create `OpenMBeanAttributeInfo` objects using the first constructor of `OpenMBeanAttributeInfoSupport`. The `DefaultValue`, `LegalValues`, `MinValue`, and `MaxValue` attributes are all set to `null` in this case. Now suppose we want to specify a range of permissible values for `QueueSize`:

```
OpenMBeanAttributeInfo[] attributes = new OpenMBeanAttributeInfo[2];
attributes[0] = new OpenMBeanAttributeInfoSupport(
  "QueueSize",
  "Number of items the Queue can hold.",
  SimpleType.INTEGER,
  true,
  true,
  false,
  null,             // no default value
  new Integer(3), // min value
  new Integer(12) // max value
);
// . . .
```

In this example, there is no default value, and the `QueueSize` attribute may take on any value from 3 to 12. Now suppose that there are particular values that we don't want `QueueSize` to take on—say, 4, 7, and 10. In that case, we would use a set of legal values to indicate this:

```
OpenMBeanAttributeInfo[] attributes = new OpenMBeanAttributeInfo[2];
attributes[0] = new OpenMBeanAttributeInfoSupport(
  "QueueSize",
  "Number of items the Queue can hold.",
  SimpleType.INTEGER,
  true,
  true,
  false,
  null,        // no default value
```

```
    new Object[] {
      new Integer[3],
      new Integer[5],
      new Integer[6],
      new Integer[8],
      new Integer[9],
      new Integer[11],
      new Integer[12],
    }
  );
  // . . .
```

OpenMBeanConstructorInfo

This interface is used to deal with open MBean constructor information and is defined as:

```
public interface OpenMBeanConstructorInfo {
  public String getDescription();
  public String getName();
  public MBeanParameterInfo[] getSignature();
  public boolean equals(Object obj);
  public int hashCode();
  public String toString();
}
```

There are a few read-only attributes of an open MBean constructor:

Name
: The name of the constructor. This name should match the name of the class on which the constructor is defined.

Description
: A human-readable description of the constructor.

Signature
: An array of MBeanParameterInfo objects that provide information about the arguments to the constructor this OpenMBeanConstructorInfo object describes.

There are three other methods that we will describe briefly, as they function exactly the same as they do for OpenMBeanParameterInfo and OpenMBeanAttributeInfo.

equals() is used to test for equality between this OpenMBeanConstructorInfo object and another that also implements this interface. A field-by-field comparison is made, and if all fields contain the same values, this method returns true. Otherwise, it returns false.

hashCode() returns the hashcode for this OpenMBeanConstructorInfo object.

toString() returns a string representation of this OpenMBeanConstructorInfo object. The physical representation produced by calling this method depends on the underlying implementation of the OpenMBeanConstructorInfo interface.

OpenMBeanConstructorInfoSupport

This is the support class for OpenMBeanConstructorInfo and subsequently implements that interface. This class is provided so that instrumentation developers can create OpenMBeanConstructorInfo objects to describe attributes. It is declared as:

```
public class OpenMBeanConstructorInfoSupport extends MBeanConstructorInfo
    implements OpenMBeanConstructorInfo, java.io.Serializable {
// . . .
}
```

As we have already seen, all of the open MBean support classes extend their MBean*Info counterparts, and OpenMBeanConstructorInfoSupport is no exception. A single constructor is provided and is defined as:

```
public OpenMBeanConstructorInfoSupport(String name,
                                       String description,
                                       OpenMBeanParameterInfo[] signature) {
// . . .
}
```

Let's look at an example of how to use this constructor. The Queue class (from the sample application) defines two constructors, declared as:

```
public Queue( ) {
  // . . .
}
public Queue(int queueSize) {
  // . . .
}
```

The first constructor is an explicitly declared default constructor, and the second takes an int that allows us to set the initial queue capacity:

```
OpenMBeanConstructorInfo[] constructors = new OpenMBeanConstructorInfo[2];
constructors[0] = new OpenMBeanConstructorInfoSupport(
  "Queue",
  "Default Constructor",
  null
);
constructors[1] = new OpenMBeanConstructorInfoSupport(
  "Queue",
  "Alternate Constructor",
  new OpenMBeanParameterInfo[] {
    new OpenMBeanParameterInfoSupport(
      "queueSize",
      "Initial capacity of the Queue.",
      SimpleType.INTEGER
    )
  }
);
// . . .
```

To describe the first constructor, we create a new OpenMBeanConstructorInfo object and pass null to the constructor of OpenMBeanConstructorInfoSupport to indicate that there are no parameters. To describe the second constructor, we must create an OpenMBeanParameterInfo object for each parameter to the constructor. There is only one parameter, so we create an anonymous OpenMBeanParameterInfo array that contains one element: an instance of OpenMBeanParameterInfoSupport.

OpenMBeanOperationInfo

This interface is used to deal with open MBean operation information and is defined as:

```
public interface OpenMBeanOperationInfo {
    public String getName( );
    public String getDescription( );
    public MBeanParameterInfo[] getSignature( );
    public int getImpact( );
    public String getReturnType( );
    public OpenType getReturnOpenType( );
    public boolean equals(Object obj);
    public int hashCode( );
    public String toString( );
}
```

There are several read-only attributes of an open MBean operation:

Name

> The name of the operation. This name should match the name of the operation as it is handled by the DynamicMBean implementation of *invoke()*.

Description

> A human-readable description of the operation.

Signature

> An array of MBeanParameterInfo objects that provides information about the arguments to the operation.

Impact

> The impact on the state of the open MBean by invoking this method. The impact may only be read-only (i.e., no effect on the MBean's state), write-only, or read-write, as designated by the constants INFO, ACTION, and INFO_ACTION, respectively. These constants are defined on the class javax.management. MBeanOperationInfo.

ReturnType

> The string representation of the fully qualified class name of the return type. For example, java.lang.Integer.

ReturnOpenType

> The OpenType of the return type. For example, SimpleType.INTEGER.

There are three other methods that we will describe briefly, as they function exactly the same as they do for OpenMBeanParameterInfo, OpenMBeanAttributeInfo, and OpenMBeanConstructorInfo.

equals() is used to test for equality between this OpenMBeanOperationInfo object and another that also implements this interface. A field-by-field comparison is made, and if all fields contain the same values, this method returns true. Otherwise, it returns false.

hashCode() returns the hashcode for this OpenMBeanOperationInfo object.

toString() returns a string representation of this OpenMBeanOperationInfo object. The physical representation produced by calling this method depends on the underlying implementation of the OpenMBeanOperationInfo interface.

OpenMBeanOperationInfoSupport

This is the support class for OpenMBeanOperationInfo and subsequently implements that interface. This class is provided so that instrumentation developers can create OpenMBeanOperationInfo objects to describe operations. It is declared as:

```
public class OpenMBeanOperationInfoSupport extends MBeanOperationInfo
   implements OpenMBeanOperationInfo, java.io.Serializable {
// . . .
}
```

As we mentioned in the introduction to this section, all of the open MBean support classes extend their MBean*Info counterparts. As we can see, OpenMBean-OperationInfoSupport extends MBeanOperationInfo. OpenMBeanOperationInfoSupport provides a single constructor that we can use to create an OpenMBeanOperationInfo object:

```
public OpenMBeanOperationInfoSupport(String name,
                                     String description,
                                     OpenMBeanParameterInfo[] signature,
                                     OpenType returnOpenType,
                                     int impact) {

   // . . .
}
```

Let's look at an example of how to use this constructor, continuing with the *createWorker()* example from the OpenMBeanParameterInfoSupport section:

```
// Create parameter metadata
OpenMBeanParameterInfo[] params = new OpenMBeanParameterInfo[2];
params[0] = new OpenMBeanParameterInfoSupport(
   "role",
   "The type of worker to create.",
   SimpleType.STRING
);
params[1] = new OpenMBeanParameterInfoSupport(
   "workFactor",
   "The weighted work factor for this new worker thread.",
   SimpleType.INTEGER
);
// Create operation metadata
```

```
OpenMBeanOperationInfo[] operations = new OpenMBeanOperationInfo[1];
operations[0] = new OpenMBeanOperationInfoSupport(
  "createWorker",
  "Creates a new worker thread.",
  params,
  SimpleType.VOID,
  MBeanOperationInfo.ACTION
);
```

In this example, we used the simplest way possible to describe the parameters. However, we are free to give the parameters a default value and either a set of legal values or a valid-value range.

MBeanNotificationInfo

Notifications sent from an open MBean convey the same information as notifications sent from any other MBean type, so no open MBean–specific class is provided for this purpose. However, notifications sent by open MBeans still must be described using the JMX metadata class `MBeanNotificationInfo`, which is found in the `javax.management` package (see Chapter 3 for more information).

OpenMBeanInfo

This interface describes an open MBean and is defined as:

```
public interface OpenMBeanInfo {
  public String getClassName();
  public String getDescription();
  public MBeanAttributeInfo[] getAttributes();
  public MBeanOperationInfo[] getOperations();
  public MBeanConstructorInfo[] getConstructors();
  public MBeanNotificationInfo[] getNotifications();
  public boolean equals(Object obj);
  public int hashCode();
  public String toString();
}
```

There are several read-only attributes of an open MBean:

ClassName
    The string representation of the fully qualified Java class name of the resource described by this open MBean

Description
    A human-readable description of this open MBean

Attributes
    An array of `MBeanAttributeInfo` objects that describe the attributes of this open MBean

Operations

An array of `MBeanOperationInfo` objects that describe the operations of this open MBean

Constructors

An array of `MBeanConstructorInfo` objects that describe the constructors of this open MBean

Notifications

An array of `MBeanNotification` object that describe the notifications emitted by this open MBean

There are three other methods that we will describe briefly, as they function exactly the same as they do for `OpenMBeanParameterInfo`, `OpenMBeanAttributeInfo`, and `OpenMBeanConstructorInfo`.

equals() is used to test for equality between this `OpenMBeanInfo` object and another that also implements this interface. A field-by-field comparison is made, and if all fields contain the same values, this method returns `true`. Otherwise, it returns `false`.

hashCode() returns the hashcode for this `OpenMBeanInfo` object.

toString() returns a string representation of this `OpenMBeanInfo` object. The physical representation produced by calling this method depends on the underlying implementation of the `OpenMBeanInfo` interface.

OpenMBeanInfoSupport

This is the support class for `OpenMBeanInfo` and subsequently implements that interface. This class is provided so that instrumentation developers can create `OpenMBeanInfo` objects to describe operations. It is declared as:

```
public class OpenMBeanInfoSupport extends MBeanInfo
    implements OpenMBeanInfo, java.io.Serializable {
// . . .
}
```

As we mentioned in the introduction to this section, all of the open MBean support classes extend their `MBean*Info` counterparts. As we can see, `OpenMBeanInfoSupport` extends `MBeanInfo`. `OpenMBeanInfoSupport` provides a single constructor that we can use to create an `OpenMBeanInfo` object:

```
public OpenMBeanInfoSupport(String className,
                    String description,
                    OpenMBeanAttributeInfo[] openAttributes,
                    OpenMBeanConstructorInfo[] openConstructors,
                    OpenMBeanOperationInfo[] openOperations,
                    MBeanNotificationInfo[] notifications) {
    // . . .
}
```

Let's look at an example of how to use this class to describe an MBean that is an instance of the Queue class. Creating the metadata that describes the MBean itself involves pulling together the previous sections into the following steps:

1. Create metadata (i.e., OpenMBeanAttributeInfo objects) for all attributes to be exposed on the management interface, and place them into an array that will be passed to the constructor of OpenMBeanInfoSupport. If this MBean has no attributes, this parameter should be null.

2. Create metadata (i.e., OpenMBeanConstructorInfo objects) for all constructors that a management application will need to access to create instances of this MBean, and place them into an array that will be passed to the constructor of OpenMBeanInfoSupport. Make sure to fully describe any parameters using OpenMBeanParameterInfo objects. If this MBean has no constructors to be exposed to a management application, this parameter should be null.

3. Create metadata (i.e., OpenMBeanOperationInfo objects) for all operations that will be exposed on the management interface of the MBean, and place them into an array that will be passed to the constructor of OpenMBeanInfoSupport. Make sure to fully describe any parameters using OpenMBeanParameterInfo objects. If this MBean has no operations, this parameter should be null.

4. Create metadata (i.e., MBeanNotificationInfo objects) for all notifications emitted by this MBean, and place them into an array that will be passed to the constructor of OpenMBeanInfoSupport. If this MBean has no notifications, this parameter should be null.

5. Invoke the constructor of OpenMBeanInfoSupport, passing the fully qualified name of the Java class that this MBean describes, a description of this MBean, and references to the arrays created and populated in Steps 1-4.

Suppose the name of the MBean class is sample.openmbean.Queue. In that case, we would follow the steps outlined above (see the previous sections for how to do this) and then create the OpenMBeanInfo object that describes the MBean:

```
OpenMBeanInfo queueMBean = new OpenMBeanInfo(
    "sample.openmbean.Queue",
    "Queue class instrumented as an open MBean.",
    attributes,    // OpenMBeanAttributeInfo[]
    constructors,  // OpenMBeanConstructorInfo[]
    operations,    // OpenMBeanOperationInfo[]
    notifications  // MBeanNotificationInfo[]
);
```

CHAPTER 6

The MBean Server

So far, we have talked only about the instrumentation level of the JMX architecture. In this chapter, we will take a close look at the core of the JMX architecture, the agent level. This chapter is for those developers who want a deeper understanding of the JMX agent level, are responsible for developing protocol adaptors and connectors, or need to interact with a local `MBeanServer` instance.

First, we will take a quick look at the MBean server's role in the JMX agent level, how it is implemented in the RI, how to get a reference to it, and what you can do with that reference once you have it. Next, we will take a closer look at the `MBeanServerFactory` class and its various methods for obtaining references to the MBean server. Then we will look at the `MBeanServer` interface, which is how MBeans, JMX agents, and management applications interact with the MBean server. In this section, we will also explore how to register and unregister MBeans, how to use the MBean server to interact with an MBean through its `ObjectName`, how to register interest in notifications, and how to query the MBean server to return a subset of registered MBeans. This section will be followed by a discussion of the `MBeanRegistration` interface, which gives the instrumentation developer a means of control over an MBean's `ObjectName`, as well as exit points for additional processing before and after the MBean is registered and deregistered. The chapter will conclude with a look at `MBeanServerDelegate`, a class required by all JMX-compliant implementations to provide metadata about that particular JMX implementation.

What Is the MBean Server?

The MBean server is at the heart of the agent level of the JMX architecture. The primary function of the MBean server is to act as a *registry* for MBeans. It is through the MBean server that MBeans, other parts of the JMX agent, and management applications gain access to the MBeans that are registered with the MBean server. Every MBean must be registered with the MBean server in order to be managed. This is achieved by first obtaining a reference to the MBean server (we'll see how to do that later in this chapter) and then invoking the appropriate method of the MBeanServer interface. We will discuss the MBeanServer interface in more detail later in this chapter.

A secondary function of the MBean server is to act as an intermediary to allow other JMX agents, management applications, and MBeans to monitor and manage MBeans without having a reference to the MBean object. As long as the object name of the MBean is known and the MBean is registered, an MBean can be indirectly manipulated through the MBean server in which the MBean is registered.

In the RI provided with the final release of the JMX 1.0 specification, the MBeanServer interface is fully implemented in a class called MBeanServerImpl, located in the com. sun.management.jmx package. If you are using the RI and are curious about the internals of the MBean server implementation, I encourage you to look at the source code for this class.

As mentioned earlier, before an MBean can be registered with the MBean server, a reference to the MBean server must be obtained. This is achieved through MBeanServerFactory, a class located in the javax.management package that must be shipped with every compliant JMX implementation. This class contains static methods that allow you to create an instance of an MBean server and find an instance of an MBean server that has already been created. Each of the methods of the MBeanServerFactory class will be discussed later in this chapter.

The MBean server implementation class (MBeanServerImpl, in the JMX 1.0 RI) should never be instantiated directly! You should always use the static methods of MBeanServerFactory to obtain a reference to an MBean server. In addition, once you obtain a reference to an MBean server, you should never cast it to an MBeanServerImpl, even though this would work when using the RI. You should always work with the MBean server through the MBeanServer interface.

We will look at the MBeanServer interface in more detail later in this chapter. Once you have a reference to an MBean server, you can:

- Register and deregister MBeans.
- Register interest in MBean and MBean server notifications.
- Manipulate MBeans by getting and setting their attribute values and invoking their management operations.
- Query the MBean server to return subsets of the MBeans that are registered within it.

We will look at each of these actions in detail in the sections that follow.

Unless otherwise noted, we will assume that we are going to work with only a single MBean server within any given JVM.

Obtaining a Reference to the MBean Server

The under-the-hood implementation of the MBean server in the RI is com.sun.management.jmx.MBeanServerImpl, but this class should never be instantiated directly. Instead, the RI provides a factory class called MBeanServerFactory that contains various static methods that allow you to obtain a reference to the MBean server. In this section, we will describe each of those static methods and give examples of how to use them. Example 6-1 is an abbreviated version of the MBeanServerFactory class.

Example 6-1. The static methods of MBeanServerFactory

```
package javax.management;
// . . .
public class MBeanServerFactory {
// . . .
  public static MBeanServer createMBeanServer () {
    // . . .
  }

  public static MBeanServer createMBeanServer (String domain) {
    // . . .
  }

  public static MBeanServer newMBeanServer () {
    // . . .
  }

  public static MBeanServer newMBeanServer (String domain) {
    // . . .
  }

  public synchronized static ArrayList findMBeanServer (String AgentId) {
    // . . .
  }

  public static void releaseMBeanServer (MBeanServer mbeanServer) {
    // . . .
  }

// . . .
}
```

There are six static methods on MBeanServerFactory, as shown in Example 6-1. These methods allow you to create an instance, find one or more instances, and release a reference to an instance of an MBean server.

Creating the MBean Server

If no MBean server instance exists (we'll discuss how to find that out later), there are four static methods that allow you to create one. The first two, overloads of *createMBeanServer()*, allow you to create an instance of the MBean server with the default domain name and a specific domain name, respectively. When you create an instance of the MBean server, `MBeanServerFactory` maintains a reference to the MBean server that was just created, ensuring that it will not be garbage-collected. The second two methods, overloads of *newMBeanServer()*, do the same thing, but `MBeanServerFactory` does *not* maintain a reference to the newly created MBean server—it is up to the caller to maintain the reference.

If you want to create an instance of the MBean server and have `MBeanServerFactory` maintain an internal reference to it, you have two choices. The first option is to call the version of *createMBeanServer()* with no parameters, which will create an MBean server instance, store its reference inside the factory, and return an `MBeanServer` reference to you:

```
MBeanServer mbeanServer = MBeanServerFactory.createMBeanServer( );
```

Recall from Chapter 2 that every MBean has a unique `ObjectName` instance associated with it. Even though the MBean server itself is not technically a managed resource, it must still have a domain name associated with it. In the code above, the resulting MBean server would be created with the default domain name, which in the JMX 1.0 RI is "DefaultDomain". Figure 6-1 shows the management view of the MBean server when we use the no-argument version of *createMBeanServer()*.

If, however, we want to provide the MBean server with a domain name other than "DefaultDomain", we can pass a `String` argument containing that name:

```
String differentDomain = "TheTwilightZone";
MBeanServer mbeanServer = MBeanServerFactory.createMBeanServer(differentDomain);
```

The domain name of the resulting MBean server is now "TheTwilightZone". Figure 6-2 shows the management view of this MBean server. As you can see, the domain name of the MBean server is indeed what we passed to *createMBeanServer()*. But notice something interesting about Figure 6-2. When the `Queue` instance is created in the `Controller`, the default domain is used. However, the domain name of the `Queue` MBean is now "TheTwilightZone"! Passing a domain name to *createMBeanServer()* not only sets the domain name of the resulting MBean server; it also sets the default domain name for all MBeans registered within it.

The internal references to MBean servers created using the *createMBeanServer()* methods are stored within `MBeanServerFactory`. When a call to this static method is made, the MBean server is instantiated and a reference to it is added to this internal store.

However, if this is not the behavior you desire (e.g., if you don't want third-party components running within the same JVM as your MBeans to be able to find your MBean server), you can invoke one of the two static methods called *newMBeanServer()* to avoid `MBeanServerFactory`'s default behavior of keeping an internal reference to the

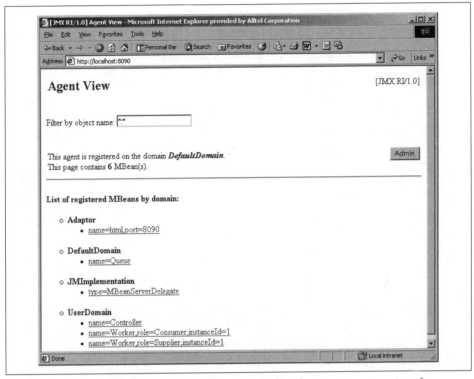

Figure 6-1. *The management view of the MBean server when the no-argument version of* createMBeanServer() *is used*

newly created MBean server. The syntax is identical to that of *createMBeanServer()* in both cases, and the resulting domain name follows the same rules as those for *createMBeanServer()*. To create an MBean server with the domain name "DefaultDomain", simply use the no-argument version of *newMBeanServer()*:

```
MBeanServer mbeanServer = MBeanServerFactory.newMBeanServer();
```

The resulting management view looks the same as the one shown in Figure 6-1. To create an MBean server with the domain name "TheTwilightZone", simply use the other version of *newMBeanServer()*:

```
String differentDomain = "TheTwilightZone";
MBeanServer mbeanServer = MBeanServerFactory.newMBeanServer(differentDomain);
```

The management view will look the same as the one shown in Figure 6-2.

 Any reference to the MBean server obtained via *newMBeanServer()* will be garbage-collected when the reference goes out of scope. You should hold the reference in an instance variable of a class that has a lifetime at least as long as that of the resulting MBean server.

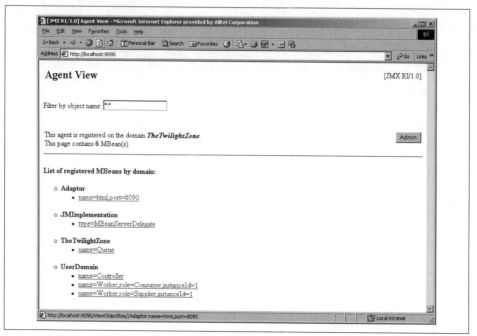

Figure 6-2. The management view of the MBean server when a domain name is supplied to createMBeanServer( )

Finding the MBean Server

To locate an existing MBean server, use MBeanServerFactory's static *findMBeanServer( )* method. Example 6-1 shows this method to be defined as:

```
public synchronized static ArrayList findMBeanServer (String AgentId) {
    // . . .
}
```

This method takes a String argument that is the "agent ID" for the MBean server you're trying to find. This terminology is rather vague, and I suspect that the designers of the specification intended there to be some latitude in how this parameter is used from implementation to implementation. According to the JMX 1.0 RI source code, the agent ID is the name of the local host machine where the JVM is running that contains the MBean server, followed by an underscore character, followed by the system time in milliseconds when the MBean server was instantiated.

For example, suppose the name of the local host is "STEVE" and the system time when the MBean server was instantiated was 1002565476994 milliseconds. The agent ID in this case would be "STEVE_ 1002565476994". Clearly, it would be very difficult (at best) to ask for a *specific* agent ID using the RI. However, if you pass null as the argument to *findMBeanServer( )*, a list of all the MBean servers in the JVM is returned. You can then iterate through the list to find the MBean server that matches the domain in which you are interested. For example, suppose we want to find the MBean server for the "TheTwilightZone" domain from earlier in this chapter. We would call the *findMBeanServer()* static method of MBeanServerFactory and then iterate through the list (we could also index through the list, because the return value is a cloned version of the ArrayList that MBeanServerFactory keeps internally) until we find the MBean server for the "TheTwilightZone" domain:

```
String agentId = null;
ArrayList mbeanServers = MBeanServerFactory.findMBeanServer(agentId);
Iterator iter = mbeanServers.iterator();
MBeanServer mbeanServer = null;
while (iter.hasNext()) {
  mbeanServer = (MBeanServer)iter.next();
  if (mbeanServer.getDefaultDomain().equals("TheTwilightZone")) {
    // found it!
    break;
  }
  else
    mbeanServer = null;
}
if (mbeanServer == null) {
  mbeanServer = MBeanServerFactory.createMBeanServer("TheTwilightZone");
}
```

If we had already created an instance of the MBean server with the domain name "TheTwilightZone" but used the static method *newMBeanServer()* to do it, this code would not find it. Recall that when we use *newMBeanServer()* to create an instance of the MBean server, MBeanServerFactory does not keep an internal reference to it. Because *findMBeanServer()* returns the ArrayList that serves as the internal reference backing store, we will never find references to MBean servers created with *newMBeanServer()*. However, the JMX RI doesn't seem to care how many instances of an MBean server are created with the same domain name, so the code above will still find the instance we created with *createMBeanServer()*. A word to the wise: if you anticipate ever needing to programmatically locate an MBean server by its domain name, make sure you create it using *createMBeanServer()*, so that MBeanServerFactory will hold a reference to it.

Releasing a Reference to the MBeanServer

Say that you need to remove the internal reference stored in MBeanServerFactory to an MBean server instance you created by calling *createMBeanServer()*. You can do so by calling *releaseMBeanServer()*, which from Example 6-1 is defined as:

```
public static void releaseMBeanServer(MBeanServer mbeanServer) {
  // . . .
}
```

Note that calling this static method does not remove the MBean server from the JVM; it simply removes it from the internal store of MBean servers maintained by MBeanServerFactory. You may call this method only with an MBeanServer reference obtained by a call to *createMBeanServer()*. The syntax is very straightforward:

```
MBeanServer mbeanServer = MBeanServerFactory.createMBeanServer();
//
// Do something with the reference
//
// Later on. . .
//
MBeanServerFactory.releaseMBeanServer(mbeanServer);
```

Once the call to *releaseMBeanServer()* is made, subsequent calls to *findMBeanServer()* will fail to locate a reference to the MBeanServer just released.

The MBeanServer Interface

In this section, we will take a close look at the MBeanServer interface, which is used to communicate with the MBeanServer implementation. First we will present the interface in its entirety, then we will proceed to dissect the interface method by method, providing examples along the way. We will also take another look at the ObjectName class, which is critical in manipulating MBeans indirectly through the MBeanServer interface (the preferred means of doing so). We have already covered what you can do through a reference to the MBeanServer interface. Let's now look more closely at this important interface. Example 6-2 shows the MBeanServer interface.

Example 6-2. The MBeanServer interface

```
package javax.management;

public interface MBeanServer {

  public Object instantiate(String className)
    throws ReflectionException, MBeanException;

  public Object instantiate(String className, ObjectName loaderName)
    throws ReflectionException, MBeanException, InstanceNotFoundException;

  public Object instantiate(String className, Object params[], String signature[])
    throws ReflectionException, MBeanException;

  public Object instantiate(String className, ObjectName loaderName,
                            Object params[], String signature[])
    throws ReflectionException, MBeanException, InstanceNotFoundException;

  public ObjectInstance registerMBean(Object object, ObjectName name)
    throws InstanceAlreadyExistsException, MBeanRegistrationException,
        NotCompliantMBeanException;
```

Example 6-2. The MBeanServer interface (continued)

```
public ObjectInstance createMBean(String className, ObjectName name)
   throws ReflectionException, InstanceAlreadyExistsException,
         MBeanRegistrationException, MBeanException, NotCompliantMBeanException;

public ObjectInstance createMBean(String className, ObjectName name,
                                 ObjectName loaderName)
   throws ReflectionException, InstanceAlreadyExistsException,
         MBeanRegistrationException, MBeanException,
         NotCompliantMBeanException, InstanceNotFoundException;

public ObjectInstance createMBean(String className, ObjectName name,
                                 Object params[], String signature[])
   throws ReflectionException, InstanceAlreadyExistsException,
         MBeanRegistrationException, MBeanException, NotCompliantMBeanException;

public ObjectInstance createMBean(String className, ObjectName name,
                                 ObjectName loaderName, Object params[],
                                 String signature[])
   throws ReflectionException, InstanceAlreadyExistsException,
         MBeanRegistrationException, MBeanException,
         NotCompliantMBeanException, InstanceNotFoundException;

public void unregisterMBean(ObjectName name)
   throws InstanceNotFoundException, MBeanRegistrationException;

public Object getAttribute(ObjectName name, String attribute)
   throws MBeanException, AttributeNotFoundException,
         InstanceNotFoundException, ReflectionException;

public AttributeList getAttributes(ObjectName name, String[] attributes)
   throws InstanceNotFoundException, ReflectionException;

public void setAttribute(ObjectName name, Attribute attribute)
   throws InstanceNotFoundException, AttributeNotFoundException,
         InvalidAttributeValueException, MBeanException, ReflectionException;

public AttributeList setAttributes(ObjectName name, AttributeList attributes)
   throws InstanceNotFoundException, ReflectionException;

public Object invoke(ObjectName name, String operationName,
                    Object params[], String signature[])
   throws InstanceNotFoundException, MBeanException, ReflectionException;

public MBeanInfo getMBeanInfo(ObjectName name)
   throws InstanceNotFoundException, IntrospectionException, ReflectionException;

public void addNotificationListener(ObjectName name, NotificationListener listener,
                                   NotificationFilter filter, Object handback)
   throws InstanceNotFoundException;
```

Example 6-2. The MBeanServer interface (continued)

```
    public void addNotificationListener(ObjectName name, ObjectName listener,
                                        NotificationFilter filter, Object handback)
        throws InstanceNotFoundException;

    public void removeNotificationListener(ObjectName name, NotificationListener listener)
        throws InstanceNotFoundException, ListenerNotFoundException;

    public void removeNotificationListener(ObjectName name, ObjectName listener)
        throws InstanceNotFoundException, ListenerNotFoundException;

    public Set queryMBeans(ObjectName name, QueryExp query);

    public Set queryNames(ObjectName name, QueryExp query);

    public ObjectInstance getObjectInstance(ObjectName name)
        throws InstanceNotFoundException;

    public boolean isRegistered(ObjectName name);

    public Integer getMBeanCount( );

    public boolean isInstanceOf(ObjectName name, String className)
        throws InstanceNotFoundException;

    public String getDefaultDomain( );

    public ObjectInputStream deserialize(ObjectName name, byte[] data)
        throws InstanceNotFoundException, OperationsException;

    public ObjectInputStream deserialize(String className, byte[] data)
        throws OperationsException, ReflectionException;

    public ObjectInputStream deserialize(String className, ObjectName loaderName,
                                         byte[] data)
        throws InstanceNotFoundException, OperationsException, ReflectionException;
}
```

As you can see from Example 6-2, the MBeanServer interface contains quite a few methods! These methods can be grouped into five distinct categories, related to the function each method performs:

Instantiation and registration
> Those methods related to instantiation of MBeans, registration of MBeans, or both

Indirect MBean manipulation
> Those methods related to manipulating MBeans through the MBean server, rather than through direct references to the MBeans themselves

Notification
> Those methods related to MBean notifications

Query

Those methods related to retrieving subsets of registered MBeans by querying the MBean server

Utility

Those methods that provide helpful functionality not directly related to any particular previous category

In this section, we will look at each method on the MBeanServer interface by category. We will start with instantiation and registration, as that category of methods is likely to be the most widely used. The other categories will follow, in the order in which they are enumerated above.

Instantiation and Registration

If you are interested only in instrumenting your application resources as MBeans, you will be concerned with only those methods of MBeanServer that allow you to instantiate and register MBeans. Two of these methods, *createMBean()* and *instantiate()*, are overloaded, with four overloads apiece. Two other methods, *registerMBean()* and *unregisterMBean()*, round out the instantiation and registration methods. These methods can be broken down into four categories:

- Instantiating an MBean
- Registering an instantiated MBean
- Combining the instantiation and registration of an MBean
- Removing a registered MBean from the MBean server

Instantiating an MBean

The four overloads of *instantiate()* are defined as:

```
public Object instantiate(String className)
    throws ReflectionException, MBeanException;

public Object instantiate(String className, Object params[], String signature[])
    throws ReflectionException, MBeanException;

public Object instantiate(String className, ObjectName loaderName)
    throws ReflectionException, MBeanException, InstanceNotFoundException;

public Object instantiate(String className, ObjectName loaderName,
                    Object params[], String signature[])
    throws ReflectionException, MBeanException, InstanceNotFoundException;
```

Each of these methods is used to create a new instance of an MBean's class, as the method name suggests. Upon creation, a reference to the newly created MBean is returned to the caller in the form of an Object reference. The caller is then responsible for registering the MBean with the MBean server.

In all cases, the String *className* parameter is the fully qualified class name of the MBean's class. For example, if the MBean class Queue to be loaded is found in the sample.mbeanserver package, the MBean would be instantiated as:

```
MBeanServer mbeanServer = MBeanServerFactory.createMBeanServer( );
String qmbeanClassName = "sample.mbeanserver.Queue";
try {
  Object qmbean = mbeanServer.instantiate(qmbeanClassName);
} catch (ReflectionException e) {
  // . . .
} catch (MBeanException e) {
  // . . .
}
```

In this case, the no-argument constructor of Queue will be called when the object is constructed. Likewise, we can use the second version of *instantiate()* to have an alternate constructor invoked when an instance of Queue is created. The alternate constructor for Queue is an int that allows you to specify the depth of the queue. The signature of the *instantiate()* method we invoke is:

```
public Object instantiate(String className, Object params[], String signature[])
    throws ReflectionException, MBeanException;
```

The first parameter is the fully qualified name of the Queue class, as mentioned earlier. The second parameter is an array of Object instances that contain the actual parameter values. Any primitive types must be wrapped in the appropriate JDK wrapper class. For our example, we must wrap the int parameter with a java.lang. Integer instance. For object types, simply pass an instance of the object that contains the parameter value. The third parameter to *instantiate()* is a String array that contains the fully qualified class names of the constructor's signature.

The alternate constructor for Queue is defined as:

```
public Queue(int queueSize) {
  // . . .
}
```

Suppose we want to use *instantiate()* to invoke this constructor when an instance of Queue is instantiated and set the *queueSize* parameter to 5:

```
MBeanServer mbeanServer = MBeanServerFactory.createMBeanServer( );
Object[] params = new Object[] {
  new Integer(5);
};
String[] signature = new String[] {
  Integer.TYPE.getName( )
};
String queueClassName = "sample.mbeanserver.Queue";
try {
  Object queue = mbeanServer.instantiate(queueClassName, params, signature);
  // . . .
} catch (ReflectionException e) {
```

```
    // . . .
} catch (MBeanException e) {
    // . . .
}
```

First we construct an array of Object instances (in this case, the array will contain only one instance), wrapping the primitive int with an instance of the JDK wrapper class Integer. Then we create an array of Strings (again, only one) containing the string representation of the Class object that corresponds to the parameter passed in the Object array. Because the parameter type is an int, we must obtain the string representation of an int. Integer.TYPE is the Class object for the primitive type int, and a call to *getName()* gives us the string representation we need. Chapter 3 contains a thorough discussion of the use of TYPE for obtaining the Class object for primitive types.

If Queue's class loader can locate and successfully load Queue, an Object reference to the newly created Queue class is returned. If the class loader cannot locate Queue, the MBeanServer implementation will use its list of class loaders to load the class. However, there are two overloaded versions of *instantiate()* that have the same signature as the two versions we just discussed, with the exception of an additional parameter that allows us to specify an ObjectName of the class loader to use when instantiating the MBean.

There is a catch, though: the class loader to be used must be an MBean and must be registered with the MBean server prior to invoking these two versions of *instantiate()*. It is beyond the scope of this book to show how to write a ClassLoader, and other than the additional parameter passed to them, the last two overloads of *instantiate()* work exactly the same way as their previous two counterparts. Be aware, though, that the ClassLoader you provide with these two overloads must be an MBean as well as an extended version of ClassLoader.

In each of the overloaded versions of *instantiate()*, it is possible for something to go wrong. Notice the exceptions that are potentially thrown from each method. The most common exception you're likely to see is a ReflectionException, which indicates that the intended constructor could not be found. For the first and third versions of *instantiate()*, it means that the no-argument constructor either was not defined on the class (but an alternate constructor was) or does not have public visibility. For the second and fourth versions, a ReflectionException means that the constructor with the specified signature either does not exist on the class or does not have public visibility.

Registering an MBean

Once *instantiate()* has been called, an Object reference to the newly created MBean is returned to the caller. It is then up to the caller to register the MBean with the MBean server (although the caller is under no obligation to do so). MBeanServer provides a method that allows you to register the MBean once it has been instantiated. This method, called *registerMBean()*, is defined as:

```
public ObjectInstance registerMBean(Object object, ObjectName name)
    throws InstanceAlreadyExistsException, MBeanRegistrationException,
        NotCompliantMBeanException;
```

The first parameter, *object*, is an Object reference to an instance of the MBean to be registered. The second parameter, *name*, is an ObjectName instance that contains the unique object name of the MBean. An MBean's object name is a String that contains the domain and the key property list and is of the form:

```
"domain:property1=value1,property2=value2,. . .,propertyN=valueN"
```

Think of the domain as the namespace mechanism for JMX. The key property list for an MBean is a comma-separated list of name/value pairs that uniquely identify an MBean within a particular domain. Refer to Chapter 2 for a more thorough discussion of the ObjectName class and its role in MBean registration.

From this point on, an MBean's *object name* is the unique string identifying the MBean, and ObjectName is a class, an instance of which is used to contain the object name. For example:

```
ObjectName name1 = new ObjectName("d1:p1=v1");
ObjectName name2 = new ObjectName("d1:p1=v1");
```

name1 and name2 are unique ObjectNames, but they contain the same object name.

If the object name is not unique, the MBean server throws an InstanceAlready-ExistsException. If the MBean is not compliant with the JMX design patterns, a NotCompliantMBeanException is thrown. If any other problems crop up during the registration process, an MBeanRegistrationException is thrown. Using the Queue example from earlier in this section, we could create an instance of Queue using *instantiate()*, then take the returned Object reference and call *registerMBean()*:

```
MBeanServer mbeanServer = MBeanServerFactory.createMBeanServer();
String qmbeanClassName = "sample.mbeanserver.Queue";
Object qmbean = null;
try {
  Object qmbean = mbeanServer.instantiate(qmbeanClassName);
} catch (ReflectionException e) {
  // . . .
} catch (MBeanException e) {
  // . . .
}
// Create an ObjectName for the MBean. . .
String domain = mbeanServer.getDefaultDomain();
String keyPropsList = "name=Queue";
ObjectName objName = new ObjectName(domainName + ":" + keyPropsList);
try {
  mbeanServer.registerMBean(qmbean, objName);
```

```
    } catch (InstanceAlreadyExistsException e) {
      // . . .
    } catch (NotCompliantMBeanException e) {
      // . . .
    } catch (MBeanRegistrationException e) {
      // . . .
    }
```

What is returned from the call to *registerMBean()* is an ObjectInstance, which encapsulates an MBean's class name and its ObjectName instance (although the resulting ObjectName may actually be different if the MBean implements the MBeanRegistration interface and provides a different ObjectName in the *preRegistration()* method). In the above code snippet, we simply ignored the return value, as we didn't need it for anything.

Instead of using *instantiate()* to register the Queue MBean, we could simply have used the new keyword to create an instance and then called *registerMBean()*:

```
MBeanServer mbeanServer = MBeanServerFactory.createMBeanServer();
String qmbeanClassName = "sample.mbeanserver.Queue";
QueueMBean qmbean = new Queue();
// Create an ObjectName for the MBean. . .
String domain = mbeanServer.getDefaultDomain();
String keyPropsList = "name=Queue";
ObjectName objName = new ObjectName(domainName + ":" + keyPropsList);
try {
  mbeanServer.registerMBean(qmbean, objName);
} catch (InstanceAlreadyExistsException e) {
  // . . .
} catch (NotCompliantMBeanException e) {
  // . . .
} catch (MBeanRegistrationException e) {
  // . . .
}
```

This is a perfectly acceptable approach to creating and registering an MBean, and one that I often use myself. There is no requirement that you instantiate your MBeans by calling *instantiate()*; this method is simply provided as a convenience.

Combining the instantiation and registration of an MBean

The MBeanServer interface provides us with a method that can combine the instantiation and registration of an MBean. This method is called *createMBean()*. *createMBean()* works in exactly the same way as *instantiate()*, but it allows you to specify an ObjectName so that the details of registering your MBean are handled behind the scenes. Just as with *instantiate()*, there are four overloads of *createMBean()*, defined as:

```
public ObjectInstance createMBean(String className, ObjectName name)
    throws ReflectionException, InstanceAlreadyExistsException,
        MBeanRegistrationException, MBeanException, NotCompliantMBeanException;
```

```
public ObjectInstance createMBean(String className, ObjectName name,
                                  ObjectName loaderName)
   throws ReflectionException, InstanceAlreadyExistsException,
          MBeanRegistrationException, MBeanException,
          NotCompliantMBeanException, InstanceNotFoundException;

public ObjectInstance createMBean(String className, ObjectName name,
                                  Object params[], String signature[])
   throws ReflectionException, InstanceAlreadyExistsException,
          MBeanRegistrationException, MBeanException, NotCompliantMBeanException;

public ObjectInstance createMBean(String className, ObjectName name,
                                  ObjectName loaderName, Object params[],
                                  String signature[])
   throws ReflectionException, InstanceAlreadyExistsException,
          MBeanRegistrationException, MBeanException,
          NotCompliantMBeanException, InstanceNotFoundException;
```

As you can see from the method signatures of the overloaded versions of
createMBean(), the possible exceptions that may be thrown are a combination of
those of the corresponding *instantiate()* and *registerMBean()* methods. Using the
Queue MBean example from earlier, we can combine the instantiation and registration processes with one call to *createMBean()*:

```
MBeanServer mbeanServer = MBeanServerFactory.createMBeanServer( );
String qmbeanClassName = "sample.mbeanserver.Queue";
String domain = mbeanServer.getDefaultDomain( );
String keyPropsList = "name=Queue";
ObjectName objName = new ObjectName(domainName + ":" + keyPropsList);
ObjectInstance objInst = null;
try {
  objInst = mbeanServer.createMBean(qmbeanClassName, objName);
} catch (ReflectionException e) {
  // . . .
} catch (InstanceAlreadyExistsException e) {
  // . . .
} catch (MBeanRegistrationException e) {
  // . . .
} catch (MBeanException e) {
  // . . .
} catch (NotCompliantMBeanException e) {
  // . . .
}
```

There is a subtle—yet important—difference between using *createMBean()* and the
other approaches we've discussed for creating and registering MBeans: when you
use *createMBean()* to instantiate and register an MBean, you will not receive a reference to the MBean object itself. This means that you will not be able to directly
manipulate the MBean, as you do not have a reference to it. Notice what is returned
from *createMBean()*: a reference to the MBean's ObjectInstance (as we've already

mentioned, every registered MBean has a corresponding ObjectInstance associated with it). This is an indirect reference to the MBean that you can use to manipulate the MBean indirectly. In the next section, we will look at how to indirectly manipulate MBeans using the MBean server and both an ObjectInstance and an ObjectName reference to the MBean.

Removing a registered MBean from the MBean server

The MBeanServer interface also provides a means to remove MBeans from the MBean server's registry. This has no effect on the object itself—if there are any valid references to it, it remains alive and well inside the JVM. However, once removed from the MBean server's internal registry, the MBean is no longer accessible through the MBean server to other MBeans, JMX agents, or management applications. The method to remove an MBean from the MBean server is called *unregisterMBean()* and is defined as:

```
public void unregisterMBean(ObjectName name)
    throws InstanceNotFoundException, MBeanRegistrationException;
```

All that is required to unregister an MBean is its object name, wrapped in an ObjectName instance. If the object name string contained within the ObjectName is not found in the MBean server's registry, an InstanceNotFoundException is thrown. If any other error occurs, the MBean server throws an MBeanRegistrationException.

Here is an example, using the Queue MBean from earlier:

```
MBeanServer mbeanServer = MBeanServerFactory.createMBeanServer();
String qmbeanClassName = "sample.mbeanserver.Queue";
String domain = mbeanServer.getDefaultDomain();
String keyPropsList = "name=Queue";
ObjectName objName = new ObjectName(domainName + ":" + keyPropsList);
// register the MBean. . .
// later on . . .
try {
  mbeanServer.unregisterMBean(objName);
} catch (InstanceNotFoundException e) {
  // . . .
} catch (MBeanRegistrationException e) {
  // . . .
}
```

If the call to *unregister()* is successful, the MBean specified by the object name string contained within the ObjectName reference passed to *unregister()* is removed from the MBean server's registry and is no longer accessible to other MBeans, JMX agents, or management applications. However, as mentioned earlier, any direct references to the MBean object will still be valid. Calling *unregister()* does not guarantee that an MBean will be eligible for garbage collection.

Indirect MBean Manipulation

The MBean server provides several methods that allow for interaction with a registered MBean through its object name. Recall that when an MBean is registered, a unique object name—a string containing the MBean's domain and key property list—is always provided by passing an instance of `ObjectName` that contains the object name. Subsequently, through an `ObjectName` instance that contains the object name of the MBean, any MBean can be manipulated through these methods on the MBean server. The MBean server looks up the MBean by its object name and, if it finds it, manipulates the MBean directly on behalf of the caller, receives the results, and returns the results to the caller. This is what is meant by indirect MBean manipulation—because the caller does not have a reference to the MBean object itself, it uses the MBean's unique object name to manipulate the MBean and uses the MBean server to broker the interaction.

By "manipulating" or "interacting with" an MBean, we mean using the management interface of an MBean to:

- Retrieve a management attribute value.
- Set a management attribute value.
- Invoke a management operation.

Through indirect MBean manipulation, only the management interface is available. For example, suppose I have a management interface defined on `MyClassMBean`:

```
public interface MyClassMBean {
  public String getStringAttribute();
  public void reset();
}
```

that's implemented on a class `MyClass` (following the standard MBean design patterns):

```
public class MyClass {
  // management interface. . .
  public String getStringAttribute() {
    return _stringAttribute;
  }
  public void reset() {
    setStringAttribute("");
  }
  // other class-related stuff. . .
  private String _stringAttribute;
  public void setStringAttribute(String value) {
    _stringAttribute = value;
  }
}
```

Notice the public setter *setStringAttribute()*. If we create an instance of `MyClass`, we are free to invoke this method because we have a reference to it:

```
MyClass myClass = new MyClass();
myClass.setAttribute("I am Roger the Shrubber.");
```

However, this method is not available through the management interface of `MyClassMBean`. The following code will not compile:

```
MyClassMBean myClass = new MyClass();
myClass.setAttribute("I\'m a lumberjack and I\'m okay.");
```

It is the same with indirect MBean manipulation. Only the management interface of the MBean can be manipulated. The MBean server provides the following methods for indirectly manipulating MBeans:

```
public Object getAttribute(ObjectName name, String attribute)
    throws MBeanException, AttributeNotFoundException,
        InstanceNotFoundException, ReflectionException;

public AttributeList getAttributes(ObjectName name, String[] attributes)
    throws InstanceNotFoundException, ReflectionException;

public void setAttribute(ObjectName name, Attribute attribute)
    throws InstanceNotFoundException, AttributeNotFoundException,
        InvalidAttributeValueException, MBeanException, ReflectionException;

public AttributeList setAttributes(ObjectName name, AttributeList attributes)
    throws InstanceNotFoundException, ReflectionException;

public Object invoke(ObjectName name, String operationName,
                    Object params[], String signature[])
    throws InstanceNotFoundException, MBeanException, ReflectionException;

public MBeanInfo getMBeanInfo(ObjectName name)
    throws InstanceNotFoundException, IntrospectionException, ReflectionException;
```

If these methods look familiar, it is because they have the same names as (and perform the same functions as) the corresponding methods on the `DynamicMBean` interface. In fact, even the parameters are the same, with the exception that the first parameter to each method above is an `ObjectName` to identify the MBean with which to interact. See Chapter 3 if you are not familiar with what these methods do and for a thorough discussion of the `Attribute`, `AttributeList`, and `MBeanInfo` classes.

The only difference between the signatures of these methods and their `DynamicMBean` counterparts is the possible exceptions that can be thrown and, as mentioned earlier, the addition of a parameter allowing you to specify the MBean's object name. For example, the *getAttribute()* method of `MBeanServer` throws an additional exception called `InstanceNotFoundException` that the *getAttribute()* method of `DynamicMBean` does not, in the event that the specified object name is not registered in the MBean server.

Notification

Through the MBean server, you can register an interest in receiving notifications from any registered MBean that is a notification broadcaster. Notification broadcasters must implement the `NotificationBroadcaster` interface. Similarly, you can unregister interest in receiving these notifications through the MBean server.

There are four methods on the `MBeanServer` interface that deal with notifications. They are defined as:

```
public void addNotificationListener(ObjectName name, NotificationListener listener,
                                    NotificationFilter filter, Object handback)
    throws InstanceNotFoundException;

public void addNotificationListener(ObjectName name, ObjectName listener,
                                    NotificationFilter filter, Object handback)
    throws InstanceNotFoundException;

public void removeNotificationListener(ObjectName name,
                                       NotificationListener listener)
    throws InstanceNotFoundException, ListenerNotFoundException;

public void removeNotificationListener(ObjectName name, ObjectName listener)
    throws InstanceNotFoundException, ListenerNotFoundException;
```

To register interest in receiving a notification, use *addNotificationListener()*. To unregister interest in receiving a notification, use *removeNotificationListener()*. There are two versions of each of these methods. The difference between the respective versions is that you can specify either an `Object` reference to a notification listener (a class that implements the `NotificationListener` interface) or the object name of the notification listener (in which case the notification listener must also be a registered MBean). We will look more closely at notification broadcasters and listeners in the next chapter.

The *name* parameter is the `ObjectName` of the notification broadcaster. The *listener* parameter is either a reference to the notification listener or, if the notification listener is an MBean, the `ObjectName` of the notification listener. Note that if you use the version of *addNotificationListener()* or *removeNotificationListener()* that takes an `ObjectName` as the *listener* parameter, the specified notification listener MBean must be registered prior to invoking the method. If it isn't, the MBean server will throw an `InstanceNotFoundException` (in the case of *addNotificationListener()*) or a `Listener-NotFoundException` (in the case of *removeNotificationListener()*). The *filter* parameter allows you to specify a notification filter, which allows you to enable only certain notifications and send only those notifications to the listener (pass null if no filtering is desired). The *handback* parameter is a reference to an opaque object to be passed unchanged by the broadcaster to the listener when the broadcaster sends a notification. Because the object is opaque, it should never be modified by the broadcaster (pass null if no handback is required). Notification filters and handback objects are covered in detail in the next chapter, so we'll skip that discussion for now—it is not important that you understand the details of notification filters and handback objects right now in order to be able to use these methods of the MBean server. In all of the example code in this chapter, we will pass null for both of these parameters.

Suppose that we want to register interest in receiving notifications from the Queue class, which emits two notifications to alert to potential stall conditions (this is covered in some detail in Chapter 3). The first notification is to alert to the possibility that the queue is stalled because it has been full for longer than the threshold value (set programmatically) and nothing has been removed. This could occur, for example, if all of the consumer threads have crashed, because nothing would be removed from the queue. The second notification is to alert the opposite condition: the queue has been empty for longer than the threshold value and nothing has been added. This could occur, for example, if all of the supplier threads have crashed and no other WorkUnits have been added since the last time the queue was signaled as empty. Also, suppose that we want the Controller to receive the notifications emitted by the Queue. Here is the relevant code:

```
Controller controller = new Controller( );
MBeanServer mbeanServer = MBeanServerFactory.createMBeanServer( );
String defaultDomain = mbeanServer.getDefaultDomain( );
ObjectName queueObjName = new ObjectName(defaultDomain + ":name=Queue");
ObjectName controllerObjName = new ObjectName(defaultDomain + ":name=Controller");
try {
  mbeanServer.createMBean(queueObjName);
  mbeanServer.registerMBean(controllerObjName);
  mbeanServer.addNotificationListener(queueObjName, controller, null, null);
  // . . .
} catch (/*all the appropriate exceptions*/) {
  // . . .
}
```

We could also pass the ObjectName for the Controller instead of its Object reference, because the Controller is also an MBean. The highlighted line above would then be:

```
mbeanServer.addNotificationListener(queueObjName, controllerObjName, null, null);
```

Now any time a potential stall condition occurs in the Queue, a notification will be broadcast by Queue and sent to Controller. It is then up to Controller to handle the notification and take the appropriate action. We will discuss some strategies for implementing notification listeners in the next chapter. For now, be aware that you can use the MBean server to register interest in receiving notifications with a broadcaster for which you do not have an Object reference. This sort of indirect interaction is what makes the MBean server so powerful. When the distributed services level of the JMX architecture gets completely specified, expect this to play a significant role in enabling distributed notifications across the network.

Query

The MBean server allows you to send it queries that return a subset of the MBeans that reside in its registry. In this section, we will look at how to build and submit queries to the MBean server and what methods are provided to allow you to submit these queries. This section will probably be most useful to those developers who are writing connectors and protocol adaptors, although it does show how to programmatically ask an MBean server for a subset of its registered MBeans, based on parameters to the methods provided by the MBean server.

There are two methods for this purpose, defined as:

```
public Set queryMBeans(ObjectName name, QueryExp query);
public Set queryNames(ObjectName name, QueryExp query);
```

The parameters to these methods define two sets of criteria: the *name* parameter defines the *scope* of the query, which in turn defines the subset of registered MBeans to which the second parameter, *query*, will be applied. The ObjectName instance passed as *name* is a pattern that somewhat resembles a regular expression. However, only two regular-expression metacharacters are recognized:

- Asterisk (*), which matches zero or more characters
- Question mark (?), which matches a single character

These metacharacters are used in building the ObjectName that defines the subset of MBeans to which the *query* parameter is applied. The simplest example is to apply the *query* parameter to all registered MBeans. The ObjectName instance that is passed would be:

```
ObjectName name = new ObjectName("*:*");
```

In this example, we have created an ObjectName pattern that matches all registered MBeans. If we then pass null as the query parameter, the subset of MBeans returned is all of the MBeans registered within the MBean server:

```
MBeanServer mbeanServer = /*obtain through some means. . .*/
ObjectName scope = new ObjectName("*:*");
QueryExp query = null;
Set results = mbeanServer.queryMBeans(name, query);
// Now look through all registered MBeans. . .
```

We could narrow the scope of the query to only domains whose names begin with "My":

```
MBeanServer mbeanServer = /*obtain through some means. . .*/
ObjectName scope = new ObjectName("My*:*");
QueryExp query = null;
Set results = mbeanServer.queryMBeans(name, query);
```

or a single domain called "MyDomain":

```
MBeanServer mbeanServer = /*obtain through some means. . .*/
ObjectName scope = new ObjectName("MyDomain:*");
QueryExp query = null;
Set results = mbeanServer.queryMBeans(name, query);
```

Similarly, we can look at all domains and narrow the scope of the query to only those MBeans that have a key property called name that has a value of Queue:

```
MBeanServer mbeanServer = /*obtain through some means. . .*/
ObjectName scope = new ObjectName("*:name=Queue,*");
QueryExp query = null;
Set results = mbeanServer.queryMBeans(name, query);
// Now look through all registered MBeans. . .
```

 If no MBeans are found in the scope of the query, an empty Set object is returned. You can test to see if the Set is empty by calling the *isEmpty()* method, which will return true if there are no Object-Instance objects in the Set, or by calling *size()* to get a count of the number of ObjectInstance objects in the Set. If the number of MBean ObjectInstance objects is zero, no MBeans were found within the scope of the query.

Once you select the scope, you can apply a query to the selected set of MBeans. Only those MBeans in the scope of the query are considered when applying the query logic. For example, if the scope of the query is set to:

```
ObjectName scope = new ObjectName(":*");
```

only those MBeans registered within the default domain will be considered when the subsequent query is applied.

A query is constructed using static methods of the Query class to create instances of QueryExp instances, which represent one or more query expressions. This query is then applied to the entire scope of the query, which is specified by the ObjectName pattern we discussed earlier. For example, to query all MBeans within the designated scope for those MBeans whose numberOfResets attributes is zero, use:

```
QueryExp = Query.eq(
  Query.attr("numberOfResets"),  // attribute name
  Query.value(0)                 // attribute value
);
```

The resulting QueryExp instance is now ready to be passed to the *queryMBeans()* method:

```
MBeanServer mbeanServer = /*obtain through some means. . .*/
ObjectName scope = new ObjectName("*:*");
QueryExp = Query.eq(
  Query.attr("numberOfResets"),  // attribute name
  Query.value(0)                 // attribute value
);
Set results = mbeanServer.queryMBeans(name, query);
```

In this example, the scope of the query is all registered MBeans whose numberOfResets attributes have a value of zero.

The Query class provides methods that allow you to build SQL-like QueryExp instances for querying MBeans that are within the scope of the query. Chapter 7 of the JMX 1.0 specification provides an excellent discussion of how to use this facility of the MBean server.

The *queryMBeans()* query returns a Set object that contains a collection of ObjectInstance objects that represent the MBeans that satisfied the query. To view the contents of the Set object, create an Iterator and then look at the resulting ObjectInstance objects one at a time:

```
MBeanServer mbeanServer = /*obtain through some means. . .*/
ObjectName scope = new ObjectName("*:*");
QueryExp = Query.match(
  Query.attr("numberOfResets"),  // attribute name
  Query.value(0)                 // attribute value
);
Set results = mbeanServer.queryMBeans(name, query);
Iterator iter = results.iterator();
while (iter.hasNext()) {
  ObjectInstance obj = (ObjectInstance)iter.next();
  // etc. . . .
}
```

Once you have an MBean's ObjectInstance, you can call the *getObjectName()* method to return an ObjectName instance that corresponds to the object name of the MBean. A more direct alternative is provided by the MBean server, which allows you to perform the same queries but have the MBean server return a Set of ObjectName instances instead. The mechanics of the query are exactly the same:

```
MBeanServer mbeanServer = /*obtain through some means. . .*/
ObjectName scope = new ObjectName("*:*");
QueryExp = Query.match(
  Query.attr("numberOfResets"),  // attribute name
  Query.value(0)                 // attribute value
);
Set results = mbeanServer.queryNames(name, query);
Iterator iter = results.iterator();
while (iter.hasNext()) {
  ObjectName objName = (ObjectName)iter.next();
  // etc. . . .
}
```

This query will return a Set object that contains the object names of all the MBeans that matched the query. If you need to use the object name of an MBean found in the query to invoke a method or retrieve or set an attribute of the MBean, this is the method you will probably want to use, as it provides you with more direct access to the ObjectName instance corresponding to the MBean.

Utility

The MBeanServer interface provides eight methods that allow you to access information about the MBeans that are registered. Three of these methods help you to deserialize the state of an MBean from a byte array.

These helper methods are defined as follows:

```
public ObjectInstance getObjectInstance(ObjectName name)
    throws InstanceNotFoundException;

public boolean isRegistered(ObjectName name);

public Integer getMBeanCount( );

public String getDefaultDomain( );

public boolean isInstanceOf(ObjectName name, String className)
    throws InstanceNotFoundException;

public ObjectInputStream deserialize(ObjectName name, byte[] data)
    throws InstanceNotFoundException, OperationsException;

public ObjectInputStream deserialize(String className, byte[] data)
    throws OperationsException, ReflectionException;

public ObjectInputStream deserialize(String className, ObjectName loaderName,
                                     byte[] data)
    throws InstanceNotFoundException, OperationsException, ReflectionException;
```

These methods allow you to:

- Retrieve an ObjectInstance object that corresponds to an ObjectName, provided the MBean identified by the ObjectName has been registered.
- Determine whether or not a particular MBean is registered.
- Obtain the number of MBeans across all domains that have been registered.
- Obtain a String containing the name of the default domain.
- Determine whether or not a particular MBean is an instance of a particular class.
- Create and return an ObjectInputStream object from which primitive types and objects can be read. This method has three versions that provide a number of ways to specify the ClassLoader to be used.

Let's look at each of these methods. First, there is *getObjectInstance()*, which takes the ObjectName of an MBean and returns the corresponding ObjectInstance for that MBean:

```
MBeanServer mbeanServer = /* obtain through some means . . . */
ObjectName objName = new ObjectName(mbeanServer.getDefaultDomain( ) +
                     ":name=Queue");
try {
  ObjectInstance objInst = mbeanServer.getObjectInstance(objName);
} catch (InstanceNotFoundException e) {
  // . . .
}
```

If the object name is not found (i.e., the MBean is not registered), an InstanceNotFoundException is thrown. In the example above, we are asking the MBean server for the ObjectInstance of the Queue MBean. This method can be useful if, for example, you need to obtain the class name of the MBean registered under the object name you provide to this method.

If you simply need to know whether a particular MBean has been registered, use the *isRegistered()* method, which takes an ObjectName that identifies the MBean. *isRegistered()* returns true if the MBean is registered and false if it is not:

```
MBeanServer mbeanServer = /* obtain through some means . . . */
ObjectName objName = new ObjectName(mbeanServer.getDefaultDomain( ) + ":name=Queue");
boolean yesOrNo = mbeanServer.isRegistered(objName);
String isOrNot = (yesOrNo) ? " is" : " is not ";
System.out.println("The MBean " + objName + isOrNot + "registered.");
```

The *getMBeanCount()* method tells you the total number of MBeans that have been registered across all domains. In other words, if two MBeans have been registered on the default domain and three MBeans have been registered under a different domain, this method will return the number 5.

```
MBeanServer mbeanServer = /* obtain through some means . . . */
Integer numberOfMBeans = mbeanServer.getMBeanCount( );
System.out.println("There are " + numberOfMBeans + " registered MBeans.");
```

We have already used the *getDefaultDomain()* method in previous examples to get a String that contains the name of the default domain. Recall from earlier in this chapter that we can set the name of the default domain to whatever we want when we create the MBean server (see Figure 6-2).

```
MBeanServer mbeanServer = MBeanServerFactory.createMBeanServer( );
String defaultDomain = mbeanServer.getDefaultDomain( );
System.out.println("The default domain is \'" + defaultDomain + "\'.");
```

The *isInstanceOf()* method allows us to determine whether an MBean is an instance of a particular class with a single method call:

```
MBeanServer mbeanServer = /* obtain through some means. . . */
String className = "sample.mbeanserver.Queue";
ObjectName objName = new ObjectName(mbeanServer.getDefaultDomain( ) + ":name=Queue");
boolean yesOrNo = mbeanServer.isInstanceOf(objName, className);
String isOrNot = (yesOrNo) ? " is " : " is not ";
System.out.println("MBean " + objName + isOrNot + "an instance of " + "class " +
                    className + ".");
```

Finally, the MBean server provides three versions of the *deserialize()* method that help deserialize objects in a byte array by setting up and returning ObjectInputStream. The ObjectInputStream object returned from *deserialize()* is then used to read primitive types and objects by calling the appropriate methods of ObjectInputStream or one of its parent classes. This class is somewhat misleadingly named—the input stream is not actually deserialized; rather, an ObjectInputStream object is returned to the caller, who is then responsible for processing the input stream through the available methods of ObjectInputStream.

Each version of *deserialize()* provides you with a different way to specify the ClassLoader that ObjectInputStream will use to locate and fetch the Java bytecode—i.e., *.class* files—and create the corresponding Class objects for the objects in the input stream when ObjectInputStream's *readObject()* method is called. These methods are provided to developers of protocol adaptors and connectors to aid, for example, in deserializing objects whose bytecode files do not reside on the same physical machine as the MBean server.

The first version of *deserialize()* allows you to use a registered MBean as the ClassLoader for classes read from the input stream when *readObject()* is called:

```
public ObjectInputStream deserialize(ObjectName name, byte[] data)
    throws InstanceNotFoundException, OperationsException;
```

The MBean specified by the *name* parameter must also extend the abstract class ClassLoader and override any methods that provide different functionality than that provided by ClassLoader. This method will search the MBean server's MBean registry for the MBean specified by *name*. If the MBean does not exist in the registry, an InstanceNotFoundException is thrown. If the *data* parameter is null or is zero bytes in length, an OperationsException is thrown.

If all goes well, an ObjectInputStream object is created using the byte array specified by *data* and returned to the caller. The caller is responsible for retrieving objects (or primitive types) from the ObjectInputStream by calling the appropriate methods of ObjectInputStream. Each time an object is read from the stream via a call to *readObject()* on the returned ObjectInputStream object, the MBean class loader specified by *name* is used to create the corresponding Class object of the object in the stream.

Through JMX instrumentation, the MBean class loader can expose a management interface that allows a management application to keep track of information such as the number of classes loaded, the number of input streams processed, and the number of serialization errors.

The second version of *deserialize()* allows you to specify the class whose class loader is to be used when loading classes for objects in the input stream:

```
public ObjectInputStream deserialize(String className, byte[] data)
    throws OperationsException, ReflectionException;
```

The *className* parameter must be a fully qualified string representation of the class whose class loader is to be used by the ObjectInputStream object. If this parameter is null, an OperationsException is thrown. Each time *readObject()* is called on the returned ObjectInputStream object, this class loader is used to load the class in the stream. If the *data* parameter is null or is zero bytes in length, an OperationsException is thrown.

If the class specified by *className* cannot be located, the MBean server will attempt to use one of the loaders in the default repository of class loaders, which is found in the com.sun.management.jmx package in the DefaultLoaderRepository class. If no suitable loader can be found, a ReflectionException is thrown.

If all goes well, an ObjectInputStream object is created, using the byte array specified by *data*, and returned to the caller. The caller is then responsible for retrieving objects (or primitive types) from the ObjectInputStream by calling the appropriate methods of ObjectInputStream. Each time an object is read from the stream via a call to *readObject()* on the returned ObjectInputStream object, the class loader of the class specified by *className* is used to retrieve the bytecode for, and create an instance of, the class of the object in the stream.

If you need to provide a class loader that must be manageable, you should instrument that class loader as an MBean and use the first version of *deserialize()*.

The third version of *deserialize()* allows you to use a registered MBean to load the specified class, whose class loader is then to be used to load classes from the input stream:

```
public ObjectInputStream deserialize(String className, ObjectName loaderName,
                                     byte[] data)
    throws InstanceNotFoundException, OperationsException, ReflectionException;
```

This version of *deserialize()* functions similarly to the second version, in that the *className* parameter is the fully qualified string representation of a class whose class loader is to be used to load classes for the objects in the input stream. However, the class specified by *className* is loaded by an MBean, which is specified by the *loaderName* parameter.

This method is provided as a convenience to developers who must provide their own class loader, when it is not necessary to manage the class loader itself. However, there may be times when it is necessary to manage the class loader that loads *className*, even though the MBean specified by *loaderName* is not the class loader that ultimately loads the class of the object in the input stream.

Controlling MBean Registration

There are times when it is necessary to perform certain activities before and after an MBean is registered and deregistered. Implementing the MBeanRegistration interface provides an MBean with four opportunities (i.e., callbacks) to perform additional processing. The MBeanRegistration interface is defined as:

```
public interface MBeanRegistration {

    public ObjectName preRegister(MBeanServer server, ObjectName name)
        throws java.lang.Exception;

    public void postRegister(Boolean registrationDone);

    public void preDeregister()
        throws java.lang.Exception;

    public void postDeregister();
}
```

Another advantage of implementing this interface is that the MBean itself can generate its own object name in *preRegister()*, which is invoked prior to registering the MBean. The first opportunity an MBean has to perform any additional processing is in *preRegister()*, which takes two parameters. The first parameter, *server*, is a reference to the MBean server in which the MBean will be registered, allowing an MBean to maintain a reference to its MBean server. The second parameter, *name*, is the object name of the MBean. The specification does not mention anything about the behavior of this method, other than that it is invoked prior to an MBean being registered. However, looking through the RI, it is clear that the designers of JMX intended that if the *name* parameter is null, the MBean will generate its own object name. Otherwise, *name* is returned unchanged.

Once the MBean has been registered, *postRegister()* is invoked with a boolean parameter, *registrationDone*, that indicates whether the registration was successful. If a problem occurred during registration, *registrationDone* will be false. Note that if an exception is thrown during the *preRegister()* callback, this method is never invoked.

If the agent that registered the MBean explicitly calls *unregister()* to deregister the MBean, the *preDeregister()* callback is invoked just prior to the MBean's deregistration. This gives the MBean the opportunity to perform any necessary cleanup, such as releasing the reference to its MBean server. This callback method can *very* loosely be thought of as a destructor in C++, with the important difference that there is no guarantee that the MBean object is going away; it simply is not going to be manageable upon its deregistration.

Finally, following successful deregistration of the MBean, *postDeregister()* is called. If the *preDeregister()* callback threw an exception, this callback method is not invoked.

An implementation of this method on an MBean may look like this:

```
// . . .
  private MBeanServer _mbeanServer;
// . . .
  public ObjectName preRegister(MBeanServer server, ObjectName name)
    throws java.lang.Exception {
    _mbeanServer = server;
    if (name == null) {
      name = new ObjectName(server.getDefaultDomain( ) + ":" +
                            "name=Queue,objNameType=self");
    }
    return name;
  }

  public void postRegister(Boolean registrationDone) {
    if (!registrationDone)
      _mbeanServer = null;
  }
```

```
    public void preDeregister( ) throws java.lang.Exception {
      _mbeanServer = null;
    }

    public void postDeregister( ) {
      // do nothing. . .
    }
// . . .
```

In this example, *preRegister()* returns the object name passed to it (indicating that the agent registering the MBean has already generated an object name for the MBean) or, if it is passed null, creates an object name—I've made up a property called objNameType and set it to a value of self, indicating to a management application, or perhaps another JMX agent, that the MBean generated its own object name. The *postRegister()* callback method releases its reference to the MBean server if the registration fails. *preDeregister()* unconditionally releases its MBean server reference, and *postDeregister()* does nothing at all.

MBeanServerDelegate

The MBean server does not directly expose a management interface, leaving manipulation of the MBeans contained in its registry to those developers who write agents, connectors, and protocol adaptors. However, information about the MBean server and some notifications can be made available to a management application through its delegate, MBeanServerDelegate. This class implements the MBeanServerDelegateMBean interface, so it is an MBean and thus is manageable. It is through this management interface that management applications can discover information about the MBean server. The string representation of the object name of the delegate MBean is "JMImplementation:type=MBeanServerDelegate".

In addition, the MBean server emits two notifications through the MBeanServerDelegate. In this section, we will look at the information about the MBean server that is exposed through the MBeanServerDelegate, as well as the notifications emitted by it on behalf of the MBean server.

MBean Server Information

The MBean server provides the following read-only String attributes through its delegate MBean:

MBeanServerId
    The unique identifier of this MBean server within the JVM. The format of this String is not dictated by the specification and is left to the implementer.

SpecificationName
    The name of the specification on which this MBean server implementation is based—must be "Java Management Extensions".

SpecificationVersion

> The version of the JMX specification on which this MBean server implementation is based—for the current release of the specification, must be "1.0 Final Release".

SpecificationVendor

> The name of the vendor of the specification on which this MBean server is based—must be "Sun Microsystems".

ImplementationName

> The implementation name of the MBean server. The vendor who implements the MBean server is free to choose the format of this attribute.

ImplementationVersion

> The version of the implementation of the MBean server. The vendor who implements the MBean server controls the value of this attribute.

The following example shows how to use the MBean server to obtain the values of these attributes programmatically:

```
MBeanServer mbeanServer = MBeanServerFactory.createMBeanServer();
ObjectName delegateObjName =
  new ObjectName("JMImplementation:type=MBeanServerDelegate");
try {
  String serverId = mbeanServer.getAttribute(delegateObjName, "MBeanServerId");
  String specName = mbeanServer.getAttribute(delegateObjName, "SpecificationName");
  String specVer = mbeanServer.getAttribute(delegateObjName, "SpecificationVersion");
  // etc. . . .
} catch (Exception e) {
  // handle. . .
}
```

MBean Server Notifications

Two notifications are emitted by the MBean server through its delegate:

jmx.mbean.created

> This notification is emitted when an MBean is registered. The object name of the MBean whose registration triggered the notification is included in the Notification object sent to the notification listener.

jmx.mbean.deleted

> This notification is emitted when an MBean is unregistered. The object name of the MBean whose deregistration triggered the notification is included in the Notification object sent to the notification listener.

> In the JMX 1.0 RI, these notifications are actually implemented as JMX.mbean.registered and JMX.mbean.unregistered, for registration and deregistration, respectively. This is in conflict with the specification and will probably be corrected in a future release of the JMX RI.

To register interest in receiving these notifications, a notification listener must be added to the list of listeners. The following example shows how to do this:

```
MBeanServer mbeanServer = MBeanServer.createMBeanServer( );
ObjectName delegateObjName =
  new ObjectName("JMImplementation:type=MBeanServerDelegate");
NotificationListener listener = /* obtain somehow */
mbeanServer.addNotificationListener(delegateObjName, listener, null, null);
```

When registration and deregistration notifications are emitted by the delegate, the listener will receive them. In the next chapter, we will cover the JMX notification model and how to write both notification listeners and broadcasters.

CHAPTER 7

JMX Notifications

The JMX specification provides a very rich, generic notification mechanism. In this chapter, we will look at the JMX notification model, which serves as the foundation for notifications. Then we will look at what a notification is and examples of different notification types. We will then take a detailed look at the different classes and interfaces that JMX provides to underpin the JMX notification model, including:

Notification

> This class represents the contents of a single notification and is sent by the broadcaster to the listener (or receiver) of the notification.

NotificationFilter

> This interface, when implemented, gives the notification listener a way to tell the JMX notification infrastructure that it is interested in only a subset of the potential notifications sent by the broadcaster. The JMX RI provides a class called NotificationFilterSupport that can be used as an off-the-shelf notification filter.

NotificationBroadcaster

> This interface must be implemented by all notification broadcasters. In addition, the RI provides an implementation of this interface called Notification-BroadcasterSupport that can be used as an off-the-shelf notification broadcaster.

NotificationListener

> This interface must be implemented by all receivers of JMX notifications.

The JMX Notification Model

A notification in the context of JMX is a unit of information sent by a broadcaster through the JMX infrastructure to a listener, which interprets and processes the notification. A notification contains, at a minimum, the notification type (a unique string that identifies the notification), an Object reference to the notification broadcaster, and a sequence number (an integer value that uniquely identifies a particular occurrence of a specific notification type). Other optional information that can be sent in a notification includes a time stamp, a human-readable text message, and a reference to an object that permits additional processing of the notification to occur. Of course, the type (and meaning) of this object must be agreed upon by the listener and the implementation of the broadcaster.

A notification broadcaster implements a special JMX interface called Notification-Broadcaster that allows any number of notification listeners to register an interest in receiving any or all of the notifications emitted by the broadcaster. Messages are sent to the listener through the JMX infrastructure using a callback mechanism. A notification listener implements a JMX interface called NotificationListener that allows the JMX infrastructure to deliver a notification on a callback method of the NotificationListener interface. The listener may, at its discretion, choose to receive only a subset of the possible notifications emitted by the broadcaster by providing a notification filter. A notification filter must implement a JMX interface called NotificationFilter.

JMX notification filtering is performed before of notifications are broadcast, so it is the broadcaster's responsibility to determine (by using the filter) whether a notification is to be sent to a listener. When the broadcaster is about to emit a particular type of notification to a listener, it checks the filter to see whether the notification is one the listener wants to receive. If the filter tells the broadcaster that the listener is interested in that notification, the broadcaster sends the notification to the listener. Otherwise, the broadcaster does not send the notification, saving the listener the trouble of receiving and ignoring notifications in which it is not interested. If no filter is present, the broadcaster sends all notifications to the listener.

In addition to a notification filter, a listener may optionally pass a reference to an object called a *handback*, an object that will be handed back to the listener when notifications are sent to that listener. This object is opaque (i.e., its contents are unknown) to the broadcaster, which simply stores the object away until a notification is broadcast to the listener, at which time the object is passed unchanged to the listener. The JMX specification does not constrain what this object must be, only implying that it is used to provide contextual information that the listener creates upon registering its interest in receiving a notification, then exploits upon receiving the notification. Notification listener developers can thus implement the handback object as their needs dictate. We will look at some examples of handback objects later in this chapter.

The relationships between the various components of the JMX notification model are shown in Figure 7-1.

When a listener wants to receive notifications, it invokes a method called *addNotificationListener()* on the broadcaster, passing it a reference to itself, a reference to the filter it wants to use, and a handback object reference (both the filter and handback references may be null). The same listener can register its interest in receiving MBean notifications from a particular broadcaster more than once, passing a different handback object to *addNotificationListener()* each time. The notification

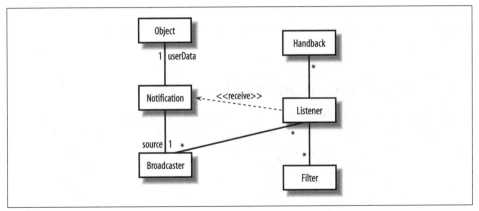

Figure 7-1. *UML diagram showing the relationships between the various components of the JMX notification model*

broadcaster keeps a table of listener/filter/handback object triplets to ensure that it passes the correct handback object upon broadcasting each notification to the listener. The listener may also pass a different filter for each handback object, allowing even more flexibility in providing contextual information when processing notifications. As Figure 7-1 also shows, each `Notification` object may only be associated with one broadcaster (the `source`) and one user-defined object (`userData`).

The key to processing notifications lies in the notification type. As we discussed in Chapter 3, a notification type is a string that may be of the form:

```
vendor[.application][.component][.eventGroup].event
```

where *vendor* is the name of your company, *application* is the name of the application (optional), *component* is the name of the component (usually the name of the MBean, also optional), *eventGroup* is the name of the group to which the event belongs (optional), and *event* is the name of the event notification. For example, the notification `"acme.OrderEntry.billing.responseTime.slow"` is defined by the company acme for the Order Entry system's billing component for a group of events related to response time to indicate that response time is slow. How this notification is handled is up to the listener. Notice, however, that only *vendor* and *event* are required, so we could have simply defined the event as `"acme.responseTimeSlow"`.

 While the above pattern is recommended by the JMX specification, this convention for defining notifications is not enforced in the RI. However, it is a good idea to follow this convention to ensure as much consistency as possible between applications from various vendors.

Why is the notification type so important? The notification type serves as the "handle" for the notification and is used in processing it. In addition, the listener is capable of processing several different notification types, and it uses the notification type as a first step in cracking into a notification to process it further.

Now that we've been introduced to the players and their respective roles in the JMX notification model, let's take a closer look at the classes provided by the JMX RI that make it all happen.

JMX Notification Classes and Interfaces

In this section, we will look at the classes that compliant implementations of JMX must supply. We will also look at examples of how to use each of these classes to create, filter, broadcast, and receive JMX notifications.

Notification

This class contains the information conveyed by a JMX notification and has the following fields:

- A notification type—a string that uniquely identifies the type of the notification
- A reference to the ObjectName of the source of the notification
- A sequence number—an integer that conveys information between the broadcaster and the listener regarding the occurrence of a notification
- A time stamp (optional) produced by the broadcaster to convey the date and time at which the notification was created
- A message (optional)—a string containing text that provides additional explanation about the notification
- User-defined data (optional)—an Object reference to an object that is used to convey richer information between broadcaster and listener than is possible through any of the other fields

Instances of this class are normally created by the notification broadcaster, which uses the following four constructors to do so:

```
public Notification(String type, Object source, long sequenceNumber) {
  // . . .
}

public Notification(String type, Object source, long sequenceNumber,
                    String message) {
  // . . .
}

public Notification(String type, Object source, long sequenceNumber,
                    long timeStamp) {
  // . . .
}

public Notification(String type, Object source, long sequenceNumber,
                    long timeStamp, String message) {
  // . . .
}
```

The parameters *type*, *source*, and *sequenceNumber* are the same across all of the constructors. The following code example shows how to use the first constructor of Notification:

```
String type = "sample.Queue.stalled.queueFull";
Object source = this;
long seq = _seq++; // increment member variable
Notification notif = new Notification(type, source, seq);
```

In this example, the sequence number is kept in a member variable. This is a reasonable approach and is common throughout the RI. We can also provide a message that gives additional information about the notification:

```
String type = "sample.Queue.stalled.queueFull";
Object source = this;
long seq = _seq++; // increment member variable
String message = "Queue is potentially stalled while full."
Notification notif = new Notification(type, source, seq, message);
```

or a time stamp, using the system clock:

```
String type = "sample.Queue.stalled.queueFull";
Object source = this;
long seq = _seq++; // increment member variable
long timeStamp = System.currentTimeMillis();
Notification notif = new Notification(type, source, seq, timeStamp);
```

Finally, we can provide all of the above information:

```
String type = "sample.Queue.stalled.queueFull";
Object source = this;
long seq = _seq++; // increment member variable
String message = "Queue is potentially stalled while full."
long timeStamp = System.currentTimeMillis();
Notification notif = new Notification(type, source, seq, timeStamp, message);
```

The Notification class also provides getters and setters for these fields. In fact, for each of the fields (with the exception of *type*) that we've already looked at, both a getter and a setter are provided. The only way to set the notification type is through the constructor, when the Notification object is created. The setters are probably provided for symmetry, as there is really no good reason for, say, a listener to modify the contents of a notification after receiving it. Note that *type* is read-only, which is a good indication that once the Notification object is created, the notification type it represents may not be altered. Once a listener receives a notification, it uses these getters to crack into the notification:

```
public void handleNotification(Notification notification, Object handback) {
    String type = notification.getType();
    Object source = notification.getSource();
    long seq = notification.getSequenceNumber();
    String message = notification.getMessage();
    Object userData = notification.getUserData();
    // Now handle the notification. . .
}
```

We will look at more examples of a listener handling a notification later in this chapter. For now, just keep in mind that it is through the getters provided by Notification that a listener accesses the contents of a notification.

You may have noticed that no constructor is provided to set the user-defined data. However, a setter is provided that allows this object to be set once an instance has been created. In the example above, we got a reference to the user-defined data object through its getter. However, this reference will be null if the broadcaster didn't use the *setUserData()* method to set this object when creating the notification. What is this user-defined object? The answer is, "it depends." Depending on what additional information must be shared between the broadcaster and the listener, this object can be any object! For example, suppose the broadcaster supplies a time stamp in the form of a Date object (an expensive way to do this) instead of explicitly setting the *timeStamp* field:

```
String type = "sample.Queue.stalled.queueFull";
Object source = this;
long seq = _seq++; // increment member variable
Notification notif = new Notification(type, source, seq);
Object timeStamp = new Date( );
notif.setUserData(timeStamp);
```

The listener must be aware of this, or a ClassCastException will be thrown when the listener tries to access the object:

```
public void handleNotification(Notification notification, Object handback) {
    String type = notification.getType( );
    Object source = notification.getSource( );
    long seq = notification.getSequenceNumber( );
    String message = notification.getMessage( );
    Date userData = (Date)notification.getUserData( );
    // Now handle the notification. . .
}
```

NotificationFilter

This is a very simple interface that must be implemented by any class that wants to be a JMX notification filter. The listener provides a notification filter to filter out notifications, such that the broadcaster sends the listener only those notifications the listener has expressed interest in receiving (through the filter). The Notification-Filter interface looks like this:

```
public interface NotificationFilter extends java.io.Serializable {
    public boolean isNotificationEnabled(Notification notification);
}
```

The interface is simple, but when a class implements this interface, there are two things it must do:

1. Store a list of notification types that are enabled by the listener (i.e., those in which the listener is interested).

2. Implement the *isNotificationEnabled()* method to allow a notification broadcaster to determine whether or not to send the notification to the listener associated with the filter.

There are several algorithms that you can use when implementing this interface. Fortunately, the RI has provided an off-the-shelf implementation of `NotificationFilter` called `NotificationFilterSupport`. In this class, the listener calls the `Notification-FilterSupport` method *enableType()*, passing a `String` argument that is the notification type in which the listener is interested. The listener repeats the call to *enableType()* for each notification type it wants to receive. Each time the *enableType()* method is called, the `NotificationFilterSupport` object adds the notification type to the collection of types in which the listener is interested.

The notification listener usually creates the `NotificationFilter` object that is used to filter its notifications. The following example shows how the listener may do this:

```
NotificationFilterSupport filter = new NotificationFilterSupport();
filter.enableType("sample.Queue.stalled.QueueFull");
filter.enableType("sample.Queue.stalled.QueueEmpty");
```

The notification listener would then use the `NotificationFilter` object as a parameter to the *addNotificationListener()* method. In this example, the only notifications that the listener would receive are the two that are listed. Regardless of which other types of notifications it can emit, the notification broadcaster with which the listener registered its interest will send only these two notifications to the listener. Because of the processing the broadcaster applies using the notification filter, the source code for the listener has to deal with only those notifications that pass the filter.

 The specification is silent with regard to how the notification filter keeps track of the notification types it allows, so you are free to implement this interface as you choose (as long as you keep track of every notification in which the listener is interested).

When *isNotificationEnabled()* is invoked, the broadcaster expects to find out whether or not the specified notification type is one in which the listener is interested. If it is, this method will return `true`, which tells the broadcaster to emit the notification.

The Handback Object

The handback object is created by the notification listener and passed to the broadcaster through the *addNotificationListener()* method. As mentioned earlier, this object provides the listener with contextual information that it can exploit when processing certain notification types. This allows the listener to process the same notification type (or group of notification types) in different ways. Just to reiterate, the notification listener can pass null if no handback object is required. The handback object is used by the notification listener to specialize its processing, but because it is an Object reference, the implementation is entirely up to the listener, as was presumably the intent of the designers of the JMX specification. So what does the handback object look like?

Suppose that the listener wants to handle a particular notification by sending an email. It might make sense, then, to use a Properties object to contain the specifics of the email—such as the recipient, the subject, and the message—so that the listener's *handleNotification()* method can remain generic. In this case, the listener would create the Properties object, set the appropriate properties, and then invoke the *addNotificationListener()* method on the broadcaster, passing the handback object as a parameter:

```
Properties props = new Properties();
props.setProperty("response", "email");
props.setProperty("smtpHost", "mail.mycompany.com");
props.setProperty("recipient", "me@mycompany.com");
props.setProperty("subject", "Queue stalled notification");
props.setProperty("message", "The queue is stalled. ");
// etc. . . .
NotificationBroadcaster broadcaster = /* obtain somehow */
broadcaster.addNotificationListener(this, null, props);
```

We don't use any filtering in this example, so the listener will receive all notifications emitted by the broadcaster. When its *handleNotification()* method is invoked, the listener can take the Properties object and then continue its processing:

```
public void handleNotification(Notification notification, Object handback) {
  // . . .
  try {
    Properties props = (Properties)handback;
    String response = (String)props.get("response");
    if (response.equals("email")) {
      // send an email, using the properties set in the handback object. . .
    } else if (response.equals("consoleMessage")) {
    } else {
      System.out.println("handleNotification: ERROR: " +
        "Unexpected response type \'" + response + "\'.");
    }
  } catch (Exception e) {
    // handle possible exceptions. . .
  }
}
```

This *handleNotification()* method is quite generic. Notice that it doesn't rely on any information to figure out how to process the notification other than the handback object it created earlier. The details of sending an email were omitted from this example for the sake of brevity. However, the sample code for this chapter includes an implementation that uses the JavaMail API for this purpose.

The significant advantage of using a handback object to provide a context for handling a notification is that the information contained in the handback object can come from practically anywhere. For example, the `Properties` handback object in the previous example was created by the listener itself, but it could have come from a configuration facility, which would allow the properties inside it to be changed outside of the application. This has significant advantages, in that the way notifications are handled can be altered without changing the source code. Another example of a handback object is an XML document that originates from a database (or from a configuration facility); the handler could parse this document to figure out how to handle the notification.

As you can see, using a handback object to provide a context for handling notifications significantly opens up your application to dynamic configuration and allows you to have as simple or complex a scheme for handling notifications as your application needs dictate.

NotificationBroadcaster

As we have already discussed, a notification broadcaster is a class that implements the `NotificationBroadcaster` interface. It is the job of a notification broadcaster to:

- Add notification listeners to an internal table of listener/filter/handback object triplets.
- Perform up-front filter processing prior to sending notifications.
- Create `Notification` objects and send these notifications to the appropriate listeners (based on the contents of the triplet table).
- Remove listeners from its internal table of listener/filter/handback object triplets as necessary.

The `NotificationBroadcaster` interface is defined as:

```
public interface NotificationBroadcaster {

    public void addNotificationListener(NotificationListener listener,
                                        NotificationFilter filter,
                                        Object handback)
        throws java.lang.IllegalArgumentException;

    public void removeNotificationListener(NotificationListener listener)
        throws ListenerNotFoundException;

    public MBeanNotificationInfo[] getNotificationInfo();

}
```

In this section, we will look at each of the methods of this interface in detail, including examples of how those methods might be implemented. Where appropriate, we will discuss how these methods are implemented by the JMX RI and how to avoid some of the pitfalls you may encounter when using the RI.

Before a notification broadcaster can send a notification to a listener, the listener must express an interest in receiving one or more of the possible notifications the broadcaster can emit. The listener does this by calling the broadcaster's *addNotificationListener()* method. As you can see from the above example, this method takes a reference to the listener, a reference to a notification filter, and a reference to a handback object. As we've mentioned, the filter and handback references may be passed as null if the listener is not interested in filtering or in receiving additional context information, respectively.

The JMX specification is clear that the notification broadcaster must maintain a table of listener/filter/handback triplets, so that the same listener can register itself with multiple handback objects. A simple implementation of this method is shown in Example 7-1.

Example 7-1. A simple implementation of addNotificationListener()

```
public class GenericBroadcaster implements NotificationBroadcaster {
// . . .
  private ArrayList _listeners = new ArrayList();
  private Hashtable _notifications = new Hashtable();
// . . .
  public void addNotificationListener(NotificationListener listener,
                                      NotificationFilter filter,
                                      Object handback) {
    _listeners.add(new ListenerFilterHandbackTriplet(listener,
                                                      filter,
                                                      handback))
  }
  private class ListenerFilterHandbackTriplet {
// . . .
    private NotificationListener _listener;
    private NotificationFilter _filter;
    private Object _handback;
// . . .
    ListenerFilterHandbackTriplet(NotificationListener listener,
                                  NotificationFilter filter,
                                  Object handback) {
      _listener = listener;
      _filter = filter;
      _handback = handback;
    }
  }
} // simple implementation of addNotification()
```

Example 7-1 is a very simple yet completely compliant implementation of this method. A private class called ListenerFilterHandbackTriplet is used to represent the triplets that are registered with the broadcaster. Each time the *addNotificationListener()* method is invoked, a new instance of this class is created and added to the private ArrayList called _listeners.

The JMX specification provides a method called *removeNotificationListener()* for removing listener/filter/handback triplets from the notification broadcaster's table. According to the specification, this method should have two types of behavior: if a handback object is supplied, only the triplet that corresponds to the listener/handback combination is removed; if no handback object is supplied, all listener/handback combinations are removed, effectively removing the listener from the broadcaster's internal table altogether. The *removeNotificationListener()* method looks like this:

```
public class GenericBroadcaster implements NotificationBroadcaster {
// . . .
  public void removeNotificationListener(NotificationListener listener) {
    removeNotificationListener(listener, null);
  }
// . . .
}
```

Looking at the signature of the *removeNotificationListener()* method that was delivered with the JMX specification, you may be asking yourself how to pass in the handback object. This was apparently an oversight on the part of the JMX expert group (and the Java community during the review process), and it will most likely be fixed in an upcoming release (either they'll make the specification match the RI, or, hopefully, vice versa). The bottom line is that there is currently an asymmetry between *addNotificationListener()* and *removeNotificationListener()*: the former allows you to add the same listener with multiple handback objects, while the latter will only allow you to remove them all. While throughout this book I have stuck with the RI's implementation, in this section I will deviate and implement the *removeNotificationListener()* method as the specification dictates, for the sake of completeness. The above implementation of *removeNotificationListener()* simply delegates to an overloaded version of this method that I added to make the code function according to the specification.

```
public class GenericBroadcaster implements NotificationBroadcaster {
// . . .
  public void removeNotificationListener(NotificationListener listener,
                                Object handback) {
    if (listener != null) {
      Iterator iter = _listeners.iterator();
      while (iter.hasNext()) {
        ListenerFilterHandbackTriplet triplet =
        (ListenerFilterHandbackTriplet)iter.next();
        if (listener == triplet.getListener() &&
        (handback == null || handback == triplet.getHandback())) {
          iter.remove();
        }
      }
    }
  }
// . . .
}
```

If the handback is passed in as null, all triplets are removed. Otherwise, only the triplets that contain the specified handback object are removed.

The final method on the NotificationBroadcaster interface is *getNotificationInfo()*, which returns an array of MBeanNotificationInfo objects. Recall from Chapter 3 that MBeanNotificationInfo is the metadata class used to describe the various notifications that can be emitted by an MBean.

 In the JMX 1.0 RI, this method, as it is implemented in Notification-BroadcasterSupport, returns an empty array of MBeanNotificationInfo objects. It's really up to the notification broadcaster implementer to implement this functionality, and we'll look at some ways to do that in this section.

The *getNotificationInfo()* method looks like this:

```
public class GenericBroadcaster implements NotificationBroadcaster {
// . . .
  private Hashtable _notifications = new Hashtable( );
// . . .
  public MBeanNotificationInfo[] getNotificationInfo( ) {
    MBeanNotificationInfo[] notifications = new MBeanNotificationInfo[1];
    String[] notificationTypes = new String[_notifications.size( )];
    Iterator iter = _notifications.keySet().iterator( );
    int aa = 0;
    while (iter.hasNext( )) {
      notificationTypes[aa] = (String)iter.next( );
      aa++;
    }
    notifications[0] = new MBeanNotificationInfo(
      notificationTypes, "NotificationTypes",
      "Types of notifications emitted by this broadcaster."
    );
    return notifications;
  }
// . . .
}
```

The notification types that are emitted by this broadcaster are stored in the Hashtable that is a member variable of the GenericBroadcaster class called _notifications. The hash table key is the notification type, a String. The object stored along with the key is an Integer object that contains the number of times the notification has been emitted. That way, if we want to make this class a managed resource, we can put an operation on the management interface that allows a management application to monitor how many times each notification type has been broadcast. However, a clean implementation of this method is no small task, because the broadcaster may not actually know up front what notifications it may send. The only way for a broadcaster to know for sure what notification types it emits is after the fact—we will look at how to exploit this knowledge later in this chapter.

We've seen one possible implementation of the NotificationBroadcaster interface, but how does a broadcaster actually send a notification? The mechanism to do this is dependent upon how the broadcaster implements this interface. In the Notification-BroadcasterSupport class of the RI, a method called *sendNotification()* is used to perform this function. I like this approach, because it gives broadcasters that extend the NotificationBroadcasterSupport class of the RI a built-in means of sending the notifications. However, the focus of this section is really on how to implement the NotificationBroadcaster interface ourselves. So how will our broadcaster actually send the notifications that it broadcasts? For the sake of consistency with the RI, let's stick with the *sendNotification()* idiom.

Recall that a broadcaster must send all notifications to all interested listeners, passing the appropriate handback objects (and filtering out unwanted notifications as necessary). Using the simple implementation from Example 7-1, *sendNotification()* looks like this:

```
public class GenericBroadcaster implements NotificationBroadcaster {
// . . .
  private Hashtable _notifications = new Hashtable();
// . . .
  public void sendNotification(Notification notification) {
    if (notification != null) {
      String notifType = notification.getType();
      if (_notifications.containsKey(notifType)) {
        Integer count = (Integer)_notifications.get(notifType);
        _notifications.put(notifType, new Integer(count.intValue()+1));
      }
      else {
        _notifications.put(notifType, new Integer(1));
      }
      // Now send the notification to all interested listeners
      for (int aa = 0; aa < _listeners.size(); aa++) {
        ListenerFilterHandbackTriplet triplet =
          (ListenerFilterHandbackTriplet)_listeners.get(aa);
        NotificationListener listener = triplet.getListener();
        NotificationFilter filter = triplet.getFilter();
        Object handback = triplet.getHandback();
        if (filter == null || filter.isNotificationEnabled(notification)) {
          listener.handleNotification(notification, handback);
        }
      }
    }
  }
// . . .
}
```

If the specified notification type contained within the *notification* parameter has already been sent, this method increments the emission count and places it back into the _notifications hash table. If the notification type has not been broadcast, a new entry in the hash table is created. This is how the *getNotificationInfo()* method gets the information to perform its processing. Because it broadcasts notifications via the *sendNotification()* method, the broadcaster itself is unaware of what notifications are sent until they are actually sent.

Next, the list of listeners is processed from beginning to end. Each listener/filter/ handback triplet in the list is sent the specified notification, unless the *isNotificationEnabled()* method of the filter in the triplet returns false, indicating that the specified notification is not one in which that listener is interested.

NotificationListener

As we have already discussed, a notification listener is a class that implements the NotificationListener interface, which is defined as:

```
public interface NotificationListener extends java.util.EventListener {
  public void handleNotification(Notification notification, Object handback);
}
```

As you can see, this interface is relatively simple—it contains a single method, *handleNotification()*. As you might expect from its name, it is the job of this method to handle any notifications that are sent to it.

Notification listeners are responsible for the following:

- Creating and populating objects that implement the NotificationFilter, if the listener desires filtering of the notifications that it will be sent

- Registering (with one or more notification broadcasters) interest in receiving notifications

- Handling any notifications sent to it

One convenient place for a notification listener to perform the first two tasks is in its constructor. To add itself to the broadcaster's list of listeners, the listener must have a reference to the broadcaster. In the examples that follow, we will assume that the listener creates the NotificationBroadcaster. Of course, the listener does not necessarily have to do anything other than implement the NotificationListener interface. In this case, an agent is responsible for creating the listener (or obtaining a reference to it somehow), in addition to performing the first two tasks listed above. My intention is not to show all of the permutations of who creates what and where, but rather to show how to register interest in receiving notifications, create notification filters, and handle notifications. For that reason, in the following examples, the listener itself will handle all of the responsibilities listed above.

To register interest in receiving notifications, the listener must obtain a reference to the broadcaster and invoke its *addNotificationListener()* method. The listener will also pass a reference to itself, an optional filter, and an optional handback object. We covered both the filter and the handback object earlier in this chapter. The following example pulls together what we have already discussed:

```
public class MyListener implements NotificationListener {
  // . . .
  private NotificationBroadcaster _broadcaster;
  // . . .
  public MyListener() {
    _broadcaster = new GenericBroadcaster();
    NotificationFilterSupport filter = new NotificationFilterSupport();
    filter.enableType("sample.Queue.stalled.QueueFull");
    filter.enableType("sample.Queue.stalled.QueueEmpty");
    Properties props = new Properties();
    props.setProperty("response", "email");
    props.setProperty("smtpHost", "mail.mycompany.com");
    props.setProperty("recipient", "me@mycompany.com");
    props.setProperty("subject", "Queue stalled notification");
    props.setProperty("message", "The queue is stalled. ");
    // etc. . . .
    _broadcaster.addNotificationListener(this, filter, props);
  }
  // . . .
}
```

All that remains is for the listener to implement the NotificationListener interface:

```
public class MyListener implements NotificationListener {
  // . . .
  public void handleNotification(Notification notification, Object handback) {
    // . . .
    try {
      Properties props = (Properties)handback;
      String response = (String)props.get("response");
      if (response.equals("email")) {
        // send an email, using the properties set in the handback object. . .
      } else if (response.equals("consoleMessage")) {
        // display a console message
      } else {
        System.out.println("handleNotification: ERROR: " +
          "Unexpected response type \'" + response + "\'.");
      }
    } catch (Exception e) {
      // handle possible exceptions. . .
    }
  }
  // . . .
}
```

The listener does not have to rely on a handback object to figure out how to handle the notification. Instead, the listener can crack into the notification by using its notification type string directly, ignoring the handback object:

```
public class MyListener implements NotificationListener {
  // . . .
  public void handleNotification(Notification notification, Object handback) {
    // . . .
```

```
    try {
      String notifType = notification.getType( );
      if (notifType.equals("sample.Queue.stalled.queueFull")) {
        // queue is full and stalled, handle it
      } else if (notifType.equals("sample.Queue.stalled.queueEmpty")) {
        // queue is empty and stalled, handle it
      } else {
        System.out.println("handleNotification: ERROR: " +
          "Unexpected response type \'" + response + "\'.");
      }
    } catch (Exception e) {
      // handle possible exceptions. . .
    }
  }
// . . .
}
```

CHAPTER 8

Dynamic Loading

In this chapter, we will discuss a facility provided by JMX that allows MBeans to be loaded into an agent dynamically. This facility, called the *M-Let* (short for *management applet*) service, is the first agent-level service we have discussed so far. There are two major sections in this chapter. The first section is an overview of the M-Let service, including the various facets of it that make it work. The second section deals with the details of the M-Let service and provides examples of code that executes in the JMX agent that uses the M-Let service.

Overview

In this section, we will look at the M-Let service, whose purpose is to provide an agent with a means to load MBeans from a Universal Resource Locator (URL). There are two ways that an agent can use the M-Let service to accomplish this. First, the agent can specify an *M-Let file* to the M-Let service, which uses the contents of this file to load the MBeans. The M-Let file is an XML-like text file that contains various tags that describe the MBeans to be loaded. The second method of loading MBeans is to use the M-Let service itself to load the MBeans without the use of an M-Let file. The M-Let service extends URLClassLoader from the java.net package and is thus capable of fetching bytecode from any valid URL into the JVM in which the agent is running.

The M-Let Service

In the RI, the M-Let service is implemented in a class called MLet, which implements an interface called MLetMBean (so it is instrumented as a standard MBean). The MLetMBean interface allows agents (and management applications) to manipulate the M-Let service to load MBeans and to manage the M-Let service itself. The MLetMBean interface is defined as:

```
public interface MLetMBean {
    public Set getMBeansFromURL(String url) throws ServiceNotFoundException;
    public Set getMBeansFromURL(URL url) throws ServiceNotFoundException;
```

```
    public void addURL(URL url);
    public void addURL(String url) throws ServiceNotFoundException;
    public URL[] getURLs();
    public URL getResource(String name);
    public InputStream getResourceAsStream(String name);
    public  Enumeration getResources(String name) throws IOException;
    public String getLibraryDirectory();
    public void setLibraryDirectory(String libdir);
}
```

In this section, we will discuss only those methods that are part of the `MLetMBean` interface. Primary emphasis will be placed on those methods that are mentioned in the specification, with secondary emphasis placed on the others.

There are two methods of primary concern when using the M-Let service: *getMBeansFromURL()* and *addURL()*. The *getMBeansFromURL()* method has two versions: the first takes a `String` that contains the URL of the text file that describes the MBeans to load, and the second takes a `URL` object that contains the URL of the M-Let file. The *addURL()* method is used to add a URL to the list of URLs that are to be searched when loading MBeans while using the M-Let service as the class loader. These two methods are the ones you will use when writing agents that use dynamic loading as a part of your MBean deployment strategy.

The other methods on the `MLetMBean` interface provide functionality that you would expect to see in a class loader. For example, the *getURLs()* method returns an array of the `URL` objects that are searched when loading classes and resources, and the *getResourceAsStream()* method takes a `String` containing the name of a resource and returns an `InputStream` object so the resource can be read.

The M-Let service must be created and registered with the MBean server before you can use it. The examples that follow assume that a reference to the MBean server has been obtained (we saw how to do this in earlier chapters) and that the M-Let service is created by simply using the Java `new` keyword on the RI class `MLet`. The `MLet` class implements the `MBeanRegistration` interface, so it is capable of creating its own object name. In the examples that follow, we will allow it to do so.

The M-Let File

The M-Let file is a text file that looks like XML but is not required to be well-formed XML. Each of the components of the M-Let file is called a *tag* (even though the "tag" may resemble an XML attribute; remember, it's not well-formed XML) The JMX specification defines several tags that are used in the M-Let file, which we will look at in this section. The format of the M-Let file is:

```
<MLET
  CODE="className" | OBJECT="serializedObjectFileName"
  ARCHIVE="classOrJarFileName"
  [CODEBASE="relativePathToArchive"]
```

```
    [NAME="mbeanObjectName"]
    [VERSION="version"]
>
[<ARG TYPE="type" VALUE="value">]
</MLET>
    .
    .
    .
```

There is one MLET tag for each MBean to be loaded. For example, if there were five MBeans to load, there would be five MLET tags in the M-Let file. Each MBean specified in the M-Let file is required to provide either the full string representation of its class name (by using the CODE tag) or the name of a file that contains the MBean's serialized state (by using the OBJECT tag). The CODE and OBJECT tags are mutually exclusive (i.e., for any given MBean, one or the other may be specified, but not both). In addition, the name of the JAR file in which the bytecode is archived must be specified. The other tags are not required. Let's look at each of these tags in detail.

MLET

As we mentioned, each MBean to be loaded by the M-Let service must have its own MLET tag in the M-Let file. It's as simple as that.

CODE

The value of this tag is designated by *className* in the example above and must be the string representation of the MBean's class name. For example, suppose the MBean's class name is sample.mlet_loadable.Queue. The CODE tag would then look like:

```
CODE="sample.mlet_loadable.Queue"
```

If we had simply specified "Queue" as the CODE value, the M-Let service would not be able to locate the bytecode for our MBean class. As you might expect, the M-Let service must be able to locate this class relative to one of the URLs that it is using as its search path. We will see how to set this URL later.

OBJECT

The value of this tag is designated by *serializedObjectFileName* in the example above and is the name of the file that contains the MBean's serialized state. Suppose that we serialized the state of the Queue class in a file named *Queue.ser*. We would then instruct the M-Let service to load the MBean from that file:

```
OBJECT="Queue.ser"
```

Of course, the M-Let service must be able to locate this file relative to one of the URLs that it is using as its search path.

ARCHIVE

The value of this tag is designated by *classOrJarFileName* in the example above and is the names of one or more JAR files, one of which contains the *.class* file for the MBean. Suppose the JAR that contains the Queue class is called *mlet_loadable.jar*. In this case, the ARCHIVE tag would look like:

```
ARCHIVE="mlet_loadable.jar"
```

Multiple JAR files are separated by commas:

```
ARCHIVE="mlet_loadable.jar,another.jar,yetanother.jar"
```

The M-Let service will search the URLs that constitute its search path for all of the JAR files that are specified by the ARCHIVE tag. At least one of the JAR files must contain the bytecode for the MBean.

CODEBASE (optional)

The value of this tag is designated by *relativePathToArchive* in the example above and is the relative path to the JAR file specified by the ARCHIVE tag. But relative to what? The M-Let service uses the URL of the M-Let file as the default URL (minus the M-Let filename, of course) to the JAR file specified by ARCHIVE. If no CODEBASE tag is specified, the default URL is used as the code base from which to load the bytecode for the MBean. This is useful when the JAR file is located in the same directory as the M-Let file.

Suppose that the URL to the M-Let file is *http://myserver/mbeans/mbeans.txt*. The default URL in this case is *http://myserver/mbeans*. Now suppose that we specify the value of the ARCHIVE tag to be *mlet_loadable.jar*, located at *http://myserver/mbeans/jars*, and we do not provide a CODEBASE tag. The M-Let service will use the default as the base URL for locating *mlet_loadable.jar*. It will try to load *http://myserver/mbeans/mlet_loadable.jar*, but it will not be able to find it.

However, if we specify a CODEBASE value relative to the default URL:

```
CODEBASE="jars"
```

the M-Let service will add the CODEBASE value to the default URL, resulting in *http://myserver/mbeans/jars/mlet_loadable.jar*, and the JAR file will be located. Because the CODEBASE value is added to the default URL, specifying:

```
CODEBASE="."
```

and omitting the CODEBASE tag altogether have the same effect. As you might expect, you can use "." and ".." to represent the current directory and parent directory, respectively. Suppose that instead of *mlet_loadble.jar* being subordinate to the M-Let file, the two files are located in peer directories, with *mlet_loadable.jar* being located at *http://myserver/jars*. In this case, the CODEBASE tag would have to be specified as:

```
CODEBASE="../jars"
```

NAME (optional)

The value of this tag is designated by *mbeanObjectName* in the example above and is the string representation of the object name for the MBean. Suppose the object name string for the Queue class is ":name=Queue,loadedFrom=MLET", where the domain is the default domain. The NAME tag could then be specified as:

```
NAME=":name=Queue,loadedFrom=MLET"
```

When the Queue MBean is loaded by the M-Let service, it will be given this object name. If the object name already exists, the MBean will not be loaded and an exception will be returned to the agent that is using the M-Let service.

If this tag is omitted, the M-Let service assumes that the MBean implements the MBeanRegistration interface and will provide its own object name.

VERSION (optional)

The value of this tag is designated by *version* in the example above and represents the version of the JAR file specified by ARCHIVE and/or the MBean to be loaded. The primary purpose of this tag is to support versioning and caching in the implementation. The format of this tag is one or more nonnegative integers separated by a dot (.):

```
VERSION="1.0.1"
```

Note that the JMX 1.0 RI does not support this tag. Support for the VERSION tag will most likely be present in a future release of the JMX RI.

ARG

This tag represents an argument that is to be passed to the constructor of the MBean when it is loaded and instantiated. The tags that accompany this tag are TYPE and VALUE, which represent the argument's data type and its value, respectively. Only fundamental types (boolean, byte, char, short, int, long, float, and double), java.lang fundamental wrapper types (Boolean, Byte, Char, Short, Int, Long, Float, Double, and String) are supported, as they may all have a string representation (unlike complex user-defined types). The ARG tag must follow the closing > of the MLET tag.

Using the Queue class, which has an alternate constructor that takes a single int to set the queue depth, we can specify a single ARG tag to set the queue depth to seven items:

```
<ARG TYPE="int" VALUE="7">
```

Multiple arguments to the MBean constructor may be specified. The order of the arguments in the M-Let file must correspond to the order of the arguments to the constructor. Suppose that a constructor takes a String, a float, and an Integer, in that order. The ARG tags must also be supplied in that order:

```
<ARG TYPE="java.lang.String" VALUE="Hello, world">
<ARG TYPE="float" VALUE="3.14159">
<ARG TYPE="java.lang.Integer" VALUE="104">
```

.at the JDK wrapper classes String and Integer must be fully qualified. If we
.ten the ARG tags as:

```
 G TYPE="String" VALUE="Hello, world">
 RG TYPE="float" VALUE="3.14159">
 ARG TYPE="Integer" VALUE="104">
```

the MBean would not be loaded, because the M-Let service cannot fetch the bytecode for the String and Integer parameters. However, fundamental types simply
require the name of the type, as that is the name of the Class object that represents
fundamental type inside the JVM.

Bringing it all together

Now that we're familiar with the tags that can be used in the M-Let file, let's look at
a simple example. Suppose that we want to load the sample.mlet_loadable.Queue
MBean from *mlet_loadable.jar*, giving it the name ":name=Queue,loadedFrom=MLET"
and passing an int argument value of 8 to its constructor:

```
<MLET
    CODE="sample.mlet_loadable.Queue"
    ARCHIVE="mlet_loadable.jar"
    NAME=":name=Queue,loadedFrom=MLET"
>
<ARG TYPE="int" VALUE="8">
</MLET>
```

We will see later exactly how to use the M-Let file, the URL describing its location,
and the *getMBeansFromURL()* method of the MLetMBean interface to load the MBeans.

What about comments in the M-Let file? The specification does not mention them,
so it's not a good idea to expect support for comments to be in every implementation of JMX. However, in the JMX 1.0 RI, the parser that reads the M-Let file allows
for any text to be placed in the file as long as it is outside of a "< . . . >" construct. In
other words, no text other than the tags we have discussed is allowed anywhere
inside the <MLET . . . > tag, the </MLET> closing tag, or the <ARG . . . > tag. You
can place whatever text you like outside of those tags. For example:

```
This text will be ignored by the parser
<MLET
    Oops, text cannot go here!
    CODE="sample.mlet_loadable.Queue"
    ARCHIVE="mlet_loadable.jar"
    NAME=":name=Queue,loadedFrom=MLET"
> This text is ignored
This text is ignored
<ARG TYPE="int" VALUE="8">
</MLET>
```

The line of text following the MLET opening tag will cause the parser to report an error
with the M-Let file. All of the other text will be ignored by the parser.

Loading MBeans Without an M-Let File

As mentioned earlier, the MLet class, which is the RI's implementation of the M-Let service, is a class loader capable of fetching bytecode from a URL and creating a Class object for an MBean. We have already looked at how the M-Let service uses its class loader functionality in conjunction with an M-Let file to load MBeans. In this section, we will see how to use the M-Let service to load MBeans without the use of an M-Let file.

The MLetMBean interface—implemented by the MLet class—provides a method that allows an agent to add one or more URLs that the M-Let service will search when loading MBeans. This method, *addURL()*, works in conjunction with the MBean server methods *instantiate()* and *createMBean()* to load MBeans from a URL. *instantiate()* and *createMBean()* each have two versions that take as a parameter the object name of the loader to be used when fetching the bytecode for the MBean to be loaded. Once the URL of the JAR file containing the MBean(s) to be loaded has been added to the M-Let service's search list of URLs, either *instantiate()* or *createMBean()* can be called to load the MBean. We will see how to do this later in this chapter.

If the MBean to be loaded exists in the same code base (i.e., one or more JAR files, specified by a URL) as any other MBean that has been loaded using an M-Let file, you do not need to specify the URL. In other words, the M-Let service remembers any URL from which it has previously loaded a class. This functionality is typical of all class loaders. We will look at an example of this later in this chapter.

How Does Dynamic Loading Work?

In this section, we will take a detailed look at the mechanics of the M-Let service. We will first look at an example of how to use an M-Let file to load an MBean from a JAR file. Then we will see how to use the M-Let service as the class loader for MBeans without the use of an M-Let file. For the sake of clarity and brevity, the examples in this section show agent-side code and do not contain complete exception-handling constructs.

We have discussed the tags used in the M-Let file, as well as the *getMBeansFromURL()* method of the M-Let service, which is used to load the MBeans specified in the M-Let file. Now let's look at a couple of code examples.

getMBeansFromURL( )

The *getMBeansFromURL()* method allows you to specify the URL of an M-Let text file that contains the information necessary for the M-Let service to load your MBeans. There are two versions of this method. The first version takes a String that contains the complete URL to the M-Let text file. (We will deal only with URLs that are of the *file* and *http* varieties here, although many other protocols are conceivably supported.) Once an MBean is loaded using *getMBeansFromURL()*, it is then registered with the same MBean server with which the M-Let service is registered.

Suppose the M-Let text file is called *MBeans.txt* and resides in the *c:\jmxbook* directory on the local Windows-based filesystem. The URL to the M-Let text file would then be *file:/c:\jmxbook*. Furthermore, suppose the contents of this file look like:

```
<MLET
  CODE="sample.mlet_loadable.Queue"
  ARCHIVE="mlet_loadable.jar"
  NAME=":name=Queue,loadedFrom=MLET"
>
<ARG TYPE="int" VALUE="10">
</MLET>
```

You may recognize this example M-Let file from earlier in this chapter. Using this M-Let file to specify the Queue MBean as the MBean to be loaded, the call to *getMBeansFromURL()* would look like this:

```
MBeanServer mbs = /* obtain somehow */
MLetMBean mletService = new MLet();
mbs.registerMBean(mletService, null);
String url = "file:/c:\jmxbook\MBeans.txt";
try {
  Set loadedMBeans = mletService.getMBeansFromURL(url);
} catch (ServiceNotFoundException e) {
  // . . .
}
```

First, we obtain a reference to the MBean server and create the M-Let service by instantiating the RI class MLet (notice that we use the M-Let service through its management interface). We then register the M-Let service with the MBean server, passing null as the second parameter to *registerMBean()*. Passing null as the object name for the M-Let service indicates that we are relying on the M-Let service to provide its own object name. As mentioned earlier, the M-Let service in the RI implements the MBeanRegistration interface, so it can do this. Next, we build the URL string and pass it to *getMBeansFromURL()*, whose return value is a java.util.Set object that contains a set of objects. For each MBean specified in the M-Let text file that was successfully loaded and registered, an ObjectInstance object will be present in the Set. For each MBean specified in the M-Let text file that was not successfully loaded and/or registered, a Throwable object (i.e., an Error or Exception) will be present in the Set. If the call to *getMBeansFromURL()* itself does not succeed, either there was a problem with the M-Let file, or the URL string could not be converted to a well-formed URL object. A ServiceNotFoundException will be thrown in either case—you should interrogate its contents to discover the exact cause of the failure.

If all goes well with the invocation of *getMBeansFromURL()*, we then walk through the returned Set by using its *iterator()* method to return a java.util.Iterator object.

When walking through the Set, you should be prepared to encounter throwables as well as ObjectInstance objects:

```
MBeanServer mbs = /* obtain somehow */
MLetMBean mletService = new MLet();
mbs.registerMBean(mletService, null);
String url = "file:/c:\jmxbook\MBeans.txt";
try {
  Set loadedMBeans = mletService.getMBeansFromURL(url);
  Iterator iter = loadedMBeans.iterator();
  while (iter.hasNext()) {
    Object o = iter.next();
    if (o instanceof ObjectInstance) {
      ObjectInstance oi = (ObjectInstance)o;
      System.out.prinln("MBean loaded: " + oi.getObjectName());
      // etc. . . .
    } else {
      ((Throwable)o).printStackTrace();
      // etc. . . .
    }
  }
} catch (ServiceNotFoundException e) {
  // . . .
}
```

The second version of *getMBeansFromURL()* takes a java.net.URL object, instead of a string representation of a URL. The URL class provides several constructors for creating a URL. The easiest constructor to use simply takes a String that contains the URL. Using this constructor, our example looks like:

```
MBeanServer mbs = /* obtain somehow */
MLetMBean mletService = new MLet();
mbs.registerMBean(mletService, null);
try {
  URL url = new URL("file:/c:\jmxbook\MBeans.txt");
  Set loadedMBeans = mletService.getMBeansFromURL(url);
} catch (ServiceNotFoundException e) {
  // . . .
}
```

Now suppose that we want to load MBeans that are on a remote machine, using the HyperText Transfer Protocol (HTTP). This requires that there be an HTTP server (usually a web server) listening on a certain port (usually port 80) on the remote machine. Suppose that the name of the machine is *myserver*, it is running a web server listening on port 80, the MBeans are located in a directory called *jmxbook*, and the M-Let file is called *MBeans.txt*:

```
MBeanServer mbs = /* obtain somehow */
MLetMBean mletService = new MLet();
mbs.registerMBean(mletService, null);
try {
  URL url = new URL("http://myserver/jmxbook/MBeans.txt");
  Set loadedMBeans = mletService.getMBeansFromURL(url);
```

```
    Iterator iter = loadedMBeans.iterator();
    while (iter.hasNext()) {
      Object o = iter.next();
      if (o instanceof ObjectInstance) {
        ObjectInstance oi = (ObjectInstance)o;
        System.out.prinln("MBean loaded: " + oi.getObjectName());
        // etc. . . .
      } else {
        ((Throwable)o).printStackTrace();
        // etc. . . .
      }
    }
  } catch (ServiceNotFoundException e) {
    // . . .
  }
```

Notice that the code to look through the Set returned from *getMBeansFromURL()* is the same regardless of what protocol we use.

In this example, the default port (80) is assumed. However, we can also specify the port on which the HTTP server is listening when we create the URL:

```
MBeanServer mbs = /* obtain somehow */
MLetMBean mletService = new MLet();
mbs.registerMBean(mletService, null);
try {
  URL url = new URL("http://myserver:8090/jmxbook/MBeans.txt");
  Set loadedMBeans = mletService.getMBeansFromURL(url);
  // same as above. . .
} catch (ServiceNotFoundException e) {
  // . . .
}
```

In this case, the M-Let service will attempt to load the MBeans by connecting to port 8090.

Once the M-Let service has loaded one or more MBeans from a given code base (i.e., a JAR file), we can use the M-Let service's class loader functionality to load other MBeans from the same code base without using the M-Let file. As an example, let's look at the *MBeans.txt* M-Let file:

```
<MLET
  CODE="sample.mlet_loadable.Queue"
  ARCHIVE="mlet_loadable.jar"
  NAME=":name=Queue,loadedFrom=MLET"
>
<ARG TYPE="int" VALUE="10">
</MLET>
```

Suppose that the JAR file *mlet_loadable.jar* contains the bytecode for both the Queue and Supplier classes. We will use the M-Let file to load the Queue class and then load the Supplier class without specifying an M-Let file:

```
MBeanServer mbs = /* obtain somehow */
MLetMBean mletService = new MLet( );
ObjectInstance mletOI = mbs.registerMBean(mletService, null);
try {
  URL url = new URL("http://myserver/jmxbook/MBeans.txt");
  Set loadedMBeans = mletService.getMBeansFromURL(url);
  Iterator iter = loadedMBeans.iterator( );
  while (iter.hasNext( )) {
    Object o = iter.next( );
    if (o instanceof ObjectInstance) {
      ObjectInstance oi = (ObjectInstance)o;
      System.out.prinln("MBean loaded: " + oi.getObjectName( ));
      // etc. . . .
    } else {
      ((Throwable)o).printStackTrace( );
      // etc. . . .
    }
  }
  ObjectName mletObjName = mletOI.getObjectName( );
  mbs.createMBean("sample.mlet_loadable.Supplier", null, mletObjName);
} catch (ServiceNotFoundException e) {
  // . . .
}
```

Recall that if no `CODEBASE` tag is specified in the M-Let file, the URL the M-Let service uses to load the JAR file is the default URL (which is the same as that of the M-Let file, minus the name of the M-Let file itself). In this example, no `CODEBASE` tag is specified in the M-Let file, so the code base from which the M-Let service loads the `Queue` class is *http://myserver/jmxbook/mlet_loadable.jar*. Notice that we must capture the return value of the *registerMBean()* call when we register the M-Let service MBean, so we have a way to get the MBean's object name. We let the M-Let service provide its own object name, and this is our one opportunity to easily record that information. We use the M-Let service to load the `Queue` MBean, then we load and register the `Supplier` MBean by invoking the version of the MBean server method *createMBean()* that takes the object name of the MBean that will act as the class loader. In this case, that loader is the M-Let service. Notice that we specified `null` as the *objectName* parameter for the `Supplier` MBean. This is because `Supplier` implements `MBean-Registration` and creates its own object name, just as the M-Let service did.

We can also use the *instantiate()* method of the MBean server to load and create an instance of the Supplier class:

```
MBeanServer mbs = /* obtain somehow */
MLetMBean mletService = new MLet( );
ObjectInstance mletOI = mbs.registerMBean(mletService, null);
try {
  URL url = new URL("http://myserver/jmxbook/MBeans.txt");
  Set loadedMBeans = mletService.getMBeansFromURL(url);
  Iterator iter = loadedMBeans.iterator( );
```

```
    while (iter.hasNext( )) {
      Object o = iter.next( );
      if (o instanceof ObjectInstance) {
        ObjectInstance oi = (ObjectInstance)o;
        System.out.prinln("MBean loaded: " + oi.getObjectName( ));
        // etc. . . .
      } else {
        ((Throwable)o).printStackTrace( );
        // etc. . . .
      }
    }
    ObjectName mletObjName = mletOI.getObjectName( );
    Object supplier = mbs.instantiate("sample.mlet_loadable.Supplier",
                                      mletObjName);
    mbs.registerMBean(supplier, null);
  } catch (ServiceNotFoundException e) {
    // . . .
  }
```

Recall that *instantiate()* does not register the MBean, but rather returns an Object reference to it. This return value is used to register the MBean. As in the previous example, we specified null as the Supplier MBean object name, letting it provide its own object name.

If we need to provide constructor arguments to an MBean, we use the version of *instantiate()* or *createMBean()* that allows us to specify these arguments in addition to the MBean class loader. For example, if we load the Queue MBean without specifying an M-Let file (assuming that the M-Let service has already loaded one or more MBeans from the code base containing the bytecode for Queue):

```
MBeanServer mbs = /* obtain somehow */
MLetMBean mletService = new MLet( );
ObjectInstance mletOI = mbs.registerMBean(mletService, null);
// . . .
try {
  Object[] params = new Object[] { new Integer(5) };
  String[] signature = new String[] { Integer.TYPE.getName( ) };
  ObjectName mletObjName = mletOI.getObjectName( );
  Object queue = mbs.instantiate("sample.mlet_loadable.Queue",
                                 mletObjName,
                                 params, signature);
  ObjectName queueObjName = new ObjectName(":name=Queue");
  mbs.registerMBean(queue, queueObjName);
} catch (ServiceNotFoundException e) {
  // . . .
}
```

After registering the M-Let service MBean, we add the URL to the JAR file that contains the Queue class, just to make sure that the code base is available to the M-Let service. Then we construct the arrays necessary to represent the constructor argument values that will be passed to Queue's constructor. Then we call *instantiate()* as before and register the Queue MBean, passing the desired object name (Queue does not implement MBeanRegistration). We could also have used *createMBean()* to accomplish this with nearly identical agent code:

```
MBeanServer mbs = /* obtain somehow */
MLetMBean mletService = new MLet( );
ObjectInstance mletOI = mbs.registerMBean(mletService, null);
// . . .
try {
  Object[] params = new Object[] { new Integer(5) };
  String[] signature = new String[] { Integer.TYPE.getName( ) };
  ObjectName queueObjName = new ObjectName(":name=Queue");
  ObjectName mletObjName = mletOI.getObjectName( );
  mbs.createMBean("sample.mlet_loadable.Queue", queueObjName,
                  mletObjName,
                  params, signature);
} catch (ServiceNotFoundException e) {
  // . . .
}
```

What if we want to use the M-Let service to load MBeans from a code base from which we have not yet loaded any MBeans? In this case, we must add the URL of the code base to the M-Let service's search list of URLs by using the *addURL()* method. Once we have added the URL, we can call *createMBean()* or *instantiate()* to load the MBean.

For example, suppose that we want to load the Queue and Supplier MBeans without the use of an M-Let file:

```
MBeanServer mbs = /* obtain somehow */
MLetMBean mletService = new MLet( );
ObjectInstance mletOI = mbs.registerMBean(mletService, null);
try {
  mletService.addURL("http://myserver/jmxbook/mlet_loadable.jar");
  ObjectName mletObjName = mletOI.getObjectName( );
  Object queue = mbs.instantiate("sample.mlet_loadble.Queue", mletObjName);
  mbs.registerMBean(queue, ":name=Queue");
  mbs.createMBean("sample.mlet_loadable.Supplier", null, mletObjName);
} catch (ServiceNotFoundException e) {
  // . . .
}
```

First, we must add the URL to the code base containing the bytecode for the Queue and Supplier classes. Suppose that these classes reside in the same JAR file, *mlet_loadable.jar*. It is then a simple matter of calling *instantiate()* and/or *createMBean()* to load the MBeans. In the example above we used both, for the purposes of illustration.

CHAPTER 9

The Monitoring Services

In Chapter 8, we looked at the JMX notification model and how to write and use notification broadcasters and listeners. In this chapter, we will look at a few off-the-shelf implementations of notification broadcasters provided by JMX, called the *monitoring services*, or *monitors*. A monitor observes the attribute value of an MBean, called the *observed object*, at specific intervals, called the *granularity period*. From this observation, the monitor calculates a value called the *derived gauge*, which is either the value of the attribute or the difference between the values of the attribute at the two most recent observations (for numerical attributes only, of course). When the derived gauge satisfies a certain condition—which varies depending on the type of monitor in use—a notification of a type that is specific to that monitor is sent to all registered notification listeners. The monitoring service can also send error notifications if a problem occurs.

The JMX specification's monitoring services provide three types of monitors:

Counter monitors
> Observe a continually increasing, nonnegative integer MBean attribute (of type byte, short, int, long, or the corresponding JDK wrapper class) and send a notification when the derived gauge exceeds a certain value, known as the *threshold*

Gauge monitors
> Observe an arbitrarily changing numeric value (of type int, long, float, double, or the corresponding JDK wrapper type) and send a notification when the derived gauge exceeds an upper limit (known as the *high threshold*) or drops below a lower limit (known as the *low threshold*)

String monitors
> Observe a String attribute of an MBean and send a notification when the derived gauge either matches (i.e., becomes equal to) or differs from (i.e., stops being equal to) a predefined string value

These three monitors are required for a JMX implementation to be compliant with the specification.

The JMX specification defines several classes that make up the monitoring services, as shown in Figure 9-1.

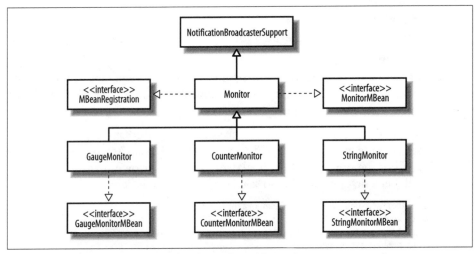

Figure 9-1. UML diagram showing the classes that make up the monitoring services

Each of the monitors is an MBean that can be managed. The base class Monitor contains functionality common to all of the monitoring services and exposes a management interface, MonitorMBean, which is defined as:

```
public interface MonitorMBean {
   public void start();
   public void stop();
   public ObjectName getObservedObject();
   public void setObservedObject(ObjectName object);
   public String getObservedAttribute();
   public void setObservedAttribute(String attribute);
   public long getGranularityPeriod();
   public void setGranularityPeriod(long period)
      throws java.lang.IllegalArgumentException;
   public boolean isActive();
}
```

Each monitor runs in its own thread of execution, so that it can monitor an MBean attribute regardless of what the MBean (or any other thread in the JVM) is doing. The *start()* method is used to start the monitor thread, and *stop()* is used to stop the thread. Once the monitor has been started, it is considered active, such that a subsequent call to *isActive()* will return true. If the monitor has been stopped or has not yet been started, *isActive()* will return false.

All monitor MBeans have three attributes in common:

ObservedObject
   The object name of the MBean that is to be monitored

ObservedAttribute

> The name of the attribute that is to be observed on the MBean designated by ObservedObject

GranularityPeriod

> The period of time that the monitor thread sleeps before calculating a new derived gauge

For each of these attributes, there is a getter and a setter. We will look at these methods in more detail—along with how they are implemented in the various monitoring service classes—later in this chapter.

The counter monitor is implemented in a class called CounterMonitor, which in turn implements an MBean interface called CounterMonitorMBean. As you can see from Figure 9-1, all of the other monitor subclasses expose their own management interfaces as well. Let's first look at CounterMonitorMBean, which is defined as:

```
public interface CounterMonitorMBean extends MonitorMBean {
    public Number getDerivedGauge();
    public long getDerivedGaugeTimeStamp();
    public Number getThreshold();
    public void setThreshold(Number value)
      throws java.lang.IllegalArgumentException;
    public Number getOffset();
    public void setOffset(Number value)
      throws java.lang.IllegalArgumentException;
    public Number getModulus();
    public void setModulus(Number value)
      throws java.lang.IllegalArgumentException;
    public boolean getNotify();
    public void setNotify(boolean value);
    public boolean getDifferenceMode();
    public void setDifferenceMode(boolean value);
}
```

This interface consists entirely of attributes. Two of these attributes—DerivedGauge and DerivedGaugeTimeStamp, which are the derived gauge and the time stamp when the gauge was derived, respectively—are read-only. The other attributes are readable and writable:

Threshold

> The counter monitor's threshold value. Default value: 0.

Offset

> A value added to the threshold each time the derived gauge exceeds the threshold. This attribute makes it possible for the notification sent when the derived gauge exceeds the threshold to be emitted more than once. Default value: 0.

Modulus

> For counters whose values wrap back to zero, this attribute is the value at which the counter is reset to zero. Default value: 0.

Notify

> A boolean attribute whose value determines whether or not a notification is sent to all registered listeners when the threshold value is exceeded. Default value: false.

DifferenceMode

> A boolean attribute whose value indicates whether the counter's derived gauge is the attribute value or the difference between the current and previous values of the attribute, for false and true, respectively. Default value: false.

Next, let's look at the GaugeMonitorMBean interface, which is implemented by GaugeMonitor. GaugeMonitorMBean is defined as:

```
public interface GaugeMonitorMBean extends MonitorMBean {
    public Number getDerivedGauge();
    public long getDerivedGaugeTimeStamp();
    public Number getHighThreshold();
    public Number getLowThreshold();
    public void setThresholds(Number highValue, Number lowValue)
        throws java.lang.IllegalArgumentException;
    public boolean getNotifyHigh();
    public void setNotifyHigh(boolean value);
    public boolean getNotifyLow();
    public void setNotifyLow(boolean value);
    public boolean getDifferenceMode();
    public void setDifferenceMode(boolean value);
}
```

The management interfaces of the gauge monitor and counter monitor services share three attributes: DerivedGauge (which is read-only), DerivedGaugeTimeStamp (also read-only), and DifferenceMode (which is readable and writable). DifferenceMode serves the same purpose for gauge monitor floating-point values as it does for counter monitor integers.

The gauge monitor has two attributes called HighThreshold and LowThreshold that represent the gauge monitor's high and low threshold values, respectively. Each attribute has a getter, but the designers of JMX decided to have one operation on the management interface—*setThresholds()*—that serves to set both attribute values at once. This is an odd choice, in that a setter takes only a single parameter, but it is completely functional.

Because there are two threshold values (high and low), there are two notifications that can be sent to indicate that those threshold values have been crossed. As a result, there are two notify methods that can be used: NotifyHigh and NotifyLow, which are used to turn on and off the high and low threshold notifications, respectively.

Finally, let's look at StringMonitorMBean, the management interface of StringMonitor. StringMonitorMBean is defined as:

```
public interface StringMonitorMBean extends MonitorMBean {
    public String getDerivedGauge();
```

```
   public long getDerivedGaugeTimeStamp( );
   public String getStringToCompare( );
   public void setStringToCompare(String value)
     throws java.lang.IllegalArgumentException;
   public boolean getNotifyMatch( );
   public void setNotifyMatch(boolean value);
   public boolean getNotifyDiffer( );
   public void setNotifyDiffer(boolean value);
}
```

In the case of the string monitor, the DerivedGauge attribute is the attribute value of
the MBean when the monitor thread checks its value. The DerivedGaugeTimeStamp has
the same purpose as the other two monitors we have already discussed. The
StringToCompare value is analogous to the threshold value of the counter monitor, in
that it serves as the reference value the derived gauge differs from or matches. When
the derived gauge differs from StringToCompare, a notification is sent to all listeners,
provided the NotifyDiffer attribute is set to true. By the same token, if the derived
gauge matches the StringToCompare attribute, a notification is sent to all listeners,
provided the NotifyMatch attribute is set to true.

The MonitorNotification Class

MonitorNotification is a subclass of the Notification class that contains attributes
specific to monitors. When a monitor sends a notification to a listener, the *notification* parameter passed to the *handleNotification()* method in the listener is actually a
MonitorNotification instance. MonitorNotification contains the following attributes
(with types in parentheses) that the listener can exploit when it receives a notification:

ObservedObject (ObjectName)
:   The object name of the MBean that is being observed

ObservedAttribute (String)
:   The MBean attribute that is being observed

DerivedGauge (Number *or* String, *depending on the monitor type*)
:   The derived gauge that resulted in the notification being sent

Trigger (Number *or* String, *depending on the monitor type*)
:   The MBean attribute value used to calculate the derived gauge at the time the
    notification was sent

One other piece of information provided by the MonitorNotification is the notification type, which tells the listener exactly what type of notification it has received.
The JMX specification defines several notification types that are specific to the monitoring services. All of these notifications are namespaced with jmx.monitor, to distin-
guish them from the other notification types defined by the JMX specification. In the
remainder of this section, we will look at the notification types that are emitted by
the monitoring services.

Error Conditions

Several notification types are defined to represent the various error conditions that occur when setting the attribute values of the different monitor types. Each of these notification types is namespaced by `jmx.monitor.error`.

The notification types are:

`jmx.monitor.error.mbean`
> Sent when the MBean to be observed is not registered in the MBean server. Always make sure before attempting to set the `ObservedObject` attribute of a monitor that the MBean is registered. When this notification is sent, the listener may interrogate the notification to identify the MBean object on which the attribute was to be monitored.

`jmx.monitor.error.attribute`
> Sent when an attribute of an MBean that was specified to be observed does not exist. Make sure that the specified attribute exists on the MBean to be monitored. When this notification is sent, the listener may interrogate the notification to see which MBean and which attribute are in error. The pertinent information contained in the notification includes the `ObservedObject` and `ObservedAttribute` attributes.

`jmx.monitor.error.type`
> Sent when the MBean attribute's type does not match that of the type of monitor in use. For example, if the monitor is a gauge monitor and the attribute is an integer type, this error will be sent to the listener. Likewise, if the monitor is a string monitor and the attribute type is `long`, this error will be sent to notify the listener that there is a mismatch. The pertinent information contained in the notification includes the `ObservedObject` and `ObservedAttribute` attributes.

`jmx.monitor.error.runtime`
> Sent as a catch-all when an error has occurred that does not fit into the other categories. If there is a problem, say, obtaining the attribute value of an MBean attribute, this exception will be thrown. The pertinent information contained in the notification depends on the monitor type and the specific error.

`jmx.monitor.error.threshold`
> Sent when the threshold value is not of the same type as the derived gauge. This error notification depends on the type of monitor in use:
>
> - If the threshold, offset, or modulus is not the same type as that of the attribute monitored by a counter monitor, this error notification will be sent.
> - If either the low or high threshold value is not of the same type as that of the attribute monitored by a gauge monitor, this error notification will be sent.

Counter Monitor Notification Types

In addition to the error notification types a counter monitor must handle, there is one other notification that deserves special mention:

`jmx.monitor.counter.threshold`
> Sent when the derived gauge has exceeded the value of the `Threshold` attribute. In essence, this means either that the attribute value of the MBean that is being monitored has exceeded the preset value of the monitor or that the derived gauge has exceeded the value of the monitor type plus the offset value. When this notification is sent, it means that the derived gauge calculated by the monitor has exceeded the current attribute value and must be handled accordingly.

Gauge Monitor Notification Types

In addition to the error notification types a gauge monitor must handle, there are two more notifications that deserve special mention:

`jmx.monitor.gauge.high`
> Sent whenever the derived gauge exceeds the value of the `HighThreshold` attribute

`jmx.monitor.gauge.low`
> Sent whenever the derived gauge drops below the value of the `LowThreshold` attribute

Once a gauge monitor notification is triggered, small oscillations around either threshold will not produce additional notifications, due to a hysteresis mechanism that is used to prevent this.

String Monitor Notification Types

In addition to the error notification types a string monitor must handle, there are two other notifications that deserve special mention:

`jmx.monitor.string.matches`
> Sent when the derived gauge first matches (i.e., becomes equal to) the `StringToCompare` attribute

`jmx.monitor.string.differs`
> Sent when the derived gauge first differs from (i.e., stops being equal to) the `StringToCompare` attribute

Counter Monitors

As mentioned in the first part of this chapter, a counter monitor is used to observe an MBean attribute that is:

- Greater than or equal to zero
- Continually increasing (i.e., never decreasing)
- One of the Java integer types (byte, short, int, or long) or one of the corresponding JDK wrapper classes (Byte, Short, Int, or Long)

In this section, we will look at the agent code that shows how to use a counter monitor. When using a counter monitor, the first thing to do is to create a new instance of the CounterMonitor class:

```
CounterMonitor monitor = new CounterMonitor();
```

After that, the following attributes of the monitor must be set:

- ObservedObject
- ObservedAttribute
- Notify (must be set to true if a notification is to be sent)
- Threshold
- GranularityPeriod
- Offset (optional)
- DifferenceMode (optional)
- Modulus (optional)

We discussed some of these attributes earlier in this chapter. If the Offset attribute is set, each time the derived gauge exceeds the threshold value, the current value of the MBean attribute is incremented by the value of Offset until the MBean attribute value is greater than the derived gauge (to prevent multiple notifications should the derived gauge spike well beyond the current MBean attribute value). When the counter monitor determines that a notification should be sent to all interested listeners, a single notification is sent, regardless of how many multiples of the threshold value the derived gauge is calculated to be.

In other words, if the previous attribute value is 1, the current MBean attribute value is 12, the Threshold value is 2, and the Offset value is 4, the JMX infrastructure will send a notification (because the threshold value has been exceeded) and will increment the threshold value until it is greater than the current attribute value. The new threshold will be 14. The previous threshold value will be incremented by 4 (the Offset) as many times as necessary to ensure that is it greater than the current MBean attribute value. So, in this example, the threshold value will be incremented from 2 to 6 to 10 to 14, when it is finally greater than the current derived gauge.

The following example shows how to create an instance of the counter monitor and set its properties.

```
ObjectName queueObjName = new ObjectName(":name=Queue");
CounterMonitor monitor = new CounterMonitor();
monitor.setObservedObject(queueObjName);
monitor.setObservedAttribute("NumberOfItemsProcessed");
monitor.setNotify(true);
monitor.setThreshold(new Long(500));
monitor.setGranularityPeriod(5000);
```

There are a couple of things to note about this example. First, the threshold type must be the same type as the attribute type (or at least the same type as its JDK wrapper), the granularity period must be in milliseconds, and the type must be long. Also, the Notify attribute must be set to true if notifications are to be sent. In the JMX 1.0 RI, the default value for this attribute is false.

Once we have created the counter monitor, we must register it with the MBean server, or a jmx.monitor.error.runtime notification will be sent:

```
ObjectName queueObjName = new ObjectName(":name=Queue");
CounterMonitor monitor = new CounterMonitor();
monitor.setObservedObject(queueObjName);
// . . .
try {
  MBeanServer server = MBeanServerFactory.createMBeanServer();
  ObjectName objName = new ObjectName("Monitor:type=Counter");
  server.registerMBean(monitor, objName);
} catch (Exception e) {
  // . . .
}
```

Finally, we must start the counter monitor's thread of execution. This is done by calling the *start()* method:

```
ObjectName queueObjName = new ObjectName(":name=Queue");
CounterMonitor monitor = new CounterMonitor();
monitor.setObservedObject(queueObjName);
// . . .
try {
  MBeanServer server = MBeanServerFactory.createMBeanServer();
  ObjectName objName = new ObjectName("Monitor:type=Counter");
  server.registerMBean(monitor, objName);
  monitor.start();
} catch (Exception e) {
  // . . .
}
```

Now that we have a running counter monitor, we need a NotificationListener implementation to handle the notifications sent by the counter monitor. As we discussed earlier in this chapter, there is a single notification type that must be handled by the listener (in addition to the standard error types): jmx.notification.monitor.threshold.

Example 9-1 shows a typical implementation of the listener's *handleNotification()* method.

Example 9-1. Typical listener implementation

```
public class Listener implements NotificationListener {
// . . .
  public Listener(NotificationBroadcaster monitor) {
    // . . .
  }
  public Listener (MBeanServer server, ObjectName monitor) {
    // . . .
  }
// . . .
  public void handleNotification(Notification notification, Object obj) {
    String type = notification.getType( );
    if (notification instanceof MonitorNotification) {
      MonitorNotification notif = (MonitorNotification)notification;
      String att = notif.getObservedAttribute( );
      ObjectName obsObj = notif.getObservedObject( );
      if (type.equals("jmx.monitor.counter.threshold")) {
        Object derivedGauge = notif.getDerivedGauge( );
        Object trigger = notif.getTrigger( );
        trace("THRESHOLD EXCEEDED: Attribute: " + att +
              ", Object: " + obsObj + ", Derived Gauge: " +
              derivedGauge + ", Trigger: " + trigger);
      } else if (type.equals("jmx.monitor.error.attribute")) {
        trace("ATTRIBUTE ERROR (" + att + "): " + notif.getMessage( ));
      } else if (type.equals("jmx.monitor.error.type")) {
        trace("ATTRIBUTE TYPE ERROR (" + att + "): " + notif.getMessage( ));
      } else if (type.equals("jmx.monitor.error.mbean")) {
        trace("OBJECT ERROR (" + obsObj + "): " + notif.getMessage( ));
      } else if (type.equals("jmx.monitor.error.runtime")) {
        trace("RUNTIME ERROR (" + obsObj + "): " + notif.getMessage( ));
      } else if (type.equals("jmx.monitor.error.threshold")) {
        trace("THRESHOLD ERROR (" + obsObj + "): " + notif.getMessage( ));
      }
    }
  }
  private void trace (String message) {
    System.out.println(message);
  }
```

In this example, we simply write the notification to System.out. When the notification is received, we make sure that it is a MonitorNotification, then proceed to exploit the information contained within it. We also want to report any errors that occur. Much of the error-handling code in this example will be repeated as we discuss the other monitor types.

Before the notification listener can receive notifications, it must be added to the list of listeners to which the monitor will send its notifications. In this example, the notification listener adds itself to the list in its constructor:

```
    // . . .
    public Listener(NotificationBroadcaster monitor) {
      NotificationFilter filter = null;
```

```
    Object handback = null;
    monitor.addNotificationListener(this, filter, handback);
  }
// . . .
```

Recall that the Monitor base class is a subclass of NotificationBroadcasterSupport and that CounterMonitor is a subclass of Monitor, so if the listener has a reference to the monitor, we can use the *addNotificationListener()* method to add the listener to the list. If the listener does not have a reference to the monitor object, it can use the MBean server to register itself with the monitor, using only the monitor's object name. To do this, we would use the alternate constructor on the Listener class:

```
// . . .
    public Listener(MBeanServer server, ObjectName monitor) {
      NotificationFilter filter = null;
      Object handback = null;
      server.addNotificationListener(monitor, this, null, null);
    }
// . . .
```

Gauge Monitors

As we mentioned in the beginning of this chapter, a gauge monitor is used to monitor an MBean attribute that is:

- Arbitrarily changing in any direction (i.e., up or down)
- One of the Java floating-point types (float or double) or one of the corresponding JDK wrapper classes (Float or Double)

In this section, we will look at the agent code that shows how to use a gauge monitor. When using a gauge monitor, the first thing to do is to create a new instance of the GaugeMonitor class:

```
GaugeMonitor monitor = new GaugeMonitor();
```

After that, the following attributes of the gauge monitor must be set:

- ObservedObject
- ObservedAttribute
- NotifyHigh (must be set to true if a notification is to be sent when the derived gauge exceeds the high threshold)
- NotifyLow (must be set to true if a notification is to be sent when the derived gauge drops below the low threshold)
- HighThreshold
- LowThreshold
- GranularityPeriod

We discussed these attributes earlier in this chapter. Recall that a notification is sent when the derived gauge exceeds the value of HighThreshold (if NotifyHigh has been explicitly set to true) or when the derived gauge drops below the value of LowThreshold (if NotifyLow is set to true). The following example shows how to create an instance of the gauge monitor, set its properties, register the gauge monitor MBean with the MBean server, and start the monitor's thread of execution:

```
ObjectName queueObjName = new ObjectName(":name=Queue");
GaugeMonitor monitor = new GaugeMonitor( );
monitor.setObservedObject(queueObjName);
monitor.setObservedAttribute("AverageUnitProcessingTime");
monitor.setNotifyHigh(true);
monitor.setNotifyLow(true);
monitor.setThresholds(new Float(500), new Float(500));
monitor.setGranularityPeriod(5000);
try {
  MBeanServer server = MBeanServerFactory.createMBeanServer( );
  ObjectName objName = new ObjectName("Monitor:type=Gauge");
  server.registerMBean(monitor, objName);
  monitor.start( );
} catch (Exception e) {
  // . . .
}
```

As with the counter monitor, we need a listener for the gauge monitor. The following example shows a typical listener implementation. The error-handling code from Example 9-1 is not repeated in this example, as it is exactly the same.

```
public class Listener implements NotificationListener {
// . . .
  public Listener(NotificationBroadcaster monitor) {
    // . . .
  }
  public Listener (MBeanServer server, ObjectName monitor) {
    // . . .
  }
// . . .
  public void handleNotification(Notification notification, Object obj) {
    String type = notification.getType();
    if (notification instanceof MonitorNotification) {
      MonitorNotification notif = (MonitorNotification)notification;
      String att = notif.getObservedAttribute( );
      ObjectName obsObj = notif.getObservedObject( );
      if (type.equals("jmx.monitor.gauge.high")) {
        Object derivedGauge = notif.getDerivedGauge( );
        Object trigger = notif.getTrigger( );
        trace("HIGH THRESHOLD EXCEEDED: Attribute: " + att +
              ", Object: " + obsObj + ", Derived Gauge: " +
              derivedGauge + ", Trigger: " + trigger);
      else if (type.equals("jmx.monitor.gauge.low")) {
        Object derivedGauge = notif.getDerivedGauge( );
```

```
        Object trigger = notif.getTrigger();
        trace("LOW THRESHOLD EXCEEDED: Attribute: " + att +
            ", Object: " + obsObj + ", Derived Gauge: " +
            derivedGauge + ", Trigger: " + trigger);
    }
    // error handling code here. . .
  }
}
private void trace (String message) {
  System.out.println(message);
}
```

In this example, we handle the two threshold notifications that are specific to gauge monitors and write the relevant information contained in the notifications to System.out. Just as with a counter monitor, the listener must register its interest in receiving notifications from the monitor. This is done in the same way regardless of the monitor type.

String Monitors

As we mentioned in the beginning of this chapter, a string monitor is used to monitor an MBean attribute that:

- Matches a predefined value
- Differs from a predefined value
- Is of type String

In this section, we will look at the agent code that shows how to use a string monitor. When using a string monitor, the first thing to do is to create a new instance of the StringMonitor class:

```
StringMonitor monitor = new StringMonitor();
```

After that, the following attributes of the string monitor must be set:

- ObservedObject
- ObservedAttribute
- StringToCompare
- NotifyMatch (must be set to true if a notification is to be sent when the derived gauge matches StringToCompare)
- NotifyDiffer (must be set to true if a notification is to be sent when the derived gauge differs from StringToCompare)
- GranularityPeriod

We discussed most of these attributes earlier in this chapter. When the derived gauge differs from StringToCompare and NotifyDiffer is set to true, a difference notification is sent. By the same token, if StringToCompare matches the derived gauge and

NotifyMatch is set to true, a match notification is sent. The following example shows how to use both of these notifications in conjunction to monitor a String attribute:

```
try {
    StringMonitor monitor = new StringMonitor();
    monitor.setObservedObject(new ObjectName("UserDomain:name=Controller"));
    monitor.setObservedAttribute("OperatorName");
    monitor.setNotifyMatch(true);
    monitor.setNotifyDiffer(true);
    monitor.setStringToCompare("Unassigned");
    monitor.setGranularityPeriod(5000);
    MBeanServer server = MBeanServerFactory.createMBeanServer();
    ObjectName objName =  new ObjectName("Monitor:type=String");
    server.registerMBean(monitor, objName);
    monitor.start();
} catch (Exception e) {
    // . . .
}
```

In this example, the Controller class has an attribute called OperatorName that designates the name of the operator watching the management console. When an instance of Controller is created, this attribute is initialized to "Unassigned", and match notifications are sent every five seconds (note the GranularityPeriod attribute). However, as soon as the operator changes the value of the OperatorName attribute, a different notification will be sent.

Other Issues

The JMX monitoring services can be very useful in providing you with an off-the-shelf implementation of a notification broadcaster that is geared for watching attribute values. However, this convenience comes at a price.

First, a monitor can be used to watch only a single attribute of a single MBean. If you would like to monitor multiple resources in your application, you must create a monitor of the appropriate type for every attribute of every MBean you want to monitor.

Second, a monitor must watch the attribute value of an MBean in its own thread of execution, so that, regardless of what the application is doing, the monitor can "spy" on the attribute value and report the results accordingly. Thus, for every monitor, a new thread in the JVM running your application must be created.

Finally, in the JMX 1.0 RI, each time the granularity period elapses and the monitor thread checks the MBean attribute, that thread is replaced with an entirely new thread! This is an odd implementation and can be fairly resource-intensive, depending on which operating system your application runs and how efficiently thread creation and scheduling occurs.

CHAPTER 10

The Timer Service

The timer service is a special-purpose notification broadcaster designed to send notifications at specific time intervals, starting at a particular date and time. Like the other agent services we have looked at, the timer service is required for all compliant JMX implementations. In addition, the timer service is an MBean, so it can be managed (although it does not have to be registered with the MBean server to be used). There are two primary uses of the timer service:

- To send a single notification to all listeners interested in that notification type
- To send multiple notifications that repeat at specific intervals for a set number of times, or indefinitely

The timer service is capable of sending any number of notifications at different intervals. Each notification that is to be sent by the timer service is given a notification type, defined by the agent that instructs the timer service to send that notification. In other words, unlike the monitoring services, the timer service does not send a predefined set of notification types. Instead, the agent tells the timer service what notification types to send, as well as when to start sending the notification, how many times the notification is to repeat, and the amount of time that is to elapse between each notification (for repeating notifications only, of course).

The timer service is implemented through the use of three classes:

Timer
> The class that contains the implementation of the timer service

TimerMBean
> The management interface of the timer service

TimerNotification
> A subclass of Notification that defines an additional field to specialize the notifications sent by the timer service

Figure 10-1 shows the relationship between these classes in UML notation.

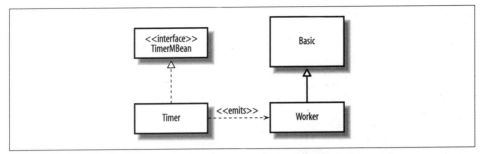

Figure 10-1. UML diagram showing the relationships between the timer service classes

In this chapter, we will look at the classes in Figure 10-1 in detail, starting with the Timer class. At the end of the chapter, we will look at two applications of the timer service:

Scheduler
A simple scheduler that kicks off the sample application after a certain date

Repeated notifications
The logging facility of the sample application, which queues the messages to be written to the log and writes them to disk each time it receives a notification

The Timer Class

The Timer class is a part of the RI and contains the implementation of the timer service. Like the monitoring service classes, the Timer class uses a separate thread of execution to perform its functions. This thread is responsible for checking the list of registered listeners, sending them notifications, and managing the parameters controlling the emission of any notifications sent. The management interface of the timer service is contained in TimerMBean and contains all of the methods necessary for manipulating the timer service.

 Unless otherwise specified, whenever we talk about certain restrictions or behavior of the timer service, we are referring to a single instance of the Timer class.

The TimerMBean interface is shown in Example 10-1.

Example 10-1. The TimerMBean interface
```
public interface TimerMBean {
  public Integer addNotification(String type, String message, Object userData, Date date)
    throws java.lang.IllegalArgumentException;
  public Integer addNotification(String type, String message, Object userData,
                      Date date, long period)
    throws java.lang.IllegalArgumentException;
```

Example 10-1. The TimerMBean interface (continued)

```
    public Integer addNotification(String type, String message, Object userData,
                                   Date date, long period, long nbOccurences)
      throws java.lang.IllegalArgumentException;
    public boolean getSendPastNotifications( );
    public void setSendPastNotifications(boolean value);
    public void removeNotification(Integer id)
      throws InstanceNotFoundException;
    public void removeNotifications(String type)
      throws InstanceNotFoundException;
    public void removeAllNotifications( );
    public void start( );
    public void stop( );
    public int getNbNotifications( );
    public Vector getAllNotificationIDs( );
    public Vector getNotificationIDs(String type);
    public String getNotificationType(Integer id);
    public String getNotificationMessage(Integer id);
    public Object getNotificationUserData(Integer id);
    public Date getDate(Integer id);
    public Long getPeriod(Integer id);
    public Long getNbOccurences(Integer id);
    public boolean isActive( );
    public boolean isEmpty( );
}
```

The first method we will look at is *addNotification()*, which is used by the agent to tell the timer service about a new notification it is to send. As you can see from Example 10-1, there are three ways to do this (i.e., there are three versions of *addNotification()*), each of which has the following parameters in common:

type

> A user-defined String that serves as the notification type and is sent along with the notification to interested listeners. Multiple notifications with the same *type* may be added.

message

> A String message that is sent along with the notification to interested listeners.

userData

> An Object that is sent along with the notification to interested listeners.

date

> A Date object that contains the date and time at which the first notification is to be sent.

These parameters are the only ones that the first version of *addNotification()* takes. A notification added using the first version of *addNotification()* will be sent only once:

```
    try {
      Timer timer = new Timer( );
      timer.addNotification("sample.timer.flushlog", null, null, new Date( ));
```

```
      timer.addNotificationListener(/* listener here */, null, null);
      timer.start( );
   } catch (IllegalArgumentException e) {
      // . . .
   }
```

Once the notification has been sent, it is removed from the list of notifications that are sent by the timer service.

The second version of *addNotification( )* takes an additional parameter, *period*, which is used to specify the amount of time that should elapse (in milliseconds) between notifications. If zero (0) is passed as this parameter, the notification will be sent only once (this has the same effect as using the first version of this method). Otherwise, the notification will repeat indefinitely at the interval specified by *period*:

```
   try {
      Timer timer = new Timer( );
      // repeat the notification every 5 seconds. . .
      timer.addNotification("sample.timer.flushlog", null, null, new Date( ), 5000);
      timer.addNotificationListener(/* listener here */, null, null);
      timer.start( );
   } catch (IllegalArgumentException e) {
      // . . .
   }
```

The third version of this method takes the *period* parameter as well as a parameter called *nbOccurences* (sic), which is the number of times the notification is to repeat at the interval specified by *period*. If the *nbOccurences* parameter is 0, the notifications will repeat indefinitely (as long as the *period* parameter is not 0), which has the same effect as using the second version of *addNotification( )*.

```
   try {
      Timer timer = new Timer( );
      // repeat the notification 10 times, 5 seconds apart
      timer.addNotification("sample.timer.flushlog", null, null, new Date( ), 5000, 10);
      timer.addNotificationListener(/* listener here */, null, null);
      timer.start( );
   } catch (IllegalArgumentException e) {
      // . . .
   }
```

Once the notification has been sent *nbOccurences* times, the notification is removed from the list of notifications sent by the timer service.

If the *date* parameter is null, or if either of the *period* or *nbOccurences* parameters are less than zero, an IllegalArgumentException will be thrown.

If the *date* parameter represents a date that is earlier than the current date, the timer service will increment *date* by *period* until the next notification date is later than the current date. If *nbOccurences* is specified, each time *period* is added to the notification date, 1 will be subtracted from *nbOccurences*. For example, suppose that *date* is 10,351 milliseconds earlier than the current date, *period* is 5000 and *nbOccurences* is

100. The timer service will add 5,000 to *date* as many times as it takes for the next notification date to be later than the current date (subject to the value of *nbOccurences*, of course). In this example, the timer service must do so three times, at which point the next notification date will be 4,649 milliseconds later than the current date. Likewise, *nbOccurences* is decremented three times, such that, after updating the notification date, 97 notifications remain.

Depending on the values of *date*, *period*, and *nbOccurences*, the notification may never be added at all. The following scenarios will result in an IllegalArgument-Exception (in each of these scenarios, the specified *date* parameter is earlier than the current date):

- *period* is zero, meaning that the notification should be sent only once. However, the notification date is earlier than the current date, so the *period* argument of zero is not allowed.

- *period* is greater than zero, meaning that the notification will repeat, but *date* is so much earlier than the current date that, after adding *period* to *date nbOccurences* times, the next notification date is still earlier than the current date.

If either of these scenarios occurs, the notification is never added to the list of notifications to be sent. The notification is added only after the notification date has successfully been updated to a date later than the current date. Once it has successfully been added, though, it is possible for the timer service to send any past notifications in order for the date represented by *date* to catch up to the current date. This may result in a flurry of notifications being sent. However, if this is the desired behavior, you can use the *setSendPastNotifications( )* method (passing true as the boolean argument) to enable this behavior. This feature of the timer service is somewhat analogous to a store-and-forward feature, guaranteeing that notifications that should have been sent (in the case of, say, a system restart) will be sent.

> The send past notifications feature applies to every notification added to the timer service instance prior to calling the timer's *start( )* method. Past notifications will not be sent for any notifications added after *start( )* is called, regardless of the notification start date. It is not possible to selectively send past notifications (i.e., for some notifications and not for others) for a particular instance of the timer service. If this sort of selective behavior is required, you must create more than once instance of the Timer object. Notifications that require this behavior will then use the Timer object that has this feature enabled.

Notice that the return value of *addNotification( )* is an Integer object. Each notification that is added is assigned a unique ID that can be used as a token to obtain information about the notification. There are several methods that require this ID as a parameter, so make sure to save the ID when you add a notification.

```
try {
    Timer timer = new Timer();
    // repeat the notification 10 times, 5 seconds apart
    Integer ID = timer.addNotification("sample.timer.flushlog", null, null,
                                    new Date(), 5000, 10);
    timer.addNotificationListener(/* listener here */, null, null);
    timer.start();
} catch (IllegalArgumentException e) {
    // . . .
}
```

 Notifications that will be sent a limited number of times (e.g., when you are using the first version of *addNotification()*, or using the third version and specifying *nbOccurences* to be greater than zero) are removed from the list of notifications sent by the timer service once that limit has been reached. Once a notification has been removed, the ID returned when the notification was added is no longer valid.

The timer service provides three methods that allow for removal of one or more notifications. The first, *removeNotification()*, removes a single notification, based on the ID that corresponds to that specific notification:

```
try {
    Timer timer = new Timer();
    // repeat the notification 10 times, 5 seconds apart
    Integer ID = timer.addNotification("sample.timer.flushlog", null, null,
                                    new Date(), 5000, 10);
    timer.addNotificationListener(/* listener here */, null, null);
    timer.start();
    // later . . .
    timer.removeNotification(ID);
} catch (IllegalArgumentException e) {
    // . . .
} catch (InstanceNotFoundException e) {
    // . . .
}
```

Of course, to use this version of *removeNotification()*, we must store the return value from *addNotification()* somewhere so that we can pass it as a parameter. In addition, we must anticipate an InstanceNotFoundException being thrown if the ID passed in does not match any notifications in the timer service's list. The most likely cause of this is that the notification has expired and been removed from the list.

The second version of *removeNotification()* takes a String that contains the notification type, so that all notifications of that type may be removed from the timer service's list of notifications. Recall that the timer service supports adding the same notification type multiple times. For example, we could add the notification type sample.timer.flushlog more than once, and pass a different user-defined object each time. This allows us to handle the same notification type in different ways.

```
try {
  Timer timer = new Timer( );
  // repeat the notification 10 times, 5 seconds apart
  timer.addNotification("sample.timer.flushlog", null, null, new Date( ), 5000, 10);
  timer.addNotificationListener(/* listener here */, null, null);
  timer.start( );
  // later . . .
  timer.removeNotification("sample.timer.flushlog");
} catch (IllegalArgumentException e) {
  // . . .
} catch (InstanceNotFoundException e) {
  // . . .
}
```

When using this method to do a wholesale removal of a particular notification type, you don't need the IDs that were generated by the timer service when the individual notifications were added; the notification type is sufficient. If the notification type string specified does not match any of the notification types in the timer service's list of notifications, an `InstanceNotFoundException` will be thrown.

The final way to remove notifications from the timer service is to use *removeAllNotifications()*, which, as its name implies, removes every notification in the timer service. Following a call to this method, the timer service will not send any further notifications, because they have all been removed! This method is very simple to use and throws no exceptions:

```
try {
  Timer timer = new Timer( );
  // repeat the notification 10 times, 5 seconds apart
  timer.addNotification("sample.timer.flushlog", null, null, new Date( ), 5000, 10);
  timer.addNotificationListener(/* listener here */, null, null);
  timer.start( );
  // later . . .
  timer.removeAllNotifications( );
} catch (IllegalArgumentException e) {
  // . . .
}
```

There are a number of utility methods provided by the timer service that allow you to get information about its current state, as well as information about a particular notification or group of notifications. If no notifications have been added, or the *removeAllNotifications()* method has been called, the *isEmpty()* method will return true. Calling this method allows agents to determine whether or not the timer service's list of notifications is empty.

The second utility method, *getSendPastNotifications()*, returns a boolean value indicating whether or not the timer service will send out past notifications when the date specified for the notification to begin is earlier than the current date. If this method returns true, the send past notifications feature is enabled.

If you need to know how many notifications are in the timer service's list of notifications, use the *getNbNotifications()* method. This method returns the number of unique notifications that will be sent, not the number of different notification types that have been added. For example, if we add the notification type `sample.timer.flushlog` three times (and no other notifications), *getNbNotifications()* will return 3.

If you need all of the notification IDs for a particular notification type that are contained in the timer service's list of notifications, use *getNotificationIDs()*. This method takes the notification type string and returns a `java.util.Vector` object. Inside the `Vector` object are the IDs (which are `Integer` objects) that were generated by the timer service for that notification type. This method is a convenient way to obtain the IDs of a particular notification type if the individual IDs were not stored somewhere following the respective calls to *addNotification()*.

The timer service also provides a method to obtain all of the notification IDs for all active notifications. This method, *getAllNotificationIDs()*, returns a `Vector` that contains the IDs for all of the notifications in the list.

If we have the ID for a particular notification, we can get detailed information about that notification. There are five pieces of information that can be provided about a notification (recall our discussion of the *addNotification()* method) and five methods that provide that information:

- *getNotificationMessage()*, which returns the notification message
- *getUserData()*, which returns the user-defined object
- *getDate()*, which returns the date the notifications are to begin
- *getPeriod()*, which returns the period of time between notifications
- *getNbOccurences()*, which returns the number of times the notification is to be sent

Whenever the timer service sends a notification to a listener, it is an instance of the `TimerNotification` class that is sent. `TimerNotification` is a subclass of `Notification` and adds an additional read-only attribute, `NotificationID`. Other than this attribute, a `TimerNotification` should be processed just like any other notification. `TimerNotification` has a single constructor, whose job is to set the `NotificationID` attribute and delegate the rest to `Notification`.

Using the Timer Service

In this section, we will look at two examples of possible applications of the timer service. We will look at enough of the source code in this chapter to discuss the fundamental concepts, but you will get the most benefit from this chapter by having the full source listings available. In the first example, we will use the timer service as a scheduler to start the sample application via a timer notification that is emitted once.

The second example shows how to use the timer service to handle repeated timer notifications to write log messages to disk.

As we've seen, the minimal steps to use the timer service are:

1. Create the timer service by instantiating the Timer class.

2. Add a notification, which includes at a minimum the notification type (which is up to you to define) and the date the notification is to start.

3. Add a notification listener to the timer service.

4. Start the timer.

Step 2 is repeated for each notification type that is to be sent by the timer service. Step 3 is repeated for as many notification listeners as are needed in the system. In the sample application code for this chapter, there are two notification types:

sample.timer.startController
> The notification type string that indicates the controller is to be started

sample.timer.flushlog
> The notification type string that indicates that any queued messages are to be written (i.e., committed) to the log

There are also two notification listeners:

sample.timer.Scheduler
> The class that is responsible for creating the timer service and adding the above notifications

sample.utility.MessageLogQueue
> The class that is used to queue log messages, listen for sample.timer.flushlog notifications, and write them to the disk-based log file

The Scheduler class acts as the JMX agent for our example. Example 10-2 shows a partial source listing for this class.

Example 10-2. Partial source listing of the Scheduler class

```
package sample.timer;
import sample.utility.*;
// . . .
public class Scheduler {
  public static void main(String[] args) {
    try {
      Properties props = new Properties();
      FileInputStream propFile = new FileInputStream("scheduler.properties");
      props.load(propFile);
      String controllerStartWaitTime = (String)props.get("controller.startWaitTime");
      long startTime = System.currentTimeMillis() +
        (new Long(controllerStartWaitTime)).longValue();
      Date startDate = new Date(startTime);
      Timer timer = new Timer();
      // Add notification that starts the controller. . .
```

Example 10-2. Partial source listing of the Scheduler class (continued)

```
            timer.addNotification("sample.timer.controllerStart",
                                  null,
                                  props,
                                  startDate);
            Listener listener = new Listener();
            timer.addNotificationListener(listener, null, null);
            // add notification that flushes the log. . .
            String logFlushWaitTime = (String)props.get("logger.flushWaitTime");
            timer.addNotification("sample.timer.flushlog",
                                  "Time to flush the log to disk.",
                                  null,
                                  new Date(),
                                  (new Long(logFlushWaitTime)).longValue());
            timer.addNotificationListener(MessageLogQueue.instance(),
                                          null,
                                          null);
            timer.start();
            ObjectName objName = new ObjectName("Timer:type=generic");
            MBeanServer mbs = MBeanServerFactory.createMBeanServer();
            mbs.registerMBean(timer, objName);
        } catch (Exception e) {
        }
    }
}
```

The *main()* method of Scheduler contains the agent code for our example and reads the following properties from the file *scheduler.properties*:

Controller start wait time

> The number of milliseconds to delay before starting the controller, used to calculate the start date for sending the sample.timer.startController notification

Log queue flush wait time

> The number of milliseconds to wait before sending the sample.timer.flushlog notifications, which results in the listener writing any queued log messages to disk

Consumer work factor

> The number of prime numbers calculated by the consumer thread for each item it removes from the queue

Supplier work factor

> The number of prime numbers calculated by the supplier thread for each item it adds to the queue

Example 10-3 shows the contents of this file.

Example 10-3. The scheduler.properties file

```
controller.startWaitTime=60000
logger.flushWaitTime=10000
controller.supplier.workFactor=150
controller.consumer.workFactor=100
```

Using the property values in this file, the controller will start in approximately one minute and the queued log messages will be written to disk every 10 seconds.

Once the start wait time for the controller is read from the properties file, that wait time is added to the current system time to calculate the date (in milliseconds) when the notification to start the controller will be sent. Next, the timer service is created and the controller start notification is added. Notice that the Properties object we created earlier is passed as the *userData* parameter to the *addNotification()* call. This allows the listener access to the properties from *scheduler.properties*. Next, we create an instance of the Listener class, which will receive the notification to start the controller. We tell the timer service to send this notification to Listener by calling the timer's *addNotificationListener()* method.

The second notification to be added is the one to flush any queued log messages to the log file on disk. Notice that we do not use a *userData* object in this case, and we indicate this by passing null on the *addNotification()* call. We indicate to the timer service that the notifications are to begin immediately by creating a new Date object, using Date's default constructor. Finally, we indicate to the timer service that this notification is to be sent repeatedly, at an interval indicated by the value of the logger.flushWaitTime property. The MessageLogQueue class acts as a queue of log messages, which are not committed to the log file until it receives a notification to do so. It is implemented as a singleton* so that it can be shared by all other objects in the system. It is the MessageLogQueue that will act as the listener for this notification, and we obtain a reference to the singleton by calling its *instance()* method.

Once the notifications and listeners have been added, the timer service is started by calling its *start()* method. The timer service is an MBean, so we create an object name for it and register it with the MBean server. This allows the timer service to be monitored and controlled.

Handling the Controller Start Notification

When the controller start notification is sent, the Listener class handles the notification:

```
package sample.timer;

import javax.management.*;

public class Listener implements NotificationListener {
  public void handleNotification(Notification notification, Object obj) {
    String type = notification.getType();
    if (notification instanceof TimerNotification) {
      TimerNotification notif = (TimerNotification)notification;
```

---

* See Gamma, et al. *Design Patterns*. Reading, MA: Addison Wesley, 1994.

```
if (type.equals("sample.timer.controllerStart")) {
    Properties props = (Properties)notif.getUserData();
    final String cwf =
        (String)props.getProperty("controller.consumer.workFactor");
    final String swf =
        (String)props.getProperty("controller.supplier.workFactor");
    Thread t = new Thread(new Runnable() {
        public void run() {
            Controller.main(new String[] {cwf, swf});
        }
    } );
    t.start();
        }
      }
    }
}
```

The code for the Listener class is relatively simple, as it has to implement only the *handleNotification()* method of NotificationListener. Recall that when the timer service sends a notification, an instance of the TimerNotification class is emitted to all interested listeners. This is the only type of notification in which Listener is interested. If the notification is not of the right type (sample.timer.controllerStart), it is ignored. If the notification type string is of the correct type, the *getUserData()* method of the Notification class (TimerNotification's parent class) is invoked to retrieve the Properties object we stored there when the controller start notification was added to the timer service. The Controller is started on a separate thread of execution, because *Controller.main()* does not terminate until all other threads in Controller (e.g., consumer and supplier threads) are finished. If we don't start the Controller on its own thread from *handleNotification()*, it may hang the timer service's notification thread if we run the code on single-processor systems, and other notifications may not be sent by the timer service until *Controller.main()* is finished executing!

Handling the Message Queue Flush Notification

When the notification to flush queued messages to disk is sent by the timer service, the MessageLogQueue class handles it:

```
package sample.utility;

import javax.management.*;
public class MessageLogQueue extends MessageLog
    implements NotificationListener {
    // singleton stuff. . .
    private static MessageLogQueue _instance = null;
    public static MessageLogQueue instance() {
        if (_instance == null)
            _instance = new MessageLogQueue();
        return _instance;
    }
```

```
  private ArrayList _store = new ArrayList(10);
  public synchronized void write(String message) {
    _store.add(message);
  }
  public synchronized void write(Throwable t) {
    _store.add(t);
  }

  public synchronized void handleNotification(Notification notification,
                                              Object obj) {
    if (notification instanceof TimerNotification) {
      String type = notification.getType();
      if (type.equals("sample.timer.flushlog")) {
        if (_store.size() > 0) {
          Iterator iter = _store.iterator();
          while (iter.hasNext()) {
            Object message = iter.next();
            if (message instanceof String)
              super.write((String)message);
            else if (message instanceof Throwable)
              super.write((Throwable)message);
          }
          _store.clear();
        }
      }
    }
  }
}
```

The emphasized lines in this code point out some of the features of the
MessageLogQueue class. First, the class is implemented using the singleton pattern, so
that there is only one instance of the class for the process (i.e., the JVM)—this allows
all classes in the JVM to write their log messages to the log file in an asynchronous
fashion. The backing store for the "queue" inside MessageLogQueue is an ArrayList,
and access to the contents of the list must be synchronized.

As we saw earlier, if the Notification object that is sent is not a TimerNotification, it
is simply ignored. This goes for the notification type as well, which must be sample.
timer.flushlog. Any messages in the backing store for the queue are written out one
at a time using an Iterator. Because both String and Throwable message types are
allowed, the Java keyword instanceof is used to determine the type of the current
entry in the list, so that it can be appropriately cast when delegating to the superclass's *write()* method. Once the contents of the queue have been written to the log
file, the backing store for the queue is emptied and is ready for the next batch of
messages.

CHAPTER 11

The Relation Service

The relation service provides a facility to associate MBeans with each other. You use the metadata classes provided by the relation service to describe and then establish *n*-ary relationships between registered MBeans, as dictated by your application policies. You then use the relation service to maintain the consistency of those relationships so that those application policies are followed. The relation service must be implemented by every compliant JMX implementation.

In this chapter, we will examine the JMX relation service and see how to write code to use it. We will begin with an overview of the concepts employed by the relation service, such as roles and relations, then we will look at the relation service classes that implement these concepts. Next, we will see how to write code to use the relation service classes to describe relationships between MBeans used in the sample application. This chapter concludes with a look at the support classes provided by the relation service, their purpose, and how to use them.

The code we will develop in this chapter to describe relations, roles, etc. runs within an agent. Thus, I will use the terms "we" and "you" synonymously with "the agent."

Introduction

To use the relation service effectively, you need to understand a few key concepts:

Role
> A named category of functionality that is performed by an MBean. For example, in the sample application, there are two subclasses of Worker whose names correspond to the roles they perform: Consumer and Supplier. A role describes the MBean objects that perform that role and is implemented by the Role class.

Role information
> Metadata about a role, such as the role name and the minimum and maximum number of MBeans that are allowed to perform that role. Role information is implemented by the RoleInfo class.

Relation type

Metadata that describes the relationships between `RoleInfo` objects. The `RelationType` interface provides information about the relation type, such as the name of the relation type and the various roles that make up that type. The relation service provides a method, *createRelationType()*, that allows the agent to easily create relation type objects that the relation service will maintain internally. Relation types created by the relation service and maintained internally are called *internal relation types*. Compliant JMX implementations of the relation service also provide a class called `RelationTypeSupport` that the agent can subclass (or use as-is) that handles relation types in a generic fashion. These relation types are called *external relation types* and are added to the relation service through its *addRelationType()* method.

Relation

An instance of a relation type. It is critical to the correct functioning of the relation service that all relation types remain *consistent*. In other words, the metadata describing the relationship between MBeans (i.e., the relation type) provides the constraints on the relation that allow the relation service to be used to ensure that the relation remains consistent at all times. Once a relation has been instantiated, it must remain consistent, or the relation service will throw an exception.

Each of these concepts is implemented in the JMX RI as a class in the `javax.management.relation` package.

The `Relation` interface provides information about the relation, such as the name of the relation (the ID, as it is called in the specification), and access to the `Role` and `RoleInfo` objects that make up the relation. As with relation types, there are two ways to create a relation. The first way is to call the *createRelation()* method of the relation service, which will create an *internal relation* (i.e., one that is maintained internally by the relation service). The second way to create a relation is to use (or subclass) the `RelationSupport` class, instantiate it, and add it to the relation service by calling the *addRelation()* method. This type of relation is referred to as an *external relation*.

It is the responsibility of the agent developer to create the necessary relation classes to describe the roles, relation types, and relations that are to be maintained by the relation service. We will discuss how to do this later in this chapter.

The Basic Relation Service Classes

The relation service classes, which were briefly mentioned in the previous section, are the basic classes needed to describe relationships between MBeans. In this section, we will take a closer look at these classes. The material here will serve as a reference for the next section, in which we will see how to write code to use the relation service. Examples will be provided in this section to point out some of the features of the various classes. In this section, we assume that the relation service has been created and has been given the variable name *relationService*. In the next section, "Using the Relation Service," we will look at more detailed examples.

RoleInfo

The `RoleInfo` class is used to describe the role that one or more MBeans (of the same Java class) perform. `RoleInfo` contains the following read-only attributes:

Name
: The name of the role. Must be unique for any given `RelationType` object.

RefMBeanClassName
: The Java class name of the MBean(s) that will act in the role described by this `RoleInfo` object.

Readable
: Indicates whether or not information about the role can be accessed.

Writable
: Indicates whether or not information about the role can be modified.

MinimumDegree
: The lower bound on the multiplicity (size) of the number of MBeans that may perform the role. Must be less than or equal to the maximum degree.

MaximumDegree
: The upper bound on the multiplicity (size) of the number of MBeans that may perform the role. Must be greater than or equal to the minimum degree.

Description
: A human-readable description of the role.

These attributes are set using one of the three constructors provided by `RoleInfo`:

```
public RoleInfo(String theName, String theRefMBeanClassName)
    throws IllegalArgumentException, ClassNotFoundException, NotCompliantException {
    // . . .
}
public RoleInfo(String theName, String theRefMBeanClassName,
                boolean theIsReadable, boolean theIsWritable)
    throws IllegalArgumentException, ClassNotFoundException, NotCompliantException {
    // . . .
}
public RoleInfo(String theName, String theRefMBeanClassName,
                boolean theIsReadable, boolean theIsWritable,
                int theMinDegree, int theMaxDegree, String theDescription)
    throws IllegalArgumentException, InvalidRoleInfoException,
        ClassNotFoundException, NotCompliantException {
    // . . .
}
```

The first constructor shows the minimum amount of information that the agent must provide about a role: the name of the role and the class names of the MBean instances that act in that role. When you use this constructor, the other values are set to default values. The current default values in the RI are listed in Table 11-1; however, these default values might change in future releases of the JMX specification, so check the Javadoc before using them.

Table 11-1. Default values for RoleInfo attributes

Attribute	Default value
Readable	true
Writable	true
MinimumDegree	1
MaximumDegree	1
Description	null

The second constructor allows the agent to set the Readable and Writable attributes of the role. MinimumDegree and MaximumDegree are set to their default values.

The third constructor allows the agent to set all of the attributes of RoleInfo.

RelationType

The RelationType interface is used to describe a relationship between one or more roles in an *n*-ary association. In this section, we will assume that we are going to use the relation service to create the RelationType object (most likely an instance of RelationSupport) on behalf of the agent, resulting in an internal relation type. To describe a relation type to the relation service, the relation service needs to know two things:

1. What is the name of the association represented by the relation type?
2. What RoleInfo objects are involved in the association?

The name of the association (i.e., the relation type) is a String that must be unique for all relation types that the relation service knows about (otherwise, an exception will be thrown). The agent must also create and pass an array of RoleInfo objects that represent the roles played by MBean instances, which may or may not have been instantiated at this point. The RelationType interface is defined as:

```
package javax.management.relation;

public interface RelationType extends Serializable {
  public String getRelationTypeName();
  public List getRoleInfo();
  public RoleInfo getRoleInfo(String theRoleInfoName)
    throws IllegalArgumentException, RoleInfoNotFoundException;
}
```

Through the RelationType interface, we can get access to the name of the relation type, a java.util.List object containing all of the RoleInfo objects that have been defined for this relation type, and a single RoleInfo object that corresponds to a specific role name. As we mentioned earlier, when discussing RoleInfo, the name given to a RoleInfo object must be unique within any instance of RelationType.

Role

A role is named collection of one or more MBean object names that corresponds to a RoleInfo object. The MBeans do not have to be registered, or even instantiated, to be added to a role. When creating a Role object, we must know the name of the RoleInfo object that describes the role the collection of MBeans will perform—otherwise, the relation service will not correctly map the Role object with its corresponding RoleInfo metadata object and will throw an exception when we attempt to create a relation. By the same token, the MBeans whose object names are part of the role must be instantiated and registered with the MBean server before we attempt to create a relation using the Role object that contains them.

A Role object is created using its lone constructor:

```
public Role(java.lang.String theRoleName, java.util.List theRoleValue)
    throws java.lang.IllegalArgumentException {
    // . . .
}
```

The first argument is the name of the role. It must match the name of a RoleInfo object that has been used to create a relation type. The second argument is a List of MBean object names (i.e., ObjectName objects) that correspond to the MBean objects that will perform the role. If either of the *theRoleName* or the *theRoleValue* parameters are null, an IllegalArgumentException will be thrown.

RoleList

The RoleList class extends java.util.ArrayList and is a list of Role objects. A RoleList object is used primarily to create a relation through the *createRelation()* method of the relation service. The RoleList class is defined as:

```
public class RoleList extends ArrayList {
    public RoleList( ) {
    // . . .
    }
    public RoleList(int theInitialCapacity) {
    // . . .
    }
    public RoleList(List theList) throws IllegalArgumentException {
    // . . .
    }
    public void add(Role theRole) throws IllegalArgumentException {
```

```
  // . . .
  }
  public void add(int theIndex, Role theRole)
    throws IllegalArgumentException, IndexOutOfBoundsException {
  // . . .
  }
  public void set(int theIndex, Role theRole)
    throws IllegalArgumentException, IndexOutOfBoundsException {
  // . . .
  }
  public boolean addAll(RoleList theRoleList)
    throws IndexOutOfBoundsException {
  // . . .
  }
  public boolean addAll(int theIndex, RoleList theRoleList)
    throws IllegalArgumentException, IndexOutOfBoundsException {
  // . . .
  }
  public Object clone( ) {
  // . . .
  }
}
```

A few convenience methods are provided on RoleList that make using it more type-safe with respect to the relation service. For example, one version of the *add()* method takes a *role* parameter, instead of the *object* parameter for the corresponding version of *add()* found in ArrayList.

RelationService

This class is at the heart of the relation service. The methods on this class allow agents to create and remove relation types and relations, find relationships between MBeans, and retrieve specific information about the relations that are maintained by the relation service. The relation service implementation class, RelationService, is too large to show a complete listing here. The methods that we will use most often are:

addRelation()
> Adds an external relation to the relation service

addRelationType()
> Adds an external relation type to the relation service

createRelation()
> Creates an internal relation

createRelationType()
> Creates an internal relation type

getRole()
> Retrieves the list of MBean object names for a specific role name within a specific internal relation

removeRelation( )
> Removes a specific internal relation from the relation service

removeRelationType( )
> Removes a specific internal relation type from the relation service

setRole( )
> Sets a writable role for a specific internal relation

You probably noticed that most of the methods on the `RelationService` class deal with internal relations. As we mentioned earlier, for external relations the relation service provides a class called `RelationSupport`, which we will discuss later in this chapter. The above list of `RelationService` methods is not exhaustive—in the interests of space, I have omitted the less frequently used methods from this discussion. All of the methods are described in the Javadoc delivered with the JMX RI. The `RelationService` class provides a single constructor:

```
public RelationService(boolean theImmediatePurgeFlg) {
    // . . .
}
```

The `boolean` argument to this constructor indicates whether or not the relation service should search for and remove invalid relations from its internal implementation immediately after an MBean that is referenced in a relation is unregistered. If the value of this parameter is `true`, as soon as any referenced MBean is unregistered, the relation service will check to see if the unregistration of the MBean causes any relations to become invalid. Any invalid relations will then be removed from the relation service. If the value of this parameter is `false`, the agent must invoke the relation service's *purgeRelations( )* method in order for this check to be made and any necessary processing to be performed.

For all internal relations, it is the job of the relation service to ensure the consistency of relations.

The `RelationService` class implements an MBean interface, which allows it to be controlled by a management application. Before the relation service can be used, the `RelationService` instance created by the agent must be registered with the MBean server.

RelationTypeSupport

This class is provided by the relation service as a convenience to agent developers so that relation types can be created that are external to the relation service. Typically, we would subclass the `RelationTypeSupport` class, provide our own constructor, and override any methods we deem necessary. For each internal relation type defined using the *createRelationType( )* method of the relation service implementation, an instance of this class is created and maintained by the relation service. However, internal relation types are not directly accessible once they are created. Creating external relation types gives us more flexibility in terms of how to create and maintain relation types. The `RelationTypeSupport` class implements the `RelationType` interface and adds a protected method called *addRoleInfo()*, which allows subclasses to add a `RoleInfo` object to the relation type. There are two constructors for `RelationTypeSupport`:

```
public RelationTypeSupport(String theRelTypeName, RoleInfo[] theRoleInfoArray)
  throws IllegalArgumentException, InvalidRelationTypeException {
  // . . .
}
protected RelationTypeSupport(String theRelTypeName) {
  // . . .
}
```

The `RelationTypeSupport` class does not have to be subclassed, and it provides a public constructor that allows us to specify the relation type name and an array of `RoleInfo` objects. We can use this constructor to create a relation type that is external to the relation service, without having to subclass `RelationTypeSupport`.

Should we choose to subclass `RelationTypeSupport`, however, there is a protected constructor that allows us to specify the name of the relation type. This constructor may be called only from a subclass. Typically we will subclass `RelationTypeSupport`, and in our subclass's constructor we will do two things:

1. Delegate the relation type name to the protected constructor of `RelationTypeSupport`.
2. Create the necessary `RoleInfo` objects and add them to the parent class one at a time, via its protected *addRoleInfo()* method.

Subclasses are also free to override the implementation of the `RelationType` interface provided by `RelationTypeSupport` as necessary.

RelationSupport

Like `RelationTypeSupport`, this class is provided by the relation service as a convenience to agent developers so that relations can be created that are external to the relation service. As with the `RelationTypeSupport` class, we subclass the `RelationSupport` class, provide our own constructor, and override any methods we deem necessary. For each internal relation defined using the *createRelation()* method of the relation service implementation, an instance of this class is created and maintained by the relation service. However, internal relations are not directly accessible once they are created. Creating external relations gives us more flexibility in terms of how to create and maintain the consistency of relations. The `RelationSupport` class implements an MBean interface—`RelationSupportMBean`—that allows external relations to be controlled by a management application. This gives external relations an advantage over internal relations when it is necessary to monitor or control MBean relationships through a management application.

RelationSupport provides two constructors, defined as:

```
public RelationSupport(String theRelId, ObjectName theRelServiceName,
                       String theRelTypeName, RoleList theRoleList)
  throws InvalidRoleValueException, IllegalArgumentException {
  // . . .
}
public RelationSupport(String theRelId, ObjectName theRelServiceName,
                       MBeanServer theRelServiceMBeanServer,
                       String theRelTypeName, RoleList theRoleList)
  throws InvalidRoleValueException, IllegalArgumentException {
  // . . .
}
```

In creating a RelationSupport instance, we must provide (at minimum) the following parameters:

theRelId
> A String that contains the name of the relation.

theRelServiceName
> The object name of the relation service.

theRelTypeName
> The name of the relation type that defines the relationship between the MBeans performing the roles that make up this relation. The relation type can be either external or internal.

theRoleList
> A List of the Role objects that make up this relation.

As we mentioned earlier, the RelationService instance created by the agent must be registered with the MBean server in order to be used. As we can see from the second parameter to both RelationSupport constructors, the object name that is assigned by the agent to the relation service is required in order to create an internal relation. In fact, not only must the object name of the relation service be provided, but the RelationService object must have been instantiated and registered with the MBean server prior to creating an external relation. This is because of certain consistency checks that the relation service makes about the external relation that is created—it cannot make these checks unless the relation service is running (and registered). In addition, the RelationSupport object maintains a reference to the MBean server with which it is registered and uses this reference to indirectly invoke methods on the relation service MBean.

The second constructor is provided only as a convenience to those agents that have not registered the external relation MBean with the MBean server, but will do so before the relation is actually referenced. The third parameter is a reference to the MBean server with which the external relation will be registered. This constructor must be used with care. Under normal circumstances, the external relation is immediately registered with the MBean server when it is created. The RelationSupport class implements the `MBeanRegistration` interface, so it has access to a reference to the MBean server in which it is registered (this reference is passed to the *preRegister()* method). Because the specification does not dictate when the initial consistency checks are made, it is safer to immediately register any external relations with the MBean server once they are instantiated.

Using the Relation Service

In the previous section, we looked at each of the relation service classes that are necessary to create internal and external relations. In this section, we will look at source code examples for creating internal relations, as these are the easiest type to create. All of the source code examples in this section are taken from the `relation` package of the sample application that we have used throughout this book.

Before we can create a relation, we have to create the MBean server and an instance of the relation service MBean, and then register the relation service MBean with the MBean server:

```
try {
  MBeanServer server = MBeanServerFactory.createMBeanServer();
  boolean purgeImmediate = true;
  RelationService rs = new RelationService(purgeImmediate);
  ObjectName rsObjName = new ObjectName("AgentServices:name=Relation");
  server.registerMBean(rs, rsObjName);
  // . . .
} catch (Exception e) {
  // . . .
}
```

Next, we describe the roles in the relation using one or more `RoleInfo` objects:

```
try {
  // . . .
  server.registerMBean(rs, rsObjName);
  RoleInfo[] roleInfo = new RoleInfo[2];
  roleInfo[0] = new RoleInfo(
    "Consumer",                  // role name
    "sample.standard.Consumer",  // class name
    true,                        // role can be read
    true,                        // role can be modified
    1,                           // must be at least one
    2,                           // no more than two
    "Consumer Role Information"  // description
  );
  roleInfo[1] = new RoleInfo(
    "Supplier",                  // role name
    "sample.standard.Supplier",  // class name
    true,                        // role can be read
    true,                        // role can be modified
    1,                           // must be at least one
```

```
      1,                          // no more than one
      "Supplier Role Information" // description
   );
} catch (Exception e) {
   // . . .
}
```

In this case, the relation consists of two roles, Consumer and Supplier, performed by two MBean classes, also called Consumer and Supplier (in the sample application, we reuse the MBean classes from the standard package). There must be at least one and no more than two Consumer MBeans in the relation. Only one Supplier MBean is allowed in the relation. Once the roles have been described using RoleInfo objects, we are ready to describe the relationship between these two roles by creating an internal relation type:

```
try {
   // . . .
   roleInfo[1] = new RoleInfo(
      "Supplier",                 // role name
      "sample.standard.Supplier", // class name
      true,                       // role can be read
      true,                       // role can be modified
      1,                          // must be at least one
      1,                          // no more than one
      "Supplier Role Information" // description
   );
   rs.createRelationType(
      "ConsumerSupplierRelationType_Internal",
      roleInfo
   );
   // . . .
} catch (Exception e) {
   // . . .
}
```

Once the relation type has been created, we instantiate the role by creating a Role object for each group of MBeans to participate in the relation:

```
try {
   // . . .
   rs.createRelationType(
      "ConsumerSupplierRelationType_Internal",
      roleInfo
   );
   // Create and register a Consumer MBean
   ObjectName consumerObjName = createWorker("Consumer", 100);
   ArrayList consumerList = new ArrayList();
   consumerList.add(consumerObjName);
   Role consumerRole = new Role("Consumer", consumerList);
   // Create and register a Supplier MBean
   ObjectName supplierObjName = createWorker("Supplier", 100);
   ArrayList supplierList = new ArrayList();
   supplierList.add(supplierObjName);
```

```
        Role supplierRole = new Role("Supplier", supplierList);
        RoleList roles = new RoleList();
        roles.add(consumerRole);
        roles.add(supplierRole);
        // . . .
    } catch (Exception e) {
        // . . .
    }
```

In this example, we use the *createWorker()* method to create and register with the MBean server an instance of each worker type. Once the Role objects are created, we create a RoleList object to contain the Role objects. The final step is to use the relation service to create an internal relation:

```
    try {
        // . . .
        RoleList roles = new RoleList();
        roles.add(consumerRole);
        roles.add(supplierRole);
        rs.createRelation(
            "ConsumerSupplierRelation_Internal",
            "ConsumerSupplierRelationType_Internal",
            roles
        );
    } catch (Exception e) {
        // . . .
    }
```

Example 11-1 shows a complete source listing of how to create the internal Consumer/Supplier relation we've been examining.

Example 11-1. Creating an internal relation

```
try {
  MBeanServer server = MBeanServerFactory.createMBeanServer();
  boolean purgeImmediate = true;
  RelationService rs = new RelationService(purgeImmediate);
  ObjectName rsObjName = new ObjectName("AgentServices:name=Relation");
  server.registerMBean(rs, rsObjName);
  RoleInfo[] roleInfo = new RoleInfo[2];
  roleInfo[0] = new RoleInfo(
    "Consumer",                 // role name
    "sample.standard.Consumer", // class name
    true,                       // role can be read
    true,                       // role can be modified
    1,                          // must be at least one
    2,                          // no more than two
    "Consumer Role Information" // description
  );
  roleInfo[1] = new RoleInfo(
    "Supplier",                 // role name
    "sample.standard.Supplier", // class name
    true,                       // role can be read
    true,                       // role can be modified
```

Example 11-1. Creating an internal relation (continued)

```
    1,                          // must be at least one
    1,                          // no more than one
    "Supplier Role Information" // description
  );
  rs.createRelationType(
    "ConsumerSupplierRelationType_Internal",
    roleInfo
  );
  // Create and register a Consumer MBean
  ObjectName consumerObjName = createWorker("Consumer", 100);
  ArrayList consumerList = new ArrayList();
  consumerList.add(consumerObjName);
  Role consumerRole = new Role("Consumer", consumerList);
  // Create and register a Supplier MBean
  ObjectName supplierObjName = createWorker("Supplier", 100);
  ArrayList supplierList = new ArrayList();
  supplierList.add(supplierObjName);
  Role supplierRole = new Role("Supplier", supplierList);
  RoleList roles = new RoleList();
  roles.add(consumerRole);
  roles.add(supplierRole);
  rs.createRelation(
    "ConsumerSupplierRelation_Internal",
    "ConsumerSupplierRelationType_Internal",
    roles
  );
} catch (Exception e) {
  // . . .
}
```

Using the Relation Service Support Classes

In the previous section, we worked through a complete example of how to create an internal relation using an internal relation type. In this section, we will look at the same example, only we will see how to create the relation as an external relation using an external relation type. As we mentioned, the relation service provides a number of support classes that can be used for this purpose. At the risk of being a bit redundant, we will repeat the flow of the previous section as closely as possible so you can compare the internal and external relations and relation types.

Before we can create a relation, we have to create the MBean server and an instance of the relation service MBean, and then register the relation MBean with the MBean server:

```
try {
  MBeanServer server = MBeanServerFactory.createMBeanServer();
  boolean purgeImmediate = true;
  RelationService rs = new RelationService(purgeImmediate);
  ObjectName rsObjName = new ObjectName("AgentServices:name=Relation");
```

```
    server.registerMBean(rs, rsObjName);
    // . . .
  } catch (Exception e) {
    // . . .
  }
```

As we saw with an internal relation type, we next describe the roles in the relation using one or more RoleInfo objects. However, to create an external relation type, we subclass the RelationTypeSupport class and add code to the subclass constructor to create the RoleInfo objects:

```
public class ConsumerSupplierRelationType extends RelationTypeSupport {
  public ConsumerSupplierRelationType () {
    super("ConsumerSupplierRelationType_External");
    try {
      addRoleInfo(new RoleInfo("Consumer",
                               "sample.standard.Consumer",
                               true,
                               false,
                               1,
                               2,
                               "Consumer Role Information"));
      addRoleInfo(new RoleInfo("Supplier",
                               "sample.standard.Supplier",
                               true,
                               false,
                               1,
                               1,
                               "Supplier Role Information"));
    } catch (Exception e) {
      throw  new RuntimeException(e.getMessage( ));
    }
  }
}
```

The emphasized lines point out some of the things we have to do in preparation for creating an external relation type. First, we subclass RelationTypeSupport with a class called ConsumerSupplierRelationType. In the subclass constructor, we delegate to one of the constructors of RelationTypeSupport, passing the name of the relation type. Then we call the *addRoleInfo()* method, passing in a new RoleInfo instance for each of the roles in the relation type.

This time, instead of using the relation service to create the relation type, we will do it explicitly by instantiating the ConsumerSupplierRelationType class. Once we instantiate the class representing the external relation type, we add the relation type to the relation service via the *addRelationType()* method:

```
  try {
    MBeanServer server = MBeanServerFactory.createMBeanServer( );
    boolean purgeImmediate = true;
    RelationService rs = new RelationService(purgeImmediate);
```

```
      ObjectName rsObjName = new ObjectName("AgentServices:name=Relation");
      server.registerMBean(rs, rsObjName);
      ConsumerSupplierRelationType rt = new ConsumerSupplierRelationType( );
      rs.addRelationType(rt);
      // . . .
   } catch (Exception e) {
      // . . .
   }
```

Before we continue, I should point out that you can use RelationTypeSupport on its own (i.e., without subclassing it). You may have noticed in the example above that we don't do much with the relation type subclass, other than delegate to the parent. Subclassing RelationTypeSupport is a way to encapsulate role information inside a class, and it offers us a way to separate concerns in the design of our agents. However, if this separation of concerns is not strictly necessary, we can still create an external relation type without using a subclass:

```
   try {
      MBeanServer server = MBeanServerFactory.createMBeanServer( );
      boolean purgeImmediate = true;
      RelationService rs = new RelationService(purgeImmediate);
      ObjectName rsObjName = new ObjectName("AgentServices:name=Relation");
      server.registerMBean(rs, rsObjName);
      RoleInfo[] roleInfo = new RoleInfo[2];
      roleInfo[0] = new RoleInfo(
         Consumer.ROLE,              // role name
         "sample.standard.Consumer", // class name
         true,                       // role can be read
         true,                       // role can be modified
         1,                          // must be at least one
         2,                          // no more than two
         "Consumer Role Information" // description
      );
      roleInfo[1] = new RoleInfo(
         Supplier.ROLE,              // role name
         "sample.standard.Supplier", // class name
         true,                       // role can be read
         true,                       // role can be modified
         1,                          // must be at least one
         1,                          // no more than two
         "Supplier Role Information" // description
      );
      RelationTypeSupport rt = new RelationTypeSupport(
         "ConsumerSupplierRelationType_External",
         roleInfo
      );
      rs.addRelationType(rt);
      // . . .
   } catch (Exception e) {
      // . . .
   }
```

Once we create an array of the necessary RoleInfo objects, we pass the array to the second constructor of RelationTypeSupport. Then we simply call the *addRelationType()* method of the relation service to add the standalone external relation type.

Once the relation type has been created, we instantiate the role by creating a Role object for each group of MBeans to participate in the relation:

```
try {
  // . . .
  rs.addRelationType(rts);
  // Create and register a Consumer MBean
  ObjectName consumerObjName = createWorker("Consumer", 100);
  ArrayList consumerList = new ArrayList();
  consumerList.add(consumerObjName);
  Role consumerRole = new Role("Consumer", consumerList);
  // Create and register a Supplier MBean
  ObjectName supplierObjName = createWorker("Supplier", 100);
  ArrayList supplierList = new ArrayList();
  supplierList.add(supplierObjName);
  Role supplierRole = new Role("Supplier", supplierList);
  RoleList roles = new RoleList();
  roles.add(consumerRole);
  roles.add(supplierRole);
  // . . .
} catch (Exception e) {
  // . . .
}
```

Regardless of whether the relation type is internal or external, we must still create Role objects. The final steps in creating the external relation are to instantiate and use the class representing the external relation:

```
public class ConsumerSupplierRelation extends RelationSupport
  implements ConsumerSupplierRelationMBean {

  public static final String NAME = "ConsumerSupplierRelation_External";
  public static final String OBJECT_NAME = "UserDomain:name=" + NAME;

  private String _relationTypeName;
  private String _relationServiceObjName;
  private List _roleList;

  // MBean interface
  public String getRelationTypeName () {
    return _relationTypeName;
  }
  public String getRelationServiceObjName () {
    return _relationServiceObjName;
  }
  public List retrieveRoleList () {
    return _roleList;
  }
```

```
    public String getRelationId () {
      return  NAME;
    }
    public ConsumerSupplierRelation (ObjectName relationServiceObjName,
                                     String relationTypeName,
                                     RoleList roleList)
    throws Exception {
      super(NAME, relationServiceObjName, relationTypeName, roleList);
      _relationTypeName = relationTypeName;
      _relationServiceObjName = relationServiceObjName.toString();
      _roleList = new ArrayList(roleList.size());
      _roleList.addAll(roleList);
    }
  }
```

The external relation we are going to create is ConsumerSupplierRelation, which is a subclass of RelationSupport. One immediately noticeable difference between an external relation type and an external relation is that an external relation is an MBean. Notice the MBean interface implemented by ConsumerSupplerRelation:

```
public interface ConsumerSupplierRelationMBean
    extends RelationSupportMBean {
      String getRelationTypeName ();
      String getRelationServiceObjName ();
      List retrieveRoleList ();
}
```

Once our external relation class has been instantiated, it must be registered with the MBean server and added to the relation service:

```
try {
  // . . .
  Role supplierRole = new Role("Supplier", supplierList);
  RoleList roles = new RoleList();
  roles.add(consumerRole);
  roles.add(supplierRole);
  ConsumerSupplierRelation relation = new ConsumerSupplierRelation(
    rsObjName,
    rt.getRelationTypeName(),
    roles);
  ObjectName relationObjName = new
    ObjectName("ConsumerSupplierRelation_External");
  server.registerMBean(relation, relationObjName);
  rs.addRelation(relationObjName);
} catch (Exception e) {
  // . . .
}
```

When we create an external relation by subclassing RelationSupport, it is very important to remember that the MBean interface of the subclass must extend RelationSupportMBean. Otherwise, when we attempt to add the relation, the relation service will throw an exception.

Example 11-2 shows a complete source listing of how to create the external Consumer/Supplier relation we've been studying.

Example 11-2. Creating an external relation

```
try {
  MBeanServer server = MBeanServerFactory.createMBeanServer();
  boolean purgeImmediate = true;
  RelationService rs = new RelationService(purgeImmediate);
  ObjectName rsObjName = new ObjectName("AgentServices:name=Relation");
  server.registerMBean(rs, rsObjName);
  ConsumerSupplierRelationType rt = new ConsumerSupplierRelationType();
  rs.addRelationType(rt);
  // Create and register a Consumer MBean
  ObjectName consumerObjName = createWorker("Consumer", 100);
  ArrayList consumerList = new ArrayList();
  consumerList.add(consumerObjName);
  Role consumerRole = new Role("Consumer", consumerList);
  // Create and register a Supplier MBean
  ObjectName supplierObjName = createWorker("Supplier", 100);
  ArrayList supplierList = new ArrayList();
  supplierList.add(supplierObjName);
  Role supplierRole = new Role("Supplier", supplierList);
  RoleList roles = new RoleList();
  roles.add(consumerRole);
  roles.add(supplierRole);
  ConsumerSupplierRelation relation = new ConsumerSupplierRelation(
    rsObjName,
    rt.getRelationTypeName(),
    roles);
  ObjectName relationObjName = new
    ObjectName("ConsumerSupplierRelation_External");
  server.registerMBean(relation, relationObjName);
  rs.addRelation(relationObjName);
} catch (Exception e) {
  // . . .
}
```

Modifying a Role

Suppose that we want to add another Consumer MBean thread into the system. The Controller class provides a method, *createWorker()*, that allows us to do so through a management application. We specify the worker's role name and its work factor, and *createWorker()* creates the appropriate worker MBean and starts its thread of execution. However, in order for the relation service to perform a consistency check on the relationship between the Consumer and Supplier MBeans, we must modify the Consumer role. Moreover, we must do so through the methods provided to us by the relation service.

Simply creating an MBean of a class type that has been specified to be part of a role in a relation has no effect on the relation service. In other words, if we instantiate a new Consumer worker but fail to modify the appropriate Role object, the relation service will be unaware of the new MBean and will not perform any consistency checks on the relation!

In the agent code that creates new worker MBeans and registers them with the MBean server, we must also modify the appropriate Role object within the Consumer/Supplier relation that we created. If creating the new worker MBean makes the role no longer be consistent, the relation service will throw an exception. We must be prepared to catch the exception and take any necessary steps to remove the newly created MBean from the system. Let's look at an example.

Suppose we create a new Consumer MBean, using a browser and the HTML Adaptor server (discussed in Chapter 6), as shown in Figure 11-1.

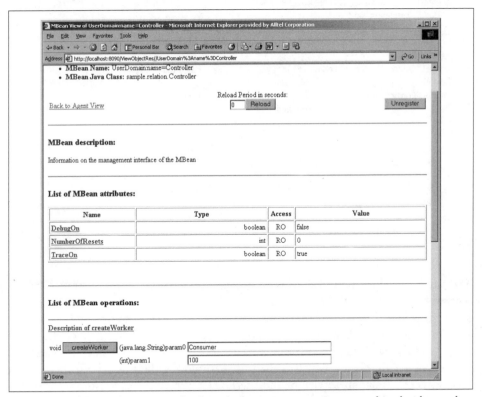

Figure 11-1. Invoking the createWorker() method to create a new Consumer thread with a work factor of 100

When we click the *createWorker* button, the *createWorker()* method of the Controller (which is the JMX agent for the sample application) is invoked. To ensure that creating the new Consumer worker thread does not violate the consistency of the relation between Consumer and Supplier, *createWorker()* must also modify the Consumer Role object so that the relation service will do a consistency check. Example 11-3 shows the code for *createWorker()*, which demonstrates how to modify the Role object and catch any exceptions that result from an inconsistent relation.

Example 11-3. Source code for createWorker()

```
public void createWorker (String role, int workFactor) {
  int index = getNumberOfWorkers(role);
  ObjectName objName = createNewWorker(role, workFactor, index + 1);
  try {
    // _relationService is a reference to the relation service MBean
    List theRoleMBeans =
      _relationService.getRole("ConsumerSupplierRelation_Internal", role);
    List theNewRoleMBeans = new ArrayList();
    theNewRoleMBeans.addAll(theRoleMBeans);
    theNewRoleMBeans.add(objName);
    _relationService.setRole(CONSUMERSUPPLIER_RELATION_NAME,
                        new Role(role, theNewRoleMBeans));
  } catch (Exception e) {
    trace("Controller.createWorker(): ERROR: " + e.getMessage());
    trace(e);
    trace("Controller.createWorker(): the MBean \'" + objName +
        "\' will be unregistered and its stop() method invoked.");
    try {
    // _server is a reference to the MBean server
      _server.invoke(objName, "stop", new Object[0], new String[0]);
      _server.unregisterMBean(objName);
    } catch (Exception e2) {
      trace("Controller.createWorker(): ERROR: " + e2.getMessage());
      trace(e2);
    }
    throw  new RuntimeException(e.getMessage());
  }
}
```

The first thing this method does is to delegate the creation and registration of the worker MBean. Once the MBean has been created and registered with the MBean server, it is added to the list of MBeans acting in that role. The first step in accomplishing this is to call the relation service method *getRole()*. A copy of the list is made, and the newly created MBean is added to the new list. This new list is used to create a new Role object, which is then used to modify the role within the relation service, via the relation service method *setRole()*. We could have simply added the new MBean to the list retrieved from the call to *getRole()*, as this would indeed have added the MBean to the role. However, no consistency check would have been made. It is only through the call to *setRole()* that the relation service will perform the necessary consistency check on the role.

Recall from earlier in this chapter that we created the Consumer RoleInfo object with a maximum degree of 2, which means that we can have two Consumer MBeans acting in that role within the Consumer/Supplier relation. As Figure 11-3 shows, the call to *createWorker()* succeeds.

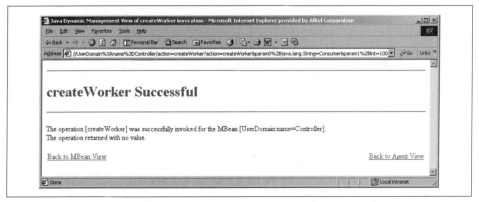

Figure 11-2. Successful invocation of the createWorker() method

However, if we invoke this method again, resulting in a third Consumer MBean, an InvalidRoleValueException will be thrown by the relation service, as shown in Figure 11-3.

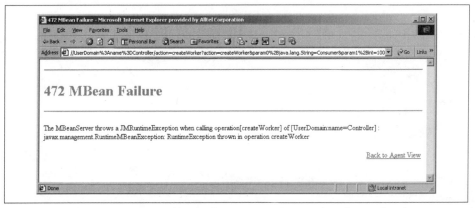

Figure 11-3. When we attempt to add a third Consumer MBean to the relation, the relation service throws an exception

The string representation of the exception looks like this:

```
javax.management.relation.InvalidRoleValueException: Consumer has a number of MBean
references greater than the expected maximum degree.
```

Upon receiving the exception, the code shown in Example 11-3 invokes the *stop()* method of the third Consumer MBean and removes it from the MBean server by calling *unregisterMBean()*.

Index

A

adaptors, compared to connectors, 20
addNotification( ) method, 252–254
addNotificationListener( ) method, 194, 208, 216
addRelation( ) method, 264, 268
addRelationType( ) method, 268, 276
addRoleInfo( ) method, 270, 276
addURL( ) method, 224
agent level, 15
Ant
  building applications with, 24–28
  targets, 25
  tasks, 26
applications
  management, 1
  policies, enforcing, 18
  sample application
    building and running, 24–28
    design, 21–23
    managing, 28
    source code, 23
architecture, JMX, 2
  agent level, 15
  distributed services level, 19
  instrumentation level, 2, 4
    dynamic MBeans, 7
    model MBeans, 9
    open MBeans, 11
    standard MBeans, 5
ARCHIVE tag, M-Let file, 226
ARG tag, M-Let file, 227

arrays
  class name format, 68
  defining, MBeanAttributeInfo objects, 69
  type string format, 67
ArrayType class, 11, 142
Attribute class (DynamicMBean interface), 88
attribute value (descriptorType field), 112
AttributeList class (DynamicMBean interface), 88
attributeNames parameter, 92
AttributeNotFoundException, 92
attributes
  DefaultValue
    OpenMBeanAttributeInfoSupport class, 166
    OpenMBeanParameterInfoSupport class, 161
  LegalValues
    OpenMBeanAttributeInfoSupport class, 166
    OpenMBeanParameterInfoSupport class, 161
  MaxValue
    OpenMBeanAttributeInfoSupport class, 166
    OpenMBeanParameterInfoSupport class, 161
  MBean class, 84
  MBeanAttributeInfo class, 65
  MBeanNotificationInfo class, 82
  MBeanOperationInfo class, 77
  MBeanParameterInfo class, 72

We'd like to hear your suggestions for improving our indexes. Send email to *index@oreilly.com*.

ReturnOpenType attribute
(OpenMBeanOperationInfo
interface), 170
ReturnType attribute
(OpenMBeanOperationInfo
interface), 170
RMI connector, 20
role field (Descriptor interface), 114
role information (relation service), 19, 263
Role objects, 267
RoleInfo class, 265
creating, 276
RoleList class, 267
roles (relation service), 19, 263
modifying, 280–283

S

sample application (see applications)
Scheduler class, 258
scripts, building applications, 24
sendNotification( ) method, 219
server parameter (preRegister( )
method), 203
setAttribute( ) method
DynamicMBean interface, 91
Queue class
explicit superclass exposure, 98, 101
superclass delegation, 105
setAttributes( ) method (DynamicMBean
interface), 93
setField( ) method, 116
setManagedResource( ) method, 134
setMethod field (Descriptor interface), 114
setModelMBeanInfo( ) method, 134
setQueueSize( ) method, 53
setRole( ) method, 269
setSendPastNotifications( ) method, 254
setter methods, 39
dynamic MBeans, referencing, 71
implementing, 52
model MBeans, operation metadata, 137
parameter errors, 48
return value type errors, 47–48
setter value (role field), 114
severity field (Descriptor interface), 114
Signature attribute
OpenMBeanConstructorInfo
interface, 168
OpenMBeanOperationInfo interface, 170

signature parameter
MBeanConstructorInfo class, 74
MBeanOperationInfo class, 77
SimpleType class, 142
size( ) method, 156
SOAP (Simple Object Access Protocol),
connectors, 21
source code (see code)
SpecificationName attribute
(MBeanServerDelegate class), 204
SpecificationVendor attribute
(MBeanServerDelegate class), 205
SpecificationVersion attribute
(MBeanServerDelegate class), 205
standard MBeans, 5
bugs, 39
defining, 36
exceptions, 54
inheritance, 40
basic, 41
compiler-enforced, 45
simple, 42–45
instrumenting, patterns, 36
introspection, 40
common mistakes, 46–49
management interface, 33–35
naming, 37
naming attributes, 38–40
public constructors, 37
string monitors, 17, 236
implementing, 248
notification types, 242
String objects, Descriptor interface field
values, 117
StringMonitorMBean interface, 239
superclass delegation, 98
dynamic MBeans, 102–104
Queue class
getAttribute( ) method, 104
invoke( ) method, 106
setAttribute( ) method, 105
Supplier class, dynamic MBeans,
management interface, 95
system management, 1

T

TabularData interface, 150–156
TabularDataSupport class, complex
data, 156

About the Author

J. Steven Perry has been a software developer for over 10 years. During that time, he's been a maintenance programmer and a systems analyst, and he is now an architect. This has given him the opportunity to see firsthand how critical the need for application management is, and the dire consequences that can result when it's absent. He currently works in the Chief Technology Office at Alltel Information Services, in Little Rock, Arkansas.

Colophon

Our look is the result of reader comments, our own experimentation, and feedback from distribution channels. Distinctive covers complement our distinctive approach to technical topics, breathing personality and life into potentially dry subjects.

The animal on the cover of *Java Management Extensions* is an octopus, an eight-armed cephalopod mollusk of the order *Octopoda*. Octopi are found worldwide in tropical and warm temperate waters. There are many species of octopus, ranging from the massive Giant Pacific octopus, which scientists believe can reach up to 30 feet in length, to the miniscule Californian octopus, which grows to be only one inch long. The common octopus is about 2–3 feet long. The octopus's brain is the most complex of the invertebrates', with long- and short-term memories, providing it with the ability to solve problems by trial-and-error methods—a trick that comes in handy when evading or robbing fishermen's traps. Octopi are completely deaf but they have complex eyes, with vision approximately as acute as a human's. The hundreds of suckers that line each of their tentacles are very sensitive and allow octopi to hold onto almost anything. If an octopus loses a tentacle, it soon grows another in its place.

Octopi feed primarily on crustaceans and mollusks, often luring their prey by wiggling the tip of a tentacle like a worm. Once it catches its victim, the octopus bites it, injecting it with a poisonous venom and digestive enzyme. It then sucks out the flesh and discards the shell (an easy way to identify an octopus's den is by the pile of shells outside its entrance). One of the octopus's defense mechanisms is the release of a purple-black ink cloud as a smokescreen or decoy. Octopi can also change color for camouflage (as well as to reflect mood change) and dart away quickly by jetting water through their siphons. These abilities keep the octopus from being an easy target for predators, even though they have no hard exterior shell. This lack of solid body matter also allows octopi to squeeze into very small spaces.

The male octopus usually dies soon after mating; the female, who usually foregoes eating for several weeks while caring for the large number of eggs she lays, often dies of starvation soon after they hatch. Only a few young out of what may be more than 200,000 eggs survive to adulthood. The lifespan of an octopus is short, ranging from 6 months to 3 years, depending on species and water temperature.

Rachel Wheeler was the production editor and copyeditor for *Java Management Extensions*. Sarah Sherman was the proofreader, Linley Dolby provided quality control, and Phil Dangler provided production assistance. Tom Dinse wrote the index.

Hanna Dyer designed the cover of this book, based on a series design by Edie Freedman. The cover image is a 19th-century engraving from *Old Fashioned Animals*. Emma Colby produced the cover layout with QuarkXPress 4.1 using Adobe's ITC Garamond font.

Melanie Wang designed the interior layout, based on a series design by David Futato. This book was converted to FrameMaker 5.5.6 with a format conversion tool created by Erik Ray, Jason McIntosh, Neil Walls, and Mike Sierra that uses Perl and XML technologies. The text font is Linotype Birka; the heading font is Adobe Myriad Condensed; and the code font is LucasFont's TheSans Mono Condensed. The illustrations that appear in the book were produced by Robert Romano and Jessamyn Read using Macromedia FreeHand 9 and Adobe Photoshop 6. The tip and warning icons were drawn by Christopher Bing. This colophon was written by Rachel Wheeler.